Intentionally blank.

(I've always wanted to say that)

- PREFACE -

Whilst living in France I met Paul Egan, someone who remains a very dear friend to this day. He had joined a well known family tree website, and when he wasn't trawling through *his* family background, had been quietly digging around mine. He'd unearthed all sorts of info which he regularly emailed over to me. Naturally, it caught my attention, and in turn, inspired me to contact some long-lost relations to further research *our* family, albeit reliant on Paul's constant help.

In an attempt to help map out my kin's narrative, relatives scraped together photos, papers and assorted tidbits which helped Paul and I build a better picture of my ancestors. Over time, a simple but fascinating tree was blossoming under which adults met, married, bore offspring (who in turn), repeated the process through the ages. However, every now and again we'd be sent scurrying down some internet rabbit hole only for the virtual footprint of the family member under the spotlight to come to an abrupt halt. How I wish that my forebears had left more evidence, more clues as to their trip through survival and to how their lives changed over time.

In September 2021, I reluctantly stepped into my 60s, and with more years behind me than I do ahead, I have yet to marry or reproduce so thought it an idea to compile a document which will serve to illustrate my *own* history.

Looking through old diaries, notes, press passes, assorted visual reminders, and after phone calls with former colleagues, it took the best part of 12 months to put this together.

By means of a disclaimer, I am not a professional writer in any sense of the word, so I make *no* excuses as to the disjointed rhythm, the typos* that slipped through, the back-tracking or some of the lengthy technical explanations that may well lose you. From start to finish, I wrote this with enormous enthusiasm and using the same narration style with which I would relate it to you face-to-face.

A note on the photographs used herein: the majority are mine, though I have (unashamedly) pinched a few from the internet. I do not claim any legal right over them as their inclusion is under the 'Fair Use' doctrine and their appearance in these pages will have no impact on the market value of the original work.

3

Finally, I have also changed the names of *some* individuals. They'll know who they are, but as to avoid any legal issues, I'll just change them as using their real names would serve no constructive purpose.

Enjoy.

Stuart
Dorking, 2022

* soz

Part One

Formative Years   6

It's Not What You Know   17

From A Prince To A Duke   27

It's Christmas In Elstree   39

A Brief Sojourn   50

The Missing Link   55

The Screening Process   65

Cutting Crew   74

Westminster Calling   76

When Three Tribes Go To War   90

Back For More   115

Madiba   127

The Management   130

Bonjour Matelot   137

Part Two

Tunnel of Love   146

Going Solo   174

Vacanza Italiana   184

One Last Time   191

Pick 'n Mix   198

Jailbird   213

Something In The Air   219

Jason and The Aeronauts   228

Strap In   233

Feet First   237

Tale End   244

Fin   251

Part One

Formative Years

To someone who's never met you, have them read page after page of your family history and it's a bit like forcing them to wade through waist-deep treacle at gun point, so I'll try to keep this introduction as brief as possible.

I was the product of a union between Joan and Duggie: my mother's second marriage but my father's first. In 1946 my mother, Joan Evans, married John Leslie Brown. A first-class rugger-bugger, John had served as a pilot with the RAF's Coastal Command during WW2. Along with his crew, they patrolled assorted Nazi submarine hunting grounds like the North Sea, in B-24 Liberators or Bristol Beauforts. The aircraft were fitted with the ASDIC system of identification (yet another toy we gifted to our American cousins), and this was key in helping them find their prey. There's a family legend which tells the story of John being 'decorated' after his crew identified a suspicious object somewhere out at sea. As John circled his aircraft, the ASDIC operator fine-tuned his readings, locked-on to the submerged target and let slip a pair of 500lb anti-submarine bombs. A few hours later, a passing Royal Navy vessel reported debris floating on the surface: whale meat.

As mentioned, John had been an enthusiastic rugby player and an even more enthusiastic beer drinker. Now back in civvy street and married to Joan, he'd often leave her with their two daughters, Jenny and Debbie, and disappear on sporting weekends with his mates. He'd play rugby in the afternoons followed by drinking bars dry from the early evenings into the early hours. So the story goes, he was friendly with Duggie McAlister (a former pilot in the Glider Pilot Regiment) and asked if he'd be so kind as to look after Joan while he was away on his weekends. This, of course, Duggie did with aplomb.

Joan and Duggie were married at London's Caxton Hall in 1959. According to my mother it had been raining that day, and as she and her betrothed made their way up steps outside, a figure bounded somewhat awkwardly past them and held open the front door: the gentleman in question was Douglas Bader. Joan had been granted a fairly painless divorce from John who remained a family friend for the rest of his life. He'd pop into whichever house we were living in and laughter would be heard throughout. It was always fun to see him.

My Mother was born in the London Borough of Paddington in 1923, one of three girls born to Peggy and Roderick Evans. Along with sisters Margaret and Muriel, the family home was in Ealing. Roderick was said to have been a very strict father, but after my mother's birth, Peggy had packed Roderick off to register my mother's birth - and this proved to be his downfall. With meticulous instructions that the new addition was to be named "Joan Dorothy", on arrival at the town hall, Roderick informed the registrar that the newborn was to be named "Dorothy Joan". For the rest of her life Mum was always known as Joan, no matter which way round her official documents recorded her name.

Muriel, the youngest of the three, worked at a record company. Demo pressings of popular singing artists of the time were always finding their way into our family collection. However, such gems were lost during our house moves but in the mid-60s I vividly remember seeing - and listening to - Ken Dodd's 'Tears' on the Columbia label. The other sibling, Margaret, was married and living elsewhere in London.

Muriel died of cancer in the mid 60s, and a few years later, Roderick was rushed to St Georges Hospital following a life-ending heart attack. My mother, her sister Margaret and mother Peggy were devastated. I don't suppose I was any more than 5 years old at the time so these were my first experiences of human grief and the effects it had on those close to me. Even at this great age, I wasn't a fan. Mum's surviving sister Margaret, now divorced, was living on the Channel Island of Guernsey, so the practical decision was taken to move Peggy over and into a small flat in St Peter Port. Peg was a wonderful woman, full of fun and would often entertain me by acting out a 1920s dance where she would pull up her skirt over her knee, 'shake a leg' and then take her false teeth out as I let rip with peals of infantile laughter. Sadly Peg had no sense of smell, and following a gas leak in her flat one night in 1976, she died in her sleep. At least she didn't know anything about it.

My father Douglas was the youngest of 4 boys born to William and Beatrice McAlister of Bray, to the south of Dublin. When my father was 2½, the Battle of Dublin was raging. The new Provisional Government battled the Irish Republican Army (IRA) that opposed the Anglo-Irish Treaty. My grandfather, William McAlister, had a sister Harriet who was holed up in her city centre lodgings when the gun battle started. With a family friend behind the wheel, 36 year old William raced to Dublin to rescue Harriet. On arrival at the rear of the property, William jumped out of the car and ran round to the front of the building where he was brought down in crossfire. We are unsure to which side fired the fatal bullet, but

William was driven (in the same car) to Meath Hospital where he died on arrival. His widow Beatrice decided to ship the boys over to relatives in the UK, removing them from the civil unrest.

Mum and Dad ... at Epsom Races?

Joan and Duggie had been married a little under 2 years when I arrived in September of 1961. My father was an advertising agent, and together with his brother Walter, had started their own agency in London's Argyll Street: Haig-McAlister Ltd. When I was born, my father was already 43 years old which, for a male in the 1960s, was quite advanced for a first-time parent. I still can't work out if he really wanted a child, as once I began to grow up, I'm not sure he was that enamoured. Like all single men, he'd done what he wanted to up until then so I'm still not convinced that family life suited him. He'd married a woman with two daughters so this 'ready-made' outfit might have been a little more than he would have cared for.

Dad commuted to London five days a week, but the priority was to house his wife, two step children and the newborn. My parents decided on 'Westdean', a house in Cobham, Surrey, so he took on a mortgage for £19,000. The house was enormous but the gardens were my Father's pride and joy. He'd spend hours behind his petrol-powered Ransome's motor-mower drawing the straightest lines on any lawn you've ever seen. The mower had a choke, a kick start and a clutch, but in the wrong hands it was a potential death trap. A gentle nudge on the throttle was all that was needed as he marched behind it, carving his way up and down the lush green Surrey turf. Even to this day, I'm drawn to the smell of freshly mown grass. The garden was populated with fruit trees: apples, pears and plums. The strawberry bed went into overdrive come the season, and inside a long wooden greenhouse, generous vines soon became heavy with fruit. Below the vines, bamboo canes overflowed with tomato plants releasing a scent and a flavour I have yet to rediscover.

Westdean.
In 1959, yours for £19,000 but today, closer to £2.3M

Every flowerbed was bordered by the sharpest of edges. My father would spend hours carefully slicing and working them with the precision of a surgeon. Hosting bloated red, white and pink roses, a riot of colour and smell. His garden was a thing of beauty, and for the mass of buzzing insects which had the run of the place, life was good and all his hard work made sure that standards were maintained.

The fog of time is one reason why I am unable to recall exactly how some relationships came about, either that or I never thought to ask my parents in later life. However, in my very early days I attended nursery school with chap called Michael, who also lived in Cobham. We would often spend our days playing at mine or I'd go to his. For some reason or another, Mum decided that she needed a housekeeper: someone to help wash up, see to the family laundry, clean the house and complete other domestic chores on a never-ending list. Of course back then one would trot down the local tobacconist, and for a minimal charge, could place a card advertising work or services in the shop window. Michael's father Dick had a wicked sense of humour, and on passing the shopfront had recognised the phone number. He'd ring my mother and put on a woman's voice, apply for the job but ask lots of irrelevant and awkward questions, often tying my mother up in knots, confusing the hell out of her. After a while she'd twig what was going on, "You utter so-and-so!" she'd squeal as the penny dropped. Michael's father was Dick Emery.

I attended Milbourne Lodge Junior school in Esher, and when the school bus dropped me off at a neighbours, I'd go through their garden and climb over the fence at the bottom and into ours. Waiting for me was Sabre, our huge black Great Dane. I'd put my forearm in his mouth, and gently closing his jaws, he'd walk me down the length of the garden and in through the back door to the kitchen. At one point I remember falling between a hedge and a wall at the front of the house and becoming stuck. Such was the bond between child and dog, that Sabre stood his ground and growled at my father, stopping him from extracting me from the tangle of thorns.

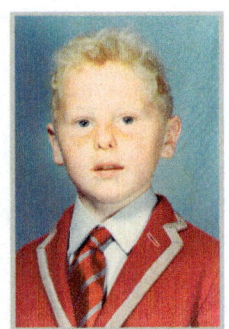

On returning from school one day, Sabre wasn't at the fence to greet me. Instead, he was lying in the back garden with adults standing around him. I was told that he was old and was going to live in Scotland but in truth, his hips were badly worn with age and he could no longer stand. Without me knowing about it, Sabre was euthanised and taken away.

At that time, the income rate was 90%, and as the 70s swept into view, my father's business suffered alarming difficulties. A much larger and competitive advertising agency was preparing a hostile takeover. Cracks began to show and the atmosphere within the family home began to sour. As the business problems worsened, my father's mood changed and my mother slowly began to lose control of her mental state. Around that time the NHS was practising (and outwardly promoting) a procedure called 'electroshock therapy' - a kind of electrical reboot type of thing - and it was decided that my mother would benefit from a course. "She'll soon be back to normal", said the doctor, and off she went. Once back at the family home in Cobham it was obvious that the therapy hadn't worked, and now a shell of her former self, she was to remain on a cocktail of medication for the rest of her natural days.

Around 1967 my father's ad agency won the account for a sports retailer called SupaSports - they sold everything the modern sportsperson would need. SupaSports had designed a track suit and had asked if 1966 World Cup hat-trick goal scorer Geoff Hurst would put his name to it: a navy blue affair with thin white pipe lines running down the arms and legs. Their shop in Walton-on-Thames had been chosen to reveal the track suit and Geoff Hurst would be there in person, but they needed a child to model the outfit. Nepotism was far from dead as the advertising agent's son was chosen: moi.

I was six years old but I clearly remember standing in the shop with my father looking on. The SupaSports hierarchy were cock-a-hoop to have scored Hurst for an hour, as the faces of the expectant public pressed against the exterior of the shop window. Hurst bounced a ball off my head and we posed for photos. As far as I can remember, I didn't get a signed football and I don't think I got to keep the tracksuit either. The photo they used was me looking up at Hurst with him smiling at the camera. A copy of the final image remained in a box at my parents' house for absolute years but heaven knows where it is now.

Shortly after that, my sister Jenny left the family home to marry Jon Clark which left my other sister Debbie and me. The atmosphere at home deteriorated even further and the family doctor, a Dr Dunlop, suggested that the young and impressionable Stuart should be spared exposure to such a toxic environment, and it was decided that he would be sent to boarding school.

In 1968, now aged 7, after months of preparation buying me a trunk and having me fitted for a uniform, one September afternoon me and my trunk were delivered inside the gates of Ripley Court School, six miles from the family home. My parents did their dutiful bit to settle me in and then they drove away. My first night at Ripley was something I will never forget: a group of wide-eyed boys guided round by a sympathetic headmaster's wife. She was at pains to show us where everything was, not that we remembered anything.

Dressed in shirt and tie, a jacket with overly long sleeves, shorts, itchy socks and shiny shoes, the gaggle of new boys was led off for their evening meal. I started my life at Ripley as a weekly boarder, allowed home at weekends. We were tucked into bed by 7.30, the sun still very much up, the evening sunlight passing easily through wafer-thin curtains. We lay there in our sturdy metal beds too frightened to even speak. As my birthday falls at the end of September, for the next fortnight I was still technically 7 years old - a fact I was to tease my parents with for years to come.

I despised boarding school, not just this one but the following one too. For nine years I loathed the education system and it is safe to say that I failed all my school exams with distinction. Dad's advertising business went through even more problems and around 1973 he was forced to sell the house in Cobham with its sumptuous gardens, tennis court and long gravel drive. At today's prices, the value of that very house is creeping towards the £3M mark. My parents, sister Debbie and I moved to a much smaller house in Milbourne Lane, Esher, a stone's throw from my junior school.

12

I was twelve, so now it was time that I moved to another school. A number of institutions were on the 'possible' list. However none of them would accept me due to my inability to pass an exam of any kind. In fact the only thing I have ever passed with any reasonable success was a kidney stone. I hadn't done very well at Ripley and there was no overnight fix. I have been and will always be a 'visual learner': if you show me how something is done then I can repeat it and I'll learn from there. However, if you write stuff on a blackboard and yell at me if I don't understand, then you'll lose my interest in whatever it is you're trying to teach me. I am someone with acute perception, which means that I notice things that others might miss. I have the ability to recognise small details with precision and spot movement around me, and this served me well in later life as you will learn.

I was classed as a pupil 'who needed a little extra help', so my next port of call was Shiplake College on the banks of the River Thames, upstream from Henley on Thames. This new establishment was around 40 miles from Esher and specialised in helping pupils who weren't naturally gifted in any sense of the word. A few of my peers went on to become rich and famous, others became something in the armed forces or even made a name for themselves in the City. I was a three-weekly boarder meaning that every 3rd weekend I was granted temporary leave, or 'exeat' as it was known: released home on the 3rd Friday afternoon and expected to report back early evening two days later on the Sunday. On each of these depressing Sundays I returned to Shiplake, engulfed in a cloud of foreboding as the very idea of going back to that place filled me with dread. There were a few boys whose parents lived within 20 minutes of mine, so from time to time the weekend driving duties were shared between them. Three small boys would be squeezed into the back of a car and we'd all travel to Shiplake together. Even to this day, a feeling of melancholy often sets in as Sunday evening arrives.

The main building at Shiplake was built in 1890 as a Victorian home for the Harrison family and bought by the BBC in 1941, using it as staff lodgings working at their nearby Caversham listening station. In 1958 it was sold to the Everett family who, a year later, turned it into the school it is today. My time at Shiplake was spent under the old regime where antiquated corporal punishment was freely administered. Upon arrival I was shown to a dormitory which I was to share with nine other boys where, after lights out one night, the 10 of us were caught talking too loudly. The door flew open and the music master burst in, flicking on the ceiling light and demanding to know who the culprit was. No one owned up, so as I was closest to the door, I was selected for exemplary punishment.

As wide eyes peered over turned-down sheets, I was ordered to bend over and grasp the metal frame of the bed. I braced to receive six of the best as the music master selected one of my slippers to administer punishment. The pain from the solid plastic heel as it made contact with my arse cheek instantly caused my eyes to fill. However at the age of 12 I wasn't ready to cry in front of my peers, no matter how much the beating hurt. The music master threw my slipper to the floor and I was ordered back into bed. He barked "Now shut up!", switched off the dormitory light and slammed the door. Muffled adolescent snorting and giggling broke out in the darkness and I briefly saw the funny side of it too, though in the dark, the tears were now flowing. On the flip side, I had won majorly in the brownie point stakes. I'd taken one for the team as I hadn't split on anyone. Just to rub it in, this was the sort of establishment where if you needed a pee in the middle of the night, you knelt over a bucket which was placed on the parquet flooring in the middle of the dormitory. We took it in turns each morning to empty this sloshing container of salts and assorted compounds.

Time went by, and my hatred for this place and everyone in it continued to grow. Corporal punishment prevailed, and as I approached the Upper 5th, I moved into a two-man study. Our cramped hovel was next to the Headmaster's study and we'd often allow friends in to listen to the thrashings that were being doled out on the other side of the wall. On the very rare occasions that I visited the Headmasters study myself, I'd have a quick look around to spot the offending weapons of discipline. Thinking that they would be hidden away in a cupboard or drawer, I was surprised to see them propped up against a wall on show to remind everyone that crime meant punishment. Before my esteemed arrival at Shiplake, the 1971 series 'Tom Brown's School Days' had been popular on television. It told the story of Brown, who as a new boy, had to contend with the school's harsh discipline and constant bullying by the older boys. The 'beating' scene stuck in my mind, though in the film it was conducted in front of the entire school.

Sister Debbie married Stephen Giles, and as our domestic numbers diminished, the house on Milbourne Lane was sold as Mum, Dad and I moved into a bungalow in Claygate. Once back at Shiplake, I sat my O-Levels which was a memorable period of abject fear and expectant failure. During the summer months, a brown envelope from the examination board landed on the doormat and with a feeling of doom, I handed it to my parents. Apart from English Language which wore a passable 'C' around its neck, every other subject received a mortifying 'U'. It was 1977 and I had finally proven to my parents that after nine years and all that money I was nothing more than an unmitigated intellectual disappointment.

My father was a heavy smoker and an even heavier drinker. We had a Bedlington terrier named Benjie who was the sweetest creature known to mankind. At precisely 9pm every night (be it high summer or darkest winter), this dog would stand by the front door and bark, prompting Dad to take him for a walk to the local pub, The Griffin. This was a two-pronged operation as the dog was exercised and emptied on the way down and my father was guaranteed a navigational aid for the trip back. Some years later Benjie was diagnosed with cancer and the vet made a home visit to put him to sleep.

My mother simply couldn't stand the grief and shut herself in her bedroom with our second Bedlington, Misty. Dad and I held Benjie as he was prepared and the vet finally injected him. "Goodbye old chap," said my father as the tears streamed down his face. "He's gone", said the vet as I too burst into floods. As the vet packed his bag and made to to leave, Dad reached inside his jacket pocket for his cheque book and tried to settle the bill there and then. The vet waved his hand, suggesting that it be done at a more appropriate time. The next day, Dad and I buried Benjie in the garden and we were all devastated.

My rave reviews from the examination board coincided with the first adult conversation I ever had with my father. We'd now moved house twice due to the decline of his business and the decision to send me to boarding school nine years ago had proven financially crippling. Since then I had single-handedly demonstrated to be a hopeless product of the private education system. I'd learnt fu*k all and had one measly 'C' grade certificate to show for it. How stupid did I feel? "So," I began, "take me out of school. You can't afford to keep me in it, I'm 16 so can legally leave." He sat, deep in thought. Mum would never go for it, or would she?

15

Behind closed doors summit meetings were held and in September I returned to Shiplake where I turned 17 at the end of the month, sat my O-Level retakes in the October and by the beginning of November I was out, back home and free as a bird. Needless to say, my retakes were a carbon copy of the originals.

So, what the hell was I going to do with myself now?

"Get yourself down to the labour exchange" I was told. So that's exactly what I did. The fact that I wasn't stepping neatly into a waiting job was an embarrassment, though I had spent a few months with my father in his office now based in Richmond. There was an outside chance that I might join the family firm and work my way up but that notion was swiftly knocked on the head as it was obvious that I didn't possess any useful abilities. The labour exchange (dole office) was a morose affair with beige, sour-faced individuals sitting behind equally beige, sour-faced desks. The available jobs were posted on handwritten cards which were placed either in the window or on easels that had been spaced at regular intervals across the floor. A young lady called me over to her desk where she noted my particulars. I was 17 and didn't have a clue as what I wanted to do which made me a perfect fit for the worldwide staffing firm, Manpower. I was given a card listing my details and told to report to the Manpower offices further along Esher high street.

Any business which required labourers, skivvies, packers or pure muscle fished in Manpower's deep and bountiful pool. In return, if you were at a loose end and needed a part-time job, then Manpower could match you with something the same day. "Can you get to Staines?" the nice lady asked me. My parents had very kindly bought me a second-hand two-stroke scooter so at least I was mobile. I confirmed that I could and was given another card with the details of a company with a household name, in whose kitchens I was now employed. I was to work from 11am until 4pm, so with a spare gallon of mixture strapped to the scooter, I set off hoping to arrive on time. It was the middle of winter, freezing cold and Staines was a stonking 9 miles away. I was assigned to a washing up detail, bending over a deep sinks scrubbing the burnt remains of lunch from the insides of even deeper kitchen pots. I lasted a week. The pitiful minimum wage was being spent on two-stroke fuel getting me there and back. Fuel for the bike had to be mixed at the petrol station: 40 parts petrol and one part semi-synthetic two-stroke oil. Pour that into the scooter's fuel tank and then prepare another gallon which was strapped to the bike behind me. All well and good but the poor thing was a logistical and mechanical disaster, so cashing in some premium bonds and part-exchanging the scooter, I bought myself Honda 250cc from a dealer in Teddington.

Back then a 17-year-old could ride a 250cc bike on a car license. I'd passed my driving test (only the second exam success in my short life to date) without a fuss a few months earlier. A friend of a schoolfriend had suggested that I join Addison Lee as a dispatch rider up in London. I'd never ridden as far as London and didn't have a clue as to what I was doing, but nevertheless, I rode through the snow, shivering uncontrollably and I presented myself at Addison Lee's West End office.

I was interviewed and given a week's probation during which I racked up a tally of evidence which was presented against any further employment. I was a country boy who simply didn't know his way around the city, regularly having to stop and thumb his way through a soaking wet A-to-Z. Despite my keenness, collections and deliveries were late and I was regularly wet through. After a week I was ordered to return the company bib to the grumpy controller who sat behind a spittle-covered plastic divider, and told to "f*ck off". My motorcycling days delivered one final straw as I had just started climbing Roehampton Vale as one of the Honda's exhaust pipes blew off and came to rest in the lane behind me. By the time I had parked up and run back to retrieve it, eight wheels of a lorry had driven over it and the pipe now resembled the lower half of a rocking horse. I strapped the hot exhaust to the back of the bike and drove off making the most awful racket. It was at this point that my life changed completely, and it was all thanks to my sister Debbie.

17

It's Not What You Know

Debbie loved singing. She'd sung since she was a teenager and she was bloody good at it. One night, while in Cobham, I remember being scooped up out of bed and driven to the village hall where a band was entertaining the locals. They launched into "Oom-Pah-Pah" from the musical 'Oliver!' and Debbie led them in a singalong and the place erupted. After WW2 Mum had been an actress and photographic model, so I'm pretty sure she'd had some input into Debbie's singing career. Mum's acting career didn't go far but she *did* appear in one film that survives to this day: "Carve Her Name With Pride". It pops up on the TV schedule from time to time. In the nightclub scene where Violette Szabo meets 'Bob' (a fellow spy) for the first time, there's Mum in close up sitting at a table. It's lovely to see her and she really was gorgeous back then. Later on I'll link the film to events in France in 2002 (along with the real-life Bob), so stick around.

Back in the day, in order to obtain professional bookings in the West End or on television or films, one needed an Equity Card: it was the industry's proof that you were a professional and had done the 'apprentice' legwork. Candidates needed *bona fide* contracts with repertory theatres or clubs, and once proof of such engagements had been submitted to Equity's applications board, you *might* be awarded your membership card. Such was the exclusivity that simply trying to join its ranks was a full-time job in itself. Nowadays, all you need is to be picked for a reality show, a couple of hundred quid and you're in.

Debbie joined a band which toured the country. They sang in theatres, bingo halls and in ice rinks, and that's how she met her husband Steve as he was out skating one afternoon. Her voice was now pro, and as she'd collected all the required paperwork as proof of her professional engagements, she applied for Equity membership. She was awarded her card, and in the late 70s, Debbie passed an audition and joined the chorus of 'Jesus Christ Superstar' at London's Palace Theatre. Once settled into the role, Mum and Dad scooped up a pair of complimentary tickets to see her perform.

It was 1978 and I was out of work, when Mum mentioned that Debbie had been talking to some colleagues. "There *might* be a job going at a neighbouring theatre". Apparently, it was something to do with the lighting crew, and Debbie had indeed been chatting to the Palace Theatre's chief electrician and told him that her brother was at a loose end and did he know of any jobs going? There was a showman's position going at the Prince Edward Theatre, 100 yards behind the Palace Theatre. "Tell your brother to ring Mick Underwood on this number" he said, handing her a piece of paper. Nervously I rang and was invited for an interview. Presenting myself at the stage door in Frith Street, Mick came to meet me, leading me down through a labyrinth of backstage passages and into the auditorium. His deputy turned up with two frothy coffees from Bar Italia, the conveniently handy (and still existing) cafe just next door. "So," said Mick, "what have you done lighting-wise?". To date my entire lighting career had been during school productions operating a pathetic lighting desk with six faders controlling a dozen coloured lights and that was it. Feeling more than a little under-experienced, I was now in the stalls of the 1700-seater Prince Edward currently home to the world's biggest musical hit, 'Evita!'. With such a production, why did they want to interview me of all people? Surely there *must* have been others with far better qualifications than I? Mick explained what the job entailed and I enthusiastically nodded my head at every detail.

Mick smiled and hired me on the spot, and ready to start my first ever proper job the next week, I skipped back to Waterloo Station for the train home to Claygate. The show was an entertainment phenomenon and the waiting list for tickets was in excess of a year. I couldn't believe it, my mother was delighted and my father relieved that I'd eventually found something more acceptable than washing up or on sitting on that bloody bike all day.

A Showman, in theatre terms, is an individual who only reports for work for the performances. They arrive before curtain up, do the job they're hired to do and go home after the final curtain. A Dayman, on the other hand, is in the theatre all day: they tend to the general electrical well-being of the theatre, maintain the equipment and *then* work on the show.

'Evita!' had 8 performances a week, with matinees on Thursday and Saturday afternoons. For now, I'd drive to Surbiton station where I could catch a 12 minute non-stopper to Waterloo, then a Northern Line tube to Leicester Square and report for duty in the crew room underneath the stage at least 30 minutes before curtain up. The show came down at 10.30, so I'd catch a train out of Waterloo around 11pm. From time to time I'd meet up with Debbie whose show at the Palace Theatre came down at the same time and we'd sit together on the train back to Surbiton. She and Steve lived in Long Ditton, not far from the station. On matinee days I'd catch a train from Surbiton around midday, do the afternoon show, spend my downtime playing the slot machines in Old Compton Street's only penny arcade and grab a sandwich for dinner. After the evening performance, I'd repeat the train routine, arriving home around 11.30.

For the first week or so at the Prince Edward, I was to shadow an experienced Showman. Here I should explain the layout of the theatre and the many functions of the lighting crew. We'll start way up in the Gods above the upper circle. Behind thick glass were 3 followspots in the limehouse. These spots were to follow the main characters of the show: Evita, Peron and Che Guevara. To operate one of these with any level competency, you had to know your stuff. The operators were a very long way from the stage and the slightest twitch of the followspot would result in the light on stage moving several feet.

Moving down to the stage area, and on each of the 4 corners (and 15 feet above the stage) were more followspots. These box lights were visible to the audience and what made these particular lights different is that they were dimmable. By slipping off a shoe and wrapping your toes around a sliding knob on the floor-mounted box, you could adjust the intensity of the light. After a while you learnt how to control these simply by the position of your foot on the dimmer. However, one of these 4 spot operators had an extra job - a small lighting desk which controlled some under-stage lights, or 'tramlines' as they were known. Squares of thick transparent perspex were incorporated into the stage flooring with Par 64s underneath (akin to aircraft landing lights). Then we move way upstage to the back wall of the building. During the show were a couple of real cine-film inserts and a two ton metal-framed cinema screen moved along rails at a 30 degree angle from the back wall to downstage where the curtain falls. On a solid shelf bolted to the back wall of the theatre was a 35mm cine projector with a fisheye lens.

In a previous life, the Prince Edward had been known as 'The London Casino', home to Cinerama. Three projectors at the back of the auditorium projected their overlapping images onto a screen that was simply enormous. In its heyday 'The London Casino' had been under the guiding hand of chief projectionist Charlie Sweeney. With his encyclopedic knowledge of the craft, Charlie had been given a second chance and was hired to run the cine projector for 'Evita!'. It was his sole responsibility and he defended his position with vigour. Already into his 70s when I knew him, and despite his grumpy outward appearance, he was only too happy to tell you about the 'good old days'.

On to stage level and the domain of the 'practicals' Showman. 'Practical' refers to any prop or piece of scenery which requires electricity to work. As such items were moved on and off stage, the connecting power cables needed to be paged in or out and their electrical connectors, then plugged or unplugged. Working in the wings meant learning muscular choreography together with the stagehands who (in near darkness) would pick up, push, roll or clear heavy props or scenery. For example, early in the first half there's a large heavy staircase festooned with coloured lights. Three members of the chorus would be positioned on the staircase, and as the scene came to an end, they'd get down off it, as simultaneously four burly stagehands released the brakes and hauled this steel structure into the wings. At the same time, the practicals Showman would pull the power cable towards him, unplug the connector and step smartly backwards as the stagehands manoeuvred the staircase through the wings and to it's storage area. The cable was coiled and stored under a hatch installed in the floor of the wings. All this has to happen in total silence, as fast as possible and without the Showman being slow or maladroit enough as to piss off the four prop-forwards dragging the wheeled staircase towards them.

Then we move out to the auditorium and a small booth (as you look towards the stage) which is attached to the right-hand wall of the stalls. The booth was split into two with the rear section being a cubby hole where the SM (stage manager) would 'call' the show using cues for the lighting and stage crews through a headset system. Up on the fly floor where splintery hemp ropes flew the scenery and curtains in and out, the team relied on a series of coloured traffic lights, also controlled by the stage manager. The front section of the booth, however, was mission control - the lighting control board. This state-of-the-art piece of kit was responsible for controlling 95% of the show. It was 'mimic memory' technology (MMS), late 1970s computerisation, and is where Mick or his deputy would sit and operate the huge lighting rig during the show. There was a huge collection of lamps hanging above the stage, mounted in the wings or strapped to the front of the dress circle. Every single lighting cue had been carefully worked out and programmed into the desk. From time to time a Showman would be promoted to Dayman and then given the opportunity to operate this modern marvel. It was a *huge* responsibility as the entire show depended on the MMS board operator hitting every cue right on the nail. Should it all go tits up, they'd also have to know how to drag it all back into line again.

Finally, we go to the crew room under the stage to find the 'Swing Showman'. Like any business, there were sicknesses, absentees and latecomers. The Swing would be able to 'stand in' or take over at any part during through the show: any of the followspots, the 'practicals' position, the cine projector and the lighting control board. On the wall of the crew room was a chart with everyone's name listed vertically and all the lighting positions horizontally. As members of the crew became more and more familiar with each position, they would fill in the relevant square with a coloured marker - just so long as they could operate whatever position without a cue sheet - and Mick would be checking. My name was added to the list as I began to learn the ropes.

I learnt all the stage followspots, then the 'practicals' position and then up to the limehouse to master the three followspots. Charlie took me under his wing and taught me the cine projector. 14 months had passed and I had learnt every position and could step in and operate the lot without needing a clue sheet. I was rewarded with a promotion to Dayman. I was now a full-time lighting technician on the biggest show in the world and earning a staggering £17 a week. Mick was now to train me up on the main lighting control board. I sat next to him and watched everything he did, soaking up as much information as I could and asking non-stop questions. I was then given two weeks to prove to him that I could operate the MMS confidently.

There's something about the buzz of a live show. It's the immediacy, the nerves, the body winding itself up into 'go' mode ... one chance to get it right and the weight of responsibility resting on your shoulders. The show crew were made up of all sorts, a former child actor, an accountant who did this in the evenings for pocket money, a couple of hippy artists, several wannabe musicians, a dancer and a stunning girl from Hornchurch with a body which could stop traffic ... and then there were the Daymen: Mick Underwood, his deputy Paul, the former child actor and myself.

This promotion turned my part time job into a career and I was cock-a-hoop to have been made up. We started work at 10.30 every morning, fixed any electrical problems in the public areas, changed faulty lightbulbs in the toilets, checked the illuminated poster displays out on Old Compton Street and of course, tended to any issues with the show's lighting rig. Using an articulated ladder (a tallescope), we worked at height changing bulbs, replacing lighting gel and swapping out duff kit for good. The theatre was lovely and quiet during the day with no show personnel around. Old Compton Street in the late 70s was heaven starting at Bar Italia for a frothy coffee, down to La Porchetta Pollo Bar (an Italian restaurant which is still there 40+ years later) and maybe 50p in the penny arcade before the show. 'Space Invaders' at 10p a shot was the game that swallowed most of our cash.

Directly opposite the stage door of the Prince Edward was the world-renowned jazz club, Ronnie Scott's. American drummer Buddy Rich was playing a late-night slot and a couple of us scampered across Frith Street on the hunt for tickets. We snaffled a couple but 'standing room only', through we were young so it didn't worry us. At 10.30 'Evita!' came down so we finished up, put the lighting kit to bed, wished our crew-mates goodnight and headed over the road. What a show! I had never seen or heard anything like it before. The Buddy Rich Orchestra was fantastic with Rich in the middle of it all, his drum riser lifting him slightly higher than the rest of the musicians. Whenever a soloist was featured, Rich would gesture towards them, inviting the soloist to take a bow. It was hot and sticky, Scott's was packed to the gunnels and I loved it.

My sister Debbie left 'Superstar' and was now part of the chorus of 'Hello Dolly' at the Theatre Royal Drury Lane, starring the legendary Carol Channing. Debs was also playing the understudy to Mrs Molloy. I remember seeing the show one night with my parents and was suitably proud of my big sister. With 8 shows a week, the matinees on Thursday and Saturday were popular (and cheaper) with group bookings as the retired and ancient could get in and out of London with comparative ease. However, these afternoon shows were notorious for snorers and the bewildered.

A short trot down the road from where I was working was the St Martin's Theatre, the forever-home of Agatha Christie's 'The Mousetrap'. The play had premiered in Nottingham back in 1952 and had transferred to London's Ambassadors the same year. In March 1974 it moved next door to a new home, the St Martin's Theatre. In the 70s, Richard Attenborough played the role of Detective Sergeant Trotter and even then the London run of 'The Mousetrap' has exceeded 26,000 performances (though not all with Dickie). Right now, the role of DS Trotter was being filled by my cousin, David McAlister.

I hadn't seen much of him since I was a kid so I'd wander down to his stage door to say hello. He'd invite me into his dressing room where we'd catch up on all things. He very kindly arranged a comp ticket for a matinee performance and I sat enthralled at this theatrical record-breaker of a show. David went on to tour all over the world with 'Annie' playing the role of Daddy Warbucks.

'Evita!' was well into its 3rd year and we'd had a number of A-Listers who'd come to marvel at this headline show. Bob Hope held up the start of one performance (and also that of the second act) so he could make an entrance through the stalls. He received a standing ovation from everyone except the dress and upper circles who hadn't a clue as to why the show was late and to why everyone was applauding. Heartthrob Paul Newman came backstage to meet the cast after one performance. I was standing not far from the door that connects prompt corner to the under-stage staircase as a buzz of excitement grew through the waiting cast. The door opened and in stepped a wizened old man with grey hair - the only giveaway being those signature blue eyes. Tremendous applause erupted.

In those days I had long(ish) curly blonde hair and blue eyes, appearing all sparkly-new and fresh - catnip to the theatre's gay community. I have always accepted people for who they are and what they want to be, but made them fully aware that I wasn't interested and didn't care for the sort of attention they were eager to thrust upon me. One night I was on the 'practicals' position and ready to page in the cable connected to the metal staircase. As the scene came to an end, I assumed my crouched position and as the stage crew hauled the staircase into the wings, one of the male chorus who'd just stepped off it, went behind me and seized a generous handful of my genitals. I was busy with electrical cable so all I could do was lash out with my foot and he backed off.

Once the cable was stored, I followed him to the under stage area and asked him not to do that again. The next night he did the exact same thing. I kicked out with my foot and he scurried off through the prompt side door and under the stage. I coiled and stored the cable, followed him to the under-stage area and issued the same request. The following night, and for the third time, he repeated his inappropriate action to which he received the same rebuttal and a carbon copy of the verbal demand. On the fourth night I was nearly sacked.

Annoyed that after three nights he'd continued his pursuit of my undercarriage, again he got off the staircase and walked into the wings and it was up with the hand for a good rummage. I threw the hastily gathered cable to one side and belted off down the stairs after him. Within seconds I'd pinned him against the wall next to the crew room as my fist made a rapid but very firm connection with his cheek. Members of the company, unaware to the previous 2 minutes, stood there agog. He burst into tears and ran away as I went back upstairs to deal with the cable.

He reported me, and after the show I was duly hauled into the stage manager's office. "We can't have people assaulting members of the company" he said. In the late 70s, sexual molestation in a theatre was common and not seen as an assault. My boss Mick came with me and I explained top both them that I had repeatedly asked the cast member in question *not* to continue with his advances and that I had been 'provoked', I was allowed to keep my job but with a warning from the Stage Manager. It upset me because the particular member of the company was a nice chap, but his urges and unwillingness to accept the word "no" had caused me to do something totally out of character. It was, and still is, the first time I've ever struck anybody. It surprised me just as much as it did him, so we apologised to each other and that was that.

Early in my training, and long before I knew all the cues of each followspot, the leading lady's regular followspot operator rang in sick. Mick looked around the room and decided that tonight was the night for me to pop my cherry on the leading lady, so to speak. I had a rough idea as to what I was doing as I was already confident with the Juan Peron and Che Guevara followspots. "Don't worry", said Mick, "I'll talk you through it." The stage manager was informed of this sudden change in personnel prior to curtain up and was currently feeling more than a little slack in the bowel department. He'd have the mother of all 4'11" temper tantrums to deal with if it all went wrong. Mick took a long satisfying draw on his Marlboro Red, smiled and told the stage manager that "everything would be OK".

Up in the limehouse I set up my followspot as a niggling feeling of both apprehension and excitement crept over me. The houselights went down, the audience chatter melted away, and over the headset, the stage manager began issuing cues to the technical personnel. After a "go" Mick would chip in with helpful nuggets of advice "The next entrance is upstage left, opposite where spot two currently is …". Of course I had an inkling of what was next having done the other 2 followspots, but it was helpful not to constantly look at the cue sheet, allowing me to concentrate on what was happening on stage. Before I knew it, the first half and the interval were done and the second half was drawing to its conclusion. The show finished, the curtain calls came and went, the applause died down, the house lights came up and the audience spilled out into the West End. The stage manager had been in to see the leading lady and had informed her that a novice had been operating her spot that night. She asked him to thank me - which was nice of her.

I continued operating the leading lady's followspot from time to time but one day the question of the wall chart came up in conversation. "Whose not filled in any boxes recently?" asked Mick. I took this opportunity to wander over to the chart and fill in my last box - Evita's followspot. Dear Mick was heartbroken as I'd beaten him. I'd beaten the department head to be the first and to have memorised every single lighting cue in the show. He laughed in defeat and was a true gent about it all.

Tickets for 'Evita!' were serious money, so if you were lucky enough to get your paws on one you'd rightfully expect to see the cast as advertised. On the rare occasion that the leading lady was off, then the stage manager had the unenviable task of picking up a microphone in prompt corner and breaking the bad news to the audience: "Ladies and Gentlemen, for tonight's performance the role of Evita will be played by …", as a wave of disappointment came thundering towards the stage. Thankfully, a number of talented understudies stepped up to the plate, and there was something fresh that they brought to the role whenever they were on.

At the point in the show where Evita pops her clogs (spoiler alert) is a heavy and emotional scene. Plum in the centre of the stage, she lies in her hospital bed. Her followspot remained steady on her head and shoulders as the last few minutes of her life are played out. The stage was washed in soft blue light as the assembled chorus and Che Guevara surrounded her bed, heads bowed. At this point, the audience are in the palm of her hand, captivated by this emotional 'goodbye', some close to tears at the very note that it strikes. Breaking away from her pillows, struggling to sit up, Evita's outstretched arm gestures to her people as she asks them to remember her fondly. At which point this hypnotic moment was shattered by one of the stage followspot operators (the girl from Hornchurch) whose foot made contact with a can of weapons grade lager she'd taken up to her lighting position. It tipped over, fell through the gap above the wings and landed on the stage with a menacing thud. The active ingredients inside the can now turned it into an alcoholic Catherine Wheel as it span in circles at breakneck speed, sending uncontrollable jets of foam in every direction before slowly running out of puff, rolling down the raked stage and disappearing over the edge into the orchestra pit. Those of us who witnessed this extraordinary display did whatever we could to continue the show with some form of professionalism.

Amongst the technical staff of the West End there was a cash prize called 'the ghoster', something everyone sought. Let's say that there was a show that was ending on a Saturday night and another opening on the Monday, or that a theatre was putting on a Sunday concert. After the Saturday evening performance, the regular theatre crew and a handpicked group of others who they knew from the pub, would work overnight to strip out the old show and install the new one. As stated earlier, I was earning a colossal £17 a week as an electrical Dayman but these 'ghosters' could net you £25 a night - cash. I was 19, made of elastic and fun, but given a £25 cash carrot I was capable of staying awake for days.

On one of these ghosters I'd become friendly with the crew from the Duke of York's in St Martin's Lane. The theatre had recently been purchased by Capital Radio, and thanks to the station's very deep pockets, the place had been beautifully refurbished. The Dukes was now looking for a Stage Dayman so I applied for the job, went to meet the Max the master carpenter, and was hired on the spot. I knew nothing about carpentry but he was willing to teach me.

At the Prince Edward, a new leading lady was now in residence and soon it was my turn to move on. So long as no production bigwigs were in attendance during a show, the orchestra also enjoyed some naughtiness from time to time. My absolute favourite was when Che sang "And the Money Kept Rolling In (And Out)" and drummer Lenny Clarke launched into a fabulous reggae beat. The rest of the orchestra played along as the musical director rolled his eyes and submitted to majority rule. My last show was on a Saturday night and I cornered Lenny, telling him I was leaving. "Could you pease give it the reggae beat tonight?" He said he'd see what he could do as he followed his mates into the orchestra pit. Lo and behold, half way through the second act, an unmistakable reggae drum riff came out of the orchestra pit as every musician adopted a Caribbean swing. It was superb and I felt very lucky.

From A Prince To A Duke

As you travel down St Martin's Lane towards Trafalgar Square, you'll find the Duke of York's Theatre on your right. Built in 1892, its new freeholders were 95.8FM's Capital Radio and they had plans for the old girl. Not only was it a superb West End theatre but Capital now had their own private concert hall to hold Sunday music events and anything else their little impresario hearts desired. After major renovations, the theatre reopened in 1980 with 'The Rose' starring Glenda Jackson and I joined just as 'The Rose' moved out and Tom Kempinski's 'Duet For One' moved in.

The 640 capacity auditorium at the Dukes was far more intimate than that of The Prince Edward. From the back of the upper circle you could see the whites of the performer's eyes, which made all the difference to an audience. Should you be on stage between performances and need to converse with a colleague at the back of the stalls, then you could talk rather than bellow like a Sergeant Major. I came to love the Dukes as it was a far smaller venue and the crews were made up of far fewer people. There was a master carpenter (my boss) and two Daymen (me and an alcoholic) then a chief electrician and an electrical Dayman. Every theatre in the West End had a fireman who'd turn up for the performances and stay overnight. West End theatre firemen were not full-timers but the roles were filled by *real* London Firemen earning extra cash nonetheless.

Looking head-on at the exterior of the theatre, down the left hand side were a pair of heavy metal gates, the long passageway enclosed by brick walls 20 feet high with the stage door tucked into a dogleg corner at the very end. Two-thirds of the way down this wall was a pair of huge 12-foot wooden dock doors through which scenery and the like could be lowered down to stage level. Any large flat pieces of scenery were manoeuvred in this exterior passageway and swung through the dock doors.

Max was the master carpenter and my new boss. Kenyan-born and of Indian extraction, I became very fond of him as he taught me woodwork, fly-work (flying scenery in and out) and all kinds of subtle stagecraft with props and the like. Taking over from where Mick Underwood at The Prince Edward left off, Max must have seen something in me which convinced him to give me a chance. I was keen, and now that I was a stage carpenter (though I'd never picked up a saw in my young life), I couldn't wait to get started. I'd been given my share of mundane tasks such as tea and coffee making, sweeping the stage, emptying rubbish bins and shuttling the 50 yards between the theatre and Robert Dyas where I'd ask for striped paint, skyhooks and left-handed screwdrivers. "You work at the Duke of York's, don't you?" said the man behind the counter. How could he tell? Like newcomers everywhere, I was made to feel welcome at a price - initiation by humiliation. I was no longer amongst the lighting fraternity, this was something completely different and I had a lot to learn.

I was shown around the set of 'Duet For One' and compared to the multitude of complex lighting and stage actions during 'Evita!', 'Duet' had virtually none: lights up at the start of act one, down for the interval, up for act two, down at the end. The two-hander transferred from the Bush Theatre (in Shepherd's Bush) to the Dukes and told the story of a world-famous violinist who's slowly consumed by multiple sclerosis, eventually becoming unable to play.

She goes to visit a depressed psychiatrist who is inadequate in helping her deal with rage and frustration. So, a happy two hours of jokes and slapstick it certainly wasn't. The set was an office in the psychiatrist's home, filled with everyday living room furniture and windows looking out over a small garden. The protagonists in this dour but gripping piece were played by Frances de la Tour and David de Keyser, the latter possessing one of the finest sets of tonsils for the richest of voice overs. He was everywhere on TV: commercials, documentaries, film trailers, you name it and a really charming man to boot. Frances de la Tour had delighted TV audiences with her portrayal of Ruth Jones, the frustrated spinster in 'Rising Damp'. Produced by Yorkshire TV, it ran for 4 years and she was now a household name so the public flocked to see her in the flesh, so to speak. The Evening Standard Award for Best Actress went to Frances for 'Rising Damp' and the same year she won the Olivier 'Best Actress' Award for 'Duet For One' … oh, and wouldn't you know it, her husband at the time was the play's author, Tom Kempinski.

A devout socialist, she joined the Workers' Revolutionary Party in the 1970s, and if there was a political drum to beat, then she'd be front and centre. I found her to be a charming lady: fun and appreciative, always stopping to say "hello" before or after a performance. Playing the role of a disabled musician meant that Ms de la Tour spent both acts sitting in a motorised wheelchair. Our pre-performance duties included cleaning the set, polishing the plastic bay windows, hoovering the carpet and making sure everything looked spick and span. Other than that, it was just a case of flying in the main drapes and fire curtain during the performances. However, when the place was empty, the crew would hold regular wheelchair races around the stage, and if we were caught, rewarded by being yelled at by the management.

Ms de la Tour would drive down into the West End from her north London home and park her battered off-white Renault 18 estate on the double yellows in front of the theatre. Early in the run she asked the stage door keeper if he could please find someone to take her keys and park the car nearby. Somehow I was volunteered for the job. For the next six months, she'd park up out front, I'd meet her at the stage door where she'd hand me the keys with "Would you be a love?" and off I'd go on parking duty. There was, however, one stipulation: "Only park in an empty meter and *not* in an NCP car park". Although Max my boss didn't mind me doing this favour for her, he wanted me back well in time for curtain up. When an empty bay couldn't be found, I'd coax her grotty car into the nearest NCP, exchange the keys for a ticket and run like the wind back to the Dukes. Needless to say, Frances wasn't at all happy but I'm fairly sure she was earning enough money to pay for it. Up the workers!

Meanwhile, the West End said 'Goodbye Dolly' in January 1980 and sister Debbie had to wait until the October for her next show 'The Streets Of London'. Unconnected to the Ralph McTell song, the Victorian London comedy musical followed the fortunes of a number of characters. It was hysterical and in the programme Debbie was credited as '1st Prostitute', a moniker I wasn't going to let her easily forget. She'd get me the odd comp ticket for a matinee show and I'd sit in the stalls tapping my foot. Debs would spot me and throw me the odd wink. Michael Carter, who went on to play Gerald Bringsley, the werewolf's underground station snack in 'American Werewolf In London' and Bib Fortuna in 'Return Of The Jedi', was a riot in his solo number. The show closed early the next year as it simply failed to attract an audience, and as far as total and utter shames go, that show was one of them.

'Duet' closed, we took the set apart, opened the dock doors and winched the set, the furniture and two knackered wheelchairs up to street level and out to the waiting scenery lorries. The new show hadn't yet been announced so we waited to learn what was happening next.

An empty theatre without a production is referred to as 'dark' and it's during these times of nothingness that theatres get down to some rigorous maintenance and everything that isn't nailed down is given a serious once-over. The grid (the metal and wooden latticework above the stage, full of pulleys and ropes which supports the lighting bars, scenery and the main curtains) is thoroughly swept to dislodge all the years of dust and crap. Of course, it all lands on the stage and has to be swept up, after which the stage would be washed, and at times, might even be treated to a fresh coat of black paint.

Dean was the lighting Dayman with whom I struck up a firm friendship. Hailing from somewhere in Yorkshire, Dean was easy to get along with, plus he had a cracking girlfriend who worked in a theatre down the road. We decided that we wanted to learn to juggle so bought tickets to see 'The Flying Karamazov Brothers'. It was a brilliant show and of course we wanted to learn how to juggle. We each bought tennis balls and took them into work where, over several weeks, we'd stand outside in the passageway by the stage door, flogging ourselves to death trying to master the art of three-ball juggling.

The lightbulb moment duly arrived. After while we could effortlessly juggle three balls for minutes on end without dropping them. Next, standing face to face, we figured out how, on the count of three, we could throw one of our balls to the other and have it seamlessly replace the missing one in the circuit. After a short while we became competent jugglers with a routine we could launch into at a moment's notice. Without batting an eyelid, we'd flip tennis balls under our legs, throw one behind the back and catch it, juggle walking backwards and on the given word, could exchange balls as the distance between us gradually became wider and wider.

We advanced to practising with weighted wooden batons, then adding material to one end, soaking it in lighter fluid and setting them alight. As we threw these flaming sticks in the passageway people walking along St Martin's Lane thought we were part of a show, would stop to watch and applaud. Long after leaving the Dukes I continued juggling and my party piece was betting someone a drink that I could keep three items of their choice in the air for 10 seconds. However, each item had to be heavier than an ounce but no bigger than a bread bin. I was challenged with house bricks, vases, super sharp kitchen knives and even clogs ... the items became more and more bizarre but I always won my drink.

Capital Radio had a little something for us: a new radio production company needed a venue for a spot of promotion. They booked the Dukes for a half day and invited the clique of London advertising agencies to a couple of performances. Naturally, these performances were expected to convince agencies with the deepest pockets into using their radio commercial services. As their presentation didn't require a set, the entire thing could be performed on the narrow strip of stage forward of the house tabs (curtains). A well-armed technical crew came in through the main foyer carrying heaps of sound equipment and selected a spot halfway up the stalls to work from. We put sheets of 6' x 8' marine ply along the backrests of the seats and the theatre's electrical department made sure that sufficient juice was available.

The visitors then busied themselves by hooking up banks of reel-to-reel tape decks, audio control boards and assorted bits and bobs so we, the theatre staff, had absolutely nothing to do but enjoy the show.

The premise was this: a man would walk onto stage, smile to the audience and explain the benefits of advertising on the radio, at which point a ghetto blaster (which was on a table next to him) would chip in and disagree with whatever he was saying and an argument would ensue.

The banks of reel-to-reel tape decks were being spun by a group of really slick operators who were following directions written in their scripts and listening to verbal cues from the director. The voice of the ghetto blaster came from one tape machine and sound effects from others. The intensity of the argument between the man and the ghetto blaster rose and the salvo of noises and sound effects increased as the man began to lose the will to live. Finally, with his temper exhausted, he delivered a wonderfully rich verbal tirade at this smug and argumentative lump of plastic, which promptly surrendered and exploded.

Uncontrollable laughter from the invitees and a thunderous round of applause followed. The ad folk had not wasted their time and were treated to the best industry presentation they were ever likely to see. The director, sitting at the back of the stalls was Griff Rhys Jones and the man on stage was Mel Smith. Together they launched 'TalkBack Productions' who were looking to transfer their creative writing skills into making slick radio ads. This they did, and since then, 'TalkBack' has grown to be one of the UK's largest producers of television comedy and light entertainment programming.

The summer of 1981 rolled around and the next full-time tenant had been announced, so we gathered around as Max briefed us. It was to be a busy show with lots to do and was a celebration of Beatles music entitled 'With A Little Help From My Friends'. The scenery arrived and as Max paced the stage marking out the positions for the scenery, flats and risers, we got to work with transferring tons of it through the dock doors - the 'get-in' as it's known (you won't be surprised to learn that when a show finishes, is being packed up and taken out of a theatre it's known as a 'get-out'. Highly imaginative, I think you'll agree).

The set was made up of six boxes which housed three or four people, mainly the musicians. The boxes were arranged three across and two up with the contents of each box hidden from the audience by electrically powered venetian blinds. Whichever number was being performed, the relevant blinds would be opened to reveal the musicians and singers inside. Seeing as the blinds fell into the field of 'electrically operated practicals', normally they should be under the authority of the lighting crew, but no, I got the job. Squeezed next to the assistant stage manager in prompt corner, we shared a somewhat cramped personal space. The stage manager would sit at a desk making sure that the show ran properly and make whispered announcements through a microphone to call cast members to the stage in advance of their entrances. Our assistant stage manager was a really very pretty blonde girl, and over the weeks of rehearsal, we shared a good laugh as we learnt the show. Things progressed from there.

After meticulous rehearsing, non-stop and exhausting night shifts along with continual problems with those sodding venetian blinds, the show previewed to a broadside of critical reprimands. I wasn't surprised. It was a terrible concept and how it got financial backing, no-one ever knew. 'With A Little Help From My Friends' opened on July 31st and closed on August 8th, but the blonde and I were quite happy. The show was packed up and bundled out of the theatre before the newspaper ink had dried.

Max had devised a temporary structure which extended the performance area of the stage by a full six feet, but it did require removing the first two rows of seats in the stalls. The alcoholic and I helped him build a selection of hinged frames which were then topped with 8' x 6' marine ply. The seats would be unscrewed and stored under stage, at which point we could begin laying out the extension stage.

The underside of these heavy sheets of marine ply had a layer of asbestos (yes kids, totally legal in the 80s) which of course made them even heavier. Max was a few inches shorter than me but was as strong as an ox. He manoeuvred one sheet of 8 x 6, stood it on end and asked me to support it. He then got a second, a third and then a fourth. I was now supporting four sheets of really heavy, asbestos-backed marine ply and Max went off to fiddle around with the hinged base frames. Convinced I could shift my weight from one foot to another, I took my eye off the ball for a second and the four sheets decided to topple towards me. Putting all my effort into keeping them vertical, they came towards me. "Max!" I yelled, but it was too late as the lot came crashing down and pinned me to the carpet. Trapped underneath, I couldn't breathe and started to panic. Max raced over as was hauling sheets off me as quick as he could. Realising I was fighting for air, he dragged me to my knees, held my hands above my head and shouted "Breathe!" It worked and the tightness in my chest subsided.

I was in pain but it wasn't my ribcage or my lungs, but a knee that was bent and currently taking most of my weight. Around the proscenium arch of the theatre are located microphones which relay audio from the stage area to speakers backstage. During a performance, the company and technical personnel can keep an ear open and ready themselves for an upcoming scene. However, front of house could also listen in with speakers in the bars, the foyer, the box office and the theatre manager's office.

Such was the noise caused by the crashing timber that the theatre manager, a tall leggy Australian woman, came rushing down from her office. By now Max and the alcoholic had transferred me into the on-stage technical area (where teas and coffees were made along with a storage space for ladders, tools and paint), and sat me in a chair. They'd cut my trouser leg open to the thigh as blood ran down into my boot. My kneecap had been split open but at least I could breathe normally. Dressed in a tight black number and high heels, the theatre manager arrived. Max briefed her on what happened and she took the first aid box out of his hands and rummaged through it. Before too long she was kneeling between my legs and attempting to clean the wound using gentle dabs of cotton wool soaked in Dettol. Quite honestly, had she finished off by simply leaning forward and kissing it better, I'm pretty sure that would have worked just as well.

At the hospital, the nurses and duty doctor who attended me dealt with the problem area swiftly. The patella wasn't broken but it was severely bruised and the joint underneath having taken somewhat of a battering too. My chest was x-rayed, the gash on my knee was closed and strapped. I was handed a pair of crutches, told to rest and shown the door. Signed off work for three weeks, I met up with the blonde from the Beatles show on frequent occasions. I hobbled my way to the train station and under a tree in Windsor Great Park, we had a lovely picnic …

Once back at work, I was given 'light duties' as another Sunday concert came to the Dukes. The Comedy Store is a late-night giggle factory on the other side of Leicester Square. Opened in 1978, the club had previously seen life as a members-only nightclub, a revue bar and a strip joint, but its latest incarnation was a venue where up-and-coming comedians could showcase their talent to a roomful of comedy-hungry punters.

The names who found fame and fortune after passing through their doors would take a month of Sundays to list, but now the Comedy Store was bringing a full show to the Dukes for 640 eager members of the public. Everything was to be performed with the house curtains down, so Max's infamous extension stage was installed. I sat watching with a cup of tea in hand as Max and the alcoholic sweated buckets putting it together. Now without crutches, I could walk, albeit with a slight limp.

I made my way up the dress circle and leant against the back wall. The ushers knew me so a nod and wink saw me installed. At boarding school one of the things that kept me sane was the weekend treat of radio comedy. Pretty much all of it was on Radio 2 on a Saturday lunchtime. I'd sit on my bed, plug my earpiece into the little battery-powered radio and was ready to be captivated by 'Morecambe and Wise', 'The News Huddlines', 'Hello Cheeky!' and more re-runs than you could wave a stick at of 'Round The Horne', 'The Goons', 'The Navy Lark', 'The Men From The Ministry' and 'Hancock's Half Hour'. Most of this comedy had derived from ex-servicemen having survived a world war, full of close-to-the-mark one liners and packed with quick delivery off-beat humour. With a smattering of armed forces in-jokes, radio was by far a wonderful medium and just listening to the sketches allowed me to enter my own little world, dreaming up whatever visuals I wanted. My favourite of them all was 'The Goons'. It was anarchic and so off-the-wall it appealed to my sense of humour in spades. By the time I was 12, I could recite whole pages of zany one-liners and jokes. Many of my school mates just didn't 'get it', only because they weren't interested in my world of radio comedy.

What I saw that night on stage at the Dukes reminded me of the audible joy that had come flooding out of that little radio years earlier. The first act that caught my attention were two chaps who came out shouting at each other. They became physical, pushing and shoving, thumping and kicking. It was as exhausting to watch as it must have been to perform, and the audience lapped it up. These two belted each other with props, each contact being exaggerated by comic sound effects. It was sheer brilliance. "Thank you very much", they said as they left the stage, "we're the Dangerous Brothers!" You'd know them as Ade Edmonson and Rik Mayall.

Later on a couple of girls took to the stage and did their thing. Not a physical act, but one filled with excellent wordplay to which the audience howled with laughter. The taller one began bullying the shorter one, who in turn, did her best to stand up for herself and reverse the insults. French and Saunders got a huge round of applause.

Channel 4 went on air in November 1982 and on its opening night saw the debut of a show comprising of those very comedians whom I saw on stage at the Dukes: 'The Comic Strip Presents' hit the screens with 'Five Go Mad In Dorset'.

The initial heat between me and the blonde slowly cooled and we went our separate ways. For now I remained in the theatre but she changed tack, drifting into television. Years later she was to produce the cult BBC classic 'Red Dwarf'.

dsfsx....... (sorry, cat on the keyboard) The next full-time show to arrive was J P Donleavy's 'The Beastly Beatitudes of Balthazar B', an odd but highly enjoyable show which was far better received by the critics than that bloody awful Beatles tribute show. The cast of 22 was headlined by Patrick Ryecart and Simon Callow and it certainly gave the stage crew something to do during the performances. Dressed in brown work coats, members of the crew appeared on stage to position and clear scenery, and in one particular scene, to push a dolly loaded with 6 theatre seats containing the two males leads. Their characters were visiting a strip club in London, and on the other side of the stage some glorious creature was divesting herself of her outer garments. In the half-light of the scene I pushed Ryecart and Callow onto the stage, applying the trolley's rubber foot brakes, then turning around and walking back into the wings. Every now and again, just as I delivered them on stage, one of them (normally Callow) would half turn towards me and make some derogatory remark which would leave the audience in hysterics. Trying my best not to break composure, I'd apply the brakes, make a swift about-turn and stifle my laughter until I was safely back in the wings.

It was during the show that I fell for 'J', another assistant stage manager. She was 14 years older than me and wore jeans and a leather jacket topped with a bob of red hair. I invited her to the Marquee club in Wardour Street one Saturday night to watch a friend's band. I knew that if she came I was going to miss my last train home but no doubt I'd return to the Dukes and plead with the nightwatchman to let me sleep in the crew room. We went to the gig, we had a laugh and I walked her back to her motorbike. "Well," she said "you can go back to the theatre or you can come home with me." She opened the top box and produced a spare helmet.

The following morning I woke in a strange flat in Highgate and to the sound of voices. Alone in bed I surveyed my surroundings, sheepishly got up and threw on my clothes. I made my way along a corridor towards the voices and I stepped into the kitchen, a cheeky feminine smile greeted me from underneath the bob of red hair. I was then introduced to the Brigadier. I should explain. The Brigadier was a character from Dr Who, and some of you of a certain age might remember that it was Nicholas Courtney who played Brigadier Lethbridge-Stewart. He was a friend who had popped round for a morning coffee and a chat with J, the bohemian assistant stage manager who'd welcomed me between the sheets the night before.

Highgate was ideal for commuting as it's on the Northern Line, and when asked if I'd like to stay for a few weeks, I certainly wasn't going to refuse. I started work at the Dukes much earlier than her so I took the tube, my red-haired lover arriving later by motorbike. After the final curtain call, we'd quietly slip away, I'd grip her tightly round the waist and she'd navigate the bike through the traffic back up to Highgate.

Other Sunday concerts were booked in and we did several overnight ghosters to dismantle the existing set, do the concert on the Sunday evening and then flog ourselves stupid returning the set to normal. We did a show with Georgie Fame and Barbara Dickson where I became a tad over-enthusiastic with the dry ice machine, flooding the stage and causing the musicians to loose sight of their colleagues. One of the visiting technicals rolled a joint which, after a few puffs, had me crawling under the stage and passing out on a pile of coconut matting. Max found me and gave me such a verbal battering that I never did it again.

Over the course of a month, J became disinterested in her plaything and I was invited to leave as she moved onto another. One good thing had come out of our exhausting Sunday concerts at work, I'd become friendly with one of the visiting concert sound and lighting crews. The in-house setup at the Dukes wasn't capable of reproducing what pro musicians expected, so an outside company was shipped in, bringing their own kit. They were a fun bunch and I instantly took to them. By now I was renting a bedsit in West Kensington and the visiting crew had a job going at their warehouse in Chelsea. My juggling mate Dean was also interested, so we were both invited to take part in the strangest of job interviews.

The outfit in question was called M.A.R.S., Mike Allen Rental Services, was owned by the late Capital Radio DJ Mike Allen. His company had the contract to supply all of Capital's outside broadcasts with lighting and sound equipment. The station had a weekly Friday night radio show called 'The Best Disco In Town' and M.A.R.S. had the job of turning the Lyceum Ballroom into a thumping disco. Greg Edwards went live on the wireless from 11pm until midnight and all the cool kids made their way to London's Strand where they'd queue for hours hoping to get in.

37

Dean and I reported to the Lyceum's back doors at midday and one of the men from M.A.R.S. let us in. We helped them unload the truck and rolled all the flight cases down the ramp and onto the stage. Under supervision we helped plug it all together, and an hour or so later a break was called and the motley crew wandered round to a pub (now long gone) on the corner of Exeter Street and The Strand where they consumed copious amounts of foaming ale. A little worse for wear, we returned to the Lyceum to finish rigging the kit, switched everything on and tested it. During our libations, engineers from Capital Radio had come down from Euston Tower and rigged a pair of turntables in the centre of the stage. One of the engineers lifted a thumb, and nodding to one of the M.A.R.S. lads, spun a disco hit of the time. The sound that emanated from those massive speakers was truly astonishing. I'd been to enough nightclubs and embarrassed myself enough at discos but never had I heard anything quite this extraordinary. If a 12" single could be made to produce a sound this good, then I wanted a job with this lot, no question. Dean and I stood with the crew boss in the middle of the dance floor as the hand gestures between him and engineer on stage signalled the gentle tweaking of knobs as they fine-tuned the sound. To Dean and I, we couldn't tell the difference, but to the crew boss he was mixing the ingredients which went to make the exacting sound he wanted.

Once the lights had been set up and pointed in the right direction, the sound had been approved by other nodding members of the crew, we all returned to the pub on Exeter Street. I was now deaf *and* pissed. Some of the crew wandered off to buy sandwiches and one disappeared for a while to 'see a man about a dog'. As the two hopefuls, we were taken up to a dressing room where the rest of the crew were relaxing, enjoying the delights of vodka with a side serving of recreational drugs. I accepted a vodka, and then another. We had a toke of whatever was being passed around and looked inquisitively at whatever powder had been spread out on a mirror.

The show began at 8pm and a wobbly collection of grinning technicians stood line abreast down the side of the stage. One by one the crew disappeared up to the dressing room and returned a little later having topped up on whatever drug took their fancy. More drink was consumed as Capital handed over a crate of lager, and by the time the live broadcast had finished at midnight, I was stoned, drunk beyond belief but still standing. But only just.

At 1am the music faded out, the disco lights were switched off and the houselights came on. Hundreds of sweaty kids left with whatever they had pulled and hit the late night kebab shops. On the other hand, we had to get all this stuff down, into flight cases then back onto the truck. By 3.30am we were done and ready to leave, but where was Dean? He'd found a wee spot under the stage and had passed out. One of the crew shook him awake and crawling out from his hidey-hole, he gathered his belongings, grunted and staggered out into the night and away home. Out of the two of us, I was the one who'd survived unscathed (kind of) so I was offered the job. On the Monday morning, I handed my notice to Max and joined the men from M.A.R.S.

It's Christmas In Elstree

My time with M.A.R.S. was brief. Apart from the regular Friday night Capital show, we operated at some private functions and some larger events around the country. The warehouse was in Lots Road was a stone's throw from the Chelsea Embankment and next door to the power station. The company was renting a small office space in the corner of a much larger warehouse belonging to Zenith Lighting, who at the time were the biggest rock 'n roll lighting company going. Pantechnicons were constantly coming and going with tours from across Europe. Flight cases with bands' names were everywhere. Whitesnake, ZZ Top, The Human League, Depeche Mode … some of the longer flight cases were full of merchandise (mainly t-shirts) and we'd make merry by helping ourselves while they were around. From my bedsit in West Kensington it was an easy commute to Chelsea. I'd always walk it, especially during my only snowy winter. The North End Road was full of slush, delivery men were pushing barrow loads of produce through shop doors … whether it was Indian clothing or fresh veg, the populace would shout morning greetings over the noise or swear at those who'd overstayed their welcome in the unloading bays. I loved it.

After 'The Best Disco In Town', the tired crew would climb up into the lorry, and at a regular point on the route, would turn left and head over Chelsea Bridge. After a 17 hour day, a well-deserved break of a hot pie and a cup of tea awaited us. The infamous pie stall on the bridge was finally shut down in 2014 after a chequered 70-year history, but in the early 80s we were tired though still capable enough to stop for a tasty meat pie of indeterminable origin and a plastic cup of piping hot brown tea. I was enjoying my time at M.A.R.S. but didn't feel as though I was learning much. For a failed public schoolboy even I knew I could do better. The hours were long - really long - and when away from home I'd spend sleepless nights on a tour bus, wedged into my cramped sleeping compartment as my mates sat at the back listening to music, smoking, drinking and farting.

I detached from M.A.R.S. orbit within the year, handed back my keys of the digs in West Ken and moved back home much to the utter joy of my parents: the prodigal son had finally made a mistake and returned to the bosom of his family. "Get yourself down to the labour exchange" I was told for a second time. We'd been here before. It was 1982 and nothing had changed in time I'd been away. The high street was exactly the same and the labour exchange was as inviting as ever, though the front door of Manpower was now giving me that 'hello sonny, we've missed you' look.

"So," said the lady who saw me, "what have you been up to?" I gave her a potted history of my theatre exploits, though I failed to mention my brief sojourn into the world of music and recreational drugs. I was invited to take a walk around the office, look at the cards and consider some of the available positions. I wasn't a tradesman, I couldn't cook and I really didn't fancy washing up again. It took a few weeks but on one visit the nice lady sat me down, opened a file and produced a card. "Looking at your history, here's one job that might be for you. There's a company in Surbiton who do something with … lighting? I'm not sure what it is exactly, but they need someone quickly. Shall I give them a call?" In those days, the labour exchange used to ring on behalf of the job seeker and sell the individual to the employer over the phone. "Yes" she said talking to someone on the other end of the line, "he's a very nice young man and seems to have what you're looking for. Would you like to see him, let's say …" looking over her glasses at me for approval "tomorrow at 10?" I returned the nod and the appointment was made.

Playlight was the lighting company in question and their warehouse, in the shadow of Berrylands railway station, was the southern branch. Their large headquarters in the People's Republic of Salford being the Mothership. They made a nice little business for themselves renting lighting equipment to theatres, conferences, product launches and to television and film studios. Mark was the man in charge 'darn saff' and he showed me around the single story unit as two scruffy young lads sorted cables and stacked boxes. I answered his questions with all the relevant information I could from my brief four year career to date. He seemed impressed with my knowledge and my enthusiasm for the subject. He brought our meeting to an end, shook my hand and asked "Can you start on Monday?"

One of my earliest jobs was transferring kit: equipment that was in the Berrylands warehouse was often needed back in Manchester, and vice versa. Berrylands is a sleepy little enclave of Surbiton and not quite as posh. To transfer kit up and down the country, Playlight had worked out a little routine: Mickey, their Mancunian warehouseman, would load up his van and drive south down the M6 and onto the M1. In Berrylands, I'd load up our bright orange Transit, travel around the North Circular Road, join the M1 and head north. In the 80s, following a motorway shunt, the cops would simply drag the wreckage to one side and keep the traffic moving. Today's horrendous lane closures now give stranded drivers ample time to learn a second language, father illegitimate children or miss out on being included in the next census. We'd worked out that the halfway point between Salford and Berrylands was Daventry, and on leaving the motorway we'd both head for a predetermined lay-by.

It was rare to keep the other one waiting more than 30 minutes unless there'd been some kind of problem en route. Way before the advent of mobile phones, if one was late, the only form of contact was ringing either office from a remote public payphone. If Mickey and I had a meet at 2pm then I knew roughly at what time I'd need to leave Berrylands; we had no advanced traffic information back then but we'd a fairly good idea of travel time needed. On arrival, we'd open our respective van rear doors, back the vehicles up to one another and start swapping equipment. It looked highly suspicious but we were never stopped or questioned by the Police and they wouldn't have found anything untoward had they done so. We'd exchange paperwork, sit and have a chat then go our separate ways.

I delivered to and rigged equipment in theatres, television and film studios, exhibition complexes and hotel function rooms. Everything that headed out of Berrylands was checked and prepared and stacked by the door, whereas returning kit was checked in, given a throughout once-over and put back into stores. The work was varied and I was enjoying myself. Playlight had a regular client in Lee Electric, the UK's largest film and TV lighting company. In those days not a film credit rolled without Lee's name on it.

An American production company was filming a series of Gilbert & Sullivan comic operas at Shepperton Studios, 18 miles south-west of London. Lee Electric were the contracted electricians and had requested a lighting board operator from Playlight, so freelancer John Lytton was sent over. After the production had been filming for a week or so, John needed more equipment so I was drove over to Shepperton to deliver it. John was a really lovely chap and we got on famously. He's sit there for eight hours a day in a small anti-room on the side of Stage B at Shepperton operating a lighting desk which controlled the vast selection of kit that hung from the roof grid in the sound stage next door.

For reference, John had a black and white monitor which relayed ghostly images of the studio set and a walkie-talkie with which the gaffer would bark instructions as to which light(s) needed to be brighter, darker or off altogether. Your average film lighting technician back then was a highly capable individual, but as dimmable lighting technology was being introduced, they needed ex-theatre types to operate it. In film, a light was either on or off and it didn't change intensity, but more and more the film world was requesting the ability to adjust the lighting during the take - and as subtly as possible. This is where Playlight made its name as they had the most powerful dimmers, the best consoles and most of their staff had theatre or 'live' experience, so who better to operate it? John sat hunched over a large green panel made up of three banks of levers, 90 levers in all:

30 on channel A, 30 on channel B and 30 on C. He was well versed with the system, how it was cabled and what went where. If he was unsure of anything, he could refer to a paper schematic of the lighting rig which had taped to the wall next to him.

Born and raised in the heart of London's West End, John had been through his own initiation with theatre lighting. Now living in Surbiton, over time he was to become a very dear and trusted friend. We'd spend hours in pubs, talking technical, comparing experiences or just having a laugh. He went on to secure a job with the BBC in their studio lighting department but a few years later his life came to an abrupt and terrible end after he'd been seconded for a period of time to work on 'Eastenders' at Elstree. Every day he'd ride his custom-built Rickman Kawasaki motorbike from Surbiton, up the North Circular Road and onwards to the studio complex, but one morning an oncoming lorry ended his hopes and dreams. The very next day he had been due to sign on the dotted line for a new home: a houseboat on the River Thames. I was in Germany on a job the day of his funeral, but I'll get to that later.

So back to Shepperton and the Gilbert & Sullivan mega-shoot: it wrapped and it was time to collect the tons of lighting dimmers and sundry control equipment. Mark packed me off to Ryder Truck Rentals and at the tender age of 22, I hired a 16-ton box lorry (it was legal to drive something quite so big on a full car license). Gingerly, I took the truck over to Shepperton where the gatekeeper lifted the security barrier and I drove round to Stage B. Backing the truck tight against the side door, we began loading it. Once was full and locked, before me, the drive up to Manchester - alone. From the lorry hire depot to Shepperton was about 7 miles, which was nerve-racking enough but before me I had a 400-mile roundtrip, including an overnight stop. It was another of life's little adventures.

Some weeks later, Mark called me into his office to tell me that Lee Electric had another film they wanted Playlight to operate and this time it was a toss-up between John and myself. He teased me with this for a good few days, but the job was confirmed so he was having a little fun at my expense. One final tease was telling me that it was two weeks up at Elstree on the new Monty Python film 'The Meaning Of Life'. Knowing how much of a Python fan I was, Mark wound me up by pretending that he couldn't make up his mind. I was fit to burst when he finally announced that John wasn't available and that I was to operate on the film.

Lee Electric sent their order through and more kit was needed, so I went up up to Daventry to meet Mickey. "You jammy sod!", he said when I told him what the job was. "All I get is a half a day on fu*king Coronation Street if I'm lucky ... and that normally gets cancelled as I'm just leaving the depot!" I commiserated, and like the cat that got the cream, set out on my return trip.

It had been decided that all our equipment should be delivered in advance to Lee's in Wembley and that they would transport and deliver it to the Elstree stage. I was to arrive later, put it together and then operate across the shooting days. The next day was a Friday so I checked and double-checked I had everything: toothbrush, travel alarm, spare undies, shirts, jeans, hairbrush (now a distant memory) and cash. Lee's had booked me a bed at the YMCA at Welwyn Garden City, so for the coming fortnight, the orange Transit was mine. With a full tank of fuel and a cheery smile, I waved goodbye to Mark and the warehouse lads and headed towards the North Circular. To reach Elstree I had to drive up to Wembley, straight past Lee Electrics and then up the Barnet Way to Elstree. Now fully conversant with a variety of lighting control boards, I felt confident that this was going to be fun. I was away on my own for the first time, responsible for the success of something major, although at the same time maybe just a little terrified.

On arrival at Elstree's main gate, my name was ticked off the list and I was handed a plan of the studio complex. A felt tipped pen marked where I should park and the location of the stage in which I would be working. I had been to quite a number of studio complexes before and although each one was different, the buzz of stepping into a new one was still a novelty. As I walked up to my stage, the huge soundproofed doors were open and I could see the set down at the other end of this vast space. The stereotypical image that filmmakers use to illustrate a working studio with people running everywhere, trolley-loads of palm trees and background actors dressed as Roman Centurions or Nazis wasn't happening today.

As I stood between the open doors, I could make out what looked like a huge staircase at the other end of the studio and a collection of circular dining tables stacked against a wall. Three-storey floor-to-ceiling scaffolding stretched the length of the back and two side walls and technicians were starting to cover it in black material. It must have been 50 feet high. I stopped one technician who was on his way out and asked him where I might find Chuck, the gaffer. He produced a walkie-talkie from his back pocket and keyed the button saying "Chuck, someone to see you at the main door". A few words came back which I didn't understand but the technician pointed me in the direction of the staircase. I thanked him and picked my way through dozens of people busily piecing together this huge set. I found Chuck and he introduced me to his team of electricians, one of whom was called Stuart, so as it was likely to cause problems over the walkie-talkies. I was to be called 'Playlight'. These boys had been in the film game since they left school, and now even in their 30s could be classed as veterans. Their grandfathers, fathers, brothers and uncles had also been in the industry, and as each male of the family came of age, they received an immediate pass into the trade. As a group they were a friendly bunch, but at 22 with a posh(ish) accent, I was regularly the butt of many a joke. It didn't matter, the youngest or newest member to join a group would cop for remorseless teasing. The trick being to give (as respectfully possible) as good as you got.

Chuck led me round behind the scaffolding on the right hand side to where all my dimmers had been placed, and from where I was to operate during the film. If I needed to change anything then I was told to help myself and do whatever it was I wanted to make it all workable. The dimmers that we had supplied were powerful enough to work lamps from 2k (2000 watts) up to 10k (10,000 watts). To give you an idea of the physical size of an old-school 10k light bulb, imagine an adult male Cocker Spaniel in the seated position. Lightbulbs at they wattage were enormous and highly fragile, and if dropped, would often explode like a small bomb. The dimmers were the size of hostess trollies (if you remember those), though you could easily put your back out if you didn't handle them properly. I arranged them in power-order (easier to problem-solve) and plugged them into the studio mains supply. After unpacking and positioning the large lighting desk, I connected the control cables to the dimmers, found a chair (uber important) and went back to the electrical team.

With the lighting plan laid out on the studio floor, Chuck took us all through what went where, which lamps needed to be connected to my dimmers and which didn't. This was more for my benefit so I needed to pay attention. The scene was the 'Restaurant in Heaven', a giant nightclub with an orchestra that came out of the floor between the diners and the stage. The central piece was an enormous staircase with a doorway at the very top. Being in heaven, the monstrous black 3-sided background played the role of 'outer space' and was to be populated with thousands of flickering stars. I was to control the orchestra lights, some of the larger lights above the stage and all of the stars. We broke for a cup of tea, Chuck folded the lighting plan and handed it to me saying "Keep a hold of this and don't lose it."

After some general organising of my area post-tea, I was told that I wasn't needed for the rest of the day and that I should go and find my digs in

Welwyn, have some dinner, get an early night and come in 'bright and breezy' at 8am tomorrow - and that went for the Sunday too. The electricians, naturally, were union members so any overtime or weekend work was very well rewarded. They were already on a good screw but in the 80s but these extra hours were counted as double bubble. On the other hand, I was on a basic salary from Playlight with no overtime incentive at all - and certainly no weekend bonus. Still, I was working at Elstree on a Python film so that was payment enough. In no way could Welwyn's YMCA be classed as luxurious. It was barely acceptable, except it was to become the bane of my life for the next two weeks. Food preparation on the premises was strictly *verboten*, the bedrooms were uncomfortably basic and there was a good chance that I might be sharing with strangers. The front door of this nocturnal respite was locked at 9pm sharp every night and no keys were issued to its clientele. "We extend a warm welcome". Yeah, right.

Early the next morning, having missed a meal the night before and breakfast, I drove through Elstree's main gate and I noticed that the canteen was open and serving breakfast. Before reporting for duty, I dived inside and bought a goodly supply of takeaway items which should see me through until lunchtime. Back on the sound stage, the job that was going to take the longest was installing the stars which were to cover the black material on three sides of the set. In the middle of the floor was a pallet loaded with boxes. As each box was opened, it revealed smaller boxes in which were hundreds of sets of white Christmas lights. Chuck told us to take as many boxes of Christmas lights as we could carry, grab a screwdriver, a roll of black gaffer tape and climb the scaffolding.

Splitting into pairs, we mounted the ladders behind the black drape and climbed to the top level. Once in position, we'd take our screwdriver and push it against the black cloth until it popped through the other side. Removing the screwdriver (leaving a hole), we'd now push a Christmas light through the hole and then apply a small strip of gaffer tape across the wire at the rear to keep the 'star' in place. Repeat.

Once you'd installed one set, throw the cardboard box down to floor level and start on another string of lights but don't bunch the lights too close together and don't put them in a straight line either. Come the end of Saturday, our team of six had installed thousands of 'stars' and covered almost half of the black cloth, but tomorrow we'd do the rest. After that, it was down to me and my little brain to wire it up and bring it all round to the dimmers. I drove back to the YMCA eager for a shower and something to eat. I can't remember exactly what I found but I'm pretty sure it was a takeaway. Banned from eating it in the hostel, I ate in the Transit as exhaustion crept over me.

Sunday afternoon revealed that our many hours of handiwork had reaped rewards, though the reverse of the black material was now a mass of dangling flimsy wires. I sat down with some of the electricians to work out the best way to get them round to the dimmers and then how to group the stars into a random order. It wouldn't look good having them in huge clumps all twinkling together as they needed to sparkle haphazardly without any repeated patterns. We grouped the wires in bunches of ten, then each bunch was connected to a junction box, which in turn, was connected to a single cable which running round to the dimmers. At the end of the day, we had an entire sky full of working stars which I programmed into smaller groups on the control board. Chuck had the studio lights switched off, and as I lifted or lowered each group of faders, the stars began to twinkle. From my position behind the backcloth, I was the only person who couldn't see what was going on but the sounds of childish 'oohs' and 'ahhs' from the electricians out on the floor was the clue that it was working nicely. I later realised that it was at this point the piss-taking was gently toned down and that 'the posh yoof' had been accepted into the team.

Monday morning saw the construction of the main theatrical set move up a notch. The orchestra scenery and lights were installed and rows of 5k (5,000 watt) lamps were loaded onto lighting bars and hoisted above the stage. All the cables were extended and brought round to me as I allotted dimmers to plug them into, then assigned them to channels on the lighting console. I made sure that everything could be operated in separate groups: the orchestra lights in one group, the lights above the stage in another and the mass of stars in a third.

During downtime I'd go for short exploratory wanders around the other Elstree stages. 'Return Of The Jedi' took up a few of the other building, and although a 'closed set', the main doors of one were open so I took a crafty peek inside. On stilts was an Ewok village with little lights flickering inside the cabins. Lighting technicians yelled from inside to their colleagues as they adjusted the colour and position of the lights. The stage directly next to ours housed another scene from the same Python film. It was a swimming pool with men dressed in suits and bowler hats which would make up part of the number we were to film next door. Running down the side of one wall was the facade of an office block covered in scaffolding and plastic sheeting. I didn't know it at the time but this was one of the buildings from 'The Crimson Permanent Assurance', a supplementary short which ran before the main film.

A visitation of bigwigs and money men arrived, including director Terry Jones. Of course, I never got to meet Jones as I was sat behind the black cloth and listening to instructions coming over my walkie-talkie. The director of photography asked to see the effect given by different lights that had been plugged into the dimmers. Using the walkie-talkie, Chuck asked me to manipulate various lights, sone to go up, some to go down. FInally, the *pièce de résistance*, "OK let's see the stars". I flicked three sets of levers as the stars twinkled away for what seemed like ages. "OK, that'll do. Go and have a cup of tea". Apparently the bigwigs were happy with our weekend's work and we were stood down.

In case you haven't seen the film, the preceding 1 hour 40 minutes had seen members of the cast (and assorted extras) killed off and their souls now assembled in the celestial reception area. On arrival, they're informed that "*It's Christmas every day here in Heaven*" and sent through to the restaurant for dinner and a cabaret. The sequence begins with a Loumacrane shot (a long arm with a camera hanging off the end), and as the timpani rolled, the camera pivots to reveal the guests seated at their tables, and pulls up as the orchestra appears from under the floor. As they arrive, from my position behind the black drapes, I lifted a group of faders on my control panel and their lights began to glow. At this point the camera tilted up and the dolly was pushed forwards. The camera tech lifted the camera higher and higher as the whole thing advanced towards the stage. Finally, the camera came to rest at the top of the central staircase to find Graham Chapman who, after a short and insincere welcome in the guise of crooner Tony Bennett, bursts into song with "It's Christmas In Heaven".

There was one irksome problem I encountered with the orchestra lights: if the faders of the control desk started at zero and were quickly lifted to the level the director of photography wanted, then the lamps would snap from 'off' to 'on'. The trick I found was to start with the faders just off zero, allowing a smidgen of electricity to gently warm the filaments but without making them glow. A smooth increase of the faders from that point and the lamps would become brighter and arrive at their predetermined level.

By the end of week one they had shot all the arrivals, the seating and cutaway shot of the cast and background artists. At one point a giant wooden television was brought in and placed behind me. During the editing process, other elements of the musical number (such as the swimming pool scene from next door) would be electronically added onto the screen. As the camera swooped towards the giant screen in one take, it was at this juncture that one of my dimmers caught fire. We were right in the middle of a take so I tried to make the gaffer aware of this issue by whispering into the microphone of my walkie-talkie. Unsurprisingly, it didn't work as the music playback was too noisy so there was no way anyone was going other me. I dealt with the now heavily smoking dimmer by ripping the cables out of it and wafting the smoke with my lighting plan - whatever good *that* did. I had no idea what it would achieve but it gave me some thinking time.

I didn't want to smother the dimmer in foam from an extinguisher just yet so decided I needed to speak louder into the mic. Chuck came running round the back, saw what was happening and shot back out onto the set bringing filming to a halt. Each take on film cost a sodding fortune with over 100 people involved in this monstrous set piece. By the time some of my electrical mates had found their way round the back with extinguishers, I had manhandled the belching dimmer away from the others and dragged it down along the dark passageway and to relative safety. I had to convince the team not to ruin it with foam arguing that as the power had been unplugged there was very little danger of it getting worse. Thankfully I had a two spare dimmers so swapped them over and filming continued a short while later. During the lunch break I wheeled the de-funked dimmer out to the car park where it sat in shame, and alone the van, for the rest of the week.

For those who have seen the film, during the musical number there's a female Quasimodo who pushes a large bell only to get hit by it on the return swing. Her name is Teresa and she was one of the chorus/dancers on 'Evita!' and it was a lovely surprise to meet up with her again. Outside I stumbled upon a former Shiplake pupil who was now working for a film transport company driving scenery all over the UK.

As time went by, the days became longer as more and more footage needed to be shot. It was a technically complex scene and they needed their money's worth. As the evenings drew longer, then the chance of getting a meal was drastically reduced. The YMCA's front door was often locked when I returned and the nightwatchman became grumpier and grumpier as I finished work later and later. As the hostel received a busy transient population, leaving my personal possessions in the room whilst I was out at work was unadvisable. So every morning I'd pack and load my luggage into the van, and every night, bring it all back in. Showers were not allowed after 10pm and there wasn't a crumb to eat anywhere, so each afternoon I'd raid the Elstree canteen and fill a bag with sandwiches and slices of cake and wolf the lot down sitting in the YMCA car park. Life in the film industry was certainly proving not be be as glamorous as advertised.

Midway through week two and it was my moment to shine, or rather the time for the stars to do their thing. As the musical number picked up speed and the chorus chimes "it's Christmas, it's Christmas in heaven … hip hip hip hip hip hooray …" those big 5k lamps above the set banged on to full power and the thousands of stars came alive, twinkling for all they were worth. The musical playback began, my cue approached so I glanced at the video playback monitor. Tapping my foot in tie to the music I'd bring up each group of stars as required. It was manic, what with me whacking faders up and down at speed but it all seemed to work.

On the last day, the final take was finished and the scene wrapped. The actors disappeared, the camera crew de-rigged and I unplugged the dimmers, packed the lighting console into its flight case and made sure all the relevant connectors were handed back to Lee Electrics. My electrical mates helped load everything into my orange Transit van, I said goodbye to all of them and headed back to the dull normality of Berrylands. It was all over far too quickly as far as I was concerned.

By the time I arrived at the depot, everyone had gone home. There wasn't a soul to talk to, though as I could have talked the hind legs off a donkey, it was a possibly a saving grace for my colleagues. I wanted to tell them all about it, what fun it had been, all the things I'd experienced, that working on a Python movie was such a blast and that Welwyn Garden City was a shithole. When the film was released I toddled off to the cinema, eager to see my name on the end credit roller. I left the cinema more than a little disappointed as the last scene had been cut short and only the Lee electricians were credited. As Playlight were sub-contractors of Lee Electrics we never got a mention, though I later got one on IMDB.

A Brief Sojourn

It was back to run-of-the-mill operations after that, I'd had my moment in the sun so my colleagues now took turns at whatever goodies came along. During my time at Playlight I'd made a ton of contacts so thought I'd take the gamble and go it alone. Besides, I'd met this girl through a colleague at work, except she lived in Leamington Spa but would I care to move up country? At that time I was driving a light blue Citroën GS, and after informing my parents I was off, filled it with luggage and fuel and hit the M40. As it happened, I was doing myself a favour as the work I was after revolved around the conference/product launch world, most of which happened in and around Birmingham, Manchester and Leeds.

I'd become friendly with the production company which handled all of Cadbury's product presentations. Although they were based in Leicester, the boss made regular trips to Bournville to visit Cadburys to discuss their next big product launch. The next big thing on the chocolate agenda was the 'Wispa' bar launch for which we travelled the length of the country. It was at this time that my father had his first stroke.

My folks were living in Claygate, Dad been taken ill at home and had been admitted to Kingston hospital. At the time I had a pager which, when it went off, sounded more like a rape alarm and frightened everyone within a half mile radius. Should it go off, I'd then ring the central number (my mother) and whatever message had arrived for me would be relayed onwards. This time she told me not to worry as Dad was awake and, although a little slow, could communicate

I was at Gleneagles at the time on another show where Ronnie Corbett was the turn. He was a huge star and a national treasure, highly approachable and a really nice chap. Behind the scenes he'd sit behind us in a chair going over his lines. In the middle of the set was a door through which he'd enter and exit, his famous armchair placed in the centre of the stage. The corporate audience adored him and it was a joy to see him in so at home, though he wasn't in his usual television studio. There was no stopping and starting and no 'second goes' at anything. This was a one-hit affair, and he had to get it right every night. Once he'd been through the usual 'my producer' jokes, he'd come off stage grinning to himself, clenching his fists and smiling, knowing that he'd done a good job. He was a charming man to have around, and in the short time he was with us, we never saw any capricious behaviour, unlike others I could mention from the entertainment profession.

51

As far back as page 8, I mentioned that my Father was a fanatical gardener and as I left Gleneagles for the long return drive down south, I spotted rolls of turf in a pile waiting to be installed somewhere on the estate. Thinking this might make an ideal present for the old man, I stopped the van and helped myself to a single roll. When I arrived at the hospital he saw me coming down the hall, gave me a weak wave and smiled. Thankfully he went on to make a full recovery. He began driving again and returned to work. Once able to do so, he dug a square out off this lawn and laid that single roll of turf. Life looked like it was returning to normal, until out of the blue, he had a second stroke.

When I was a nipper, Dad would return home from the office each evening with two newspapers: the Evening Standard and the Evening News. Being in the advertising biz, his firm would often place ads in both papers so he'd buy a copy of each just to see for himself how they looked. After dinner we'd sit and do the crosswords together. He would give me the easy clues and I would try to work out the answers. It was our nightly routine which was brought to a close at 9pm when Benjie the Bedlington wanted to go to the pub. My father's second stroke left him in a far worse condition than the first. But now here I was in my 20s, sitting next to him on the sofa and helping him hold a pen, showing him how to write his name. Those evening crossword sessions came flooding back to me as I was being torn apart from the inside. We did the same crosswords in the same newspapers, only this time it was me encouraging him to find a four letter word from a simple clue.

On returning to Leamington it soon became apparent that my girlfriend had been entertaining a number of others whilst I'd been away, so I packed my belongings and returned south, eventually finding digs in Walton-on-Thames in a charming 3-bedroomed semi owned by an even lovelier redhead. She liked me and I liked the house.

My new landlady soon decided to rent out her 3rd bedroom and another male moved in. We all got on famously, spending hours stretched out of the sofas having a laugh. My landlady's weakness was sex, though sadly not with me. She and the new lodger were at it like knives and when they weren't in physical knots together, they tied it officially.

The jobs kept rolling in, though some were a little off the beaten track. I was sent back to Scotland and to a castle which sat slap bang in the middle of a Glen (aren't they all?). In daylight hours the castle looked stunning, wrapped in its stone grey jacket with the surrounding Scots Pine-covered mountains towering over us. However, at night the place gave everyone the colley-wobbles. Battery giant Duracell was launching a new torch: a flip-lid gizmo ideal for the boot of your car or the garden shed. If you needed a hands-free light anywhere, flip open the lid of this wee torch and 'let there be light'. To illustrate the true potential of this device to its sales force, Duracell had booked this castle for a week as we, the technical crew, lit the inside of the building, the outside walls and even the grounds. We then staffed a three-day sales conference in the castle's main room, its walls decorated with coats of arms and stags heads with surprised expressions on their faces.

The cheery on the cake was not just the unveiling of this torch but how they were going to illustrate its capabilities. That afternoon the crew had been issued with dozens of these little torches along with a pile of bamboo canes and rolls of electrical tape. We sat strapping the damn things to these poles for hours, checking that they all flipped open and worked. After a generous aperitif at sundown, the invitees were ushered outside into the castle grounds and corralled into a giant circle. We ran around inside the human circle sticking these canes into the grass. The castle illuminations were extinguished, and apart from the available moonlight, it was both dark and eerily quiet. On given command we made a second circuit flipping open all the torches as the distant thump-thump of a helicopter could be heard.

The noise came louder and louder, and as the machine came into the hover overhead, the pilot could clearly see our makeshift circular landing pad. The heli's lights came on and it slowly descended as the rotor wash began blowing sales reps in all directions. The huge yellow air-sea rescue helicopter settled on the grass, the flight crew waved to the ensemble, the engine pitch changed and up it went back into the night's sky. As the sound of the helicopter faded away, the MD (pointing a torch towards his face) addressed his staff and we collected the canes and went in for dinner.

Another booking came in from a highly respected production company based in a Mayfair mews. I knew the boss well as he'd booked me several times previously and taken a shine to me (not in that way). He invited me and a few others up to his office as he took us through the job at hand. The home-video system VHS had a rival: Betamax. Sony were releasing their all-singing all-dancing tape system to the UK and were planning a country-wide launch to selected members of the public. It would be free to attend, just so long as they got their names down early. The model(s) being promoted would be connected to a video projector and hooked up to a pro sound system and the video players would be demonstrated using clips from well known films.

The audience were invited to sit through an hour long presentation hosted by Noel Edmonds while my lighting design turned the stage area into an illuminated masterpiece (he says modestly). Our Betamax show could only take place midweek as Noel was busy with his 'Late Late Breakfast Show', rehearsing on Fridays with the live hour-long broadcast on Saturdays. Therefore, we only did one show a week and the workload was bearable. It took two days to rig and an evening to pull down and pack away. Mr Edmonds proved to be funny and an utter professional. After a few weeks, when we felt that a mutual respect had been established, we'd throw in the odd curve ball during the live performance: a giant rubber spider dropping from the lighting rig, the wrong film being played or giving his microphone helium-like sound effects. The audience shrieked with laughter at all this tomfoolery, and because Noel had years of live TV experience under his belt, he handled our playful exploits with aplomb. With a huge grin and looking to us at the back of the room, "Yeah, yeah, very funny you lot!" Calm and professional, the show continued as per the script.

At the time Noel owned an Augusta helicopter with the registration G-NOEL. The show arrived in Harrogate and the hotel's front garden was large enough to accommodate his whirly bird. To the delight of those wandering through town, Noel came in low and landed on the hotel lawn. Met by the hotel manager, he was brought through to the room we were working in we began a rehearsal. Every now and again the script changed to accommodate new technical information, jokes or stage directions. As the rehearsal wound up, Noel invited us all out for a curry. The table of 9 chowed down, and as more drink arrived, the ruder the jokes became. Since then, and for the rest of my days working with or around personalities, I have never experienced such warmth, sincerity and generosity from anyone else. With four TV channels at the time, the BBC/ITV ratings war was forever ongoing, but Noel's Saturday 'Late Late Breakfast Show' was regularly pulling 18 to 20 million viewers every week, numbers that would be out of the question these days. He was the BBC's biggest primetime star, unselfish and utterly likeable to boot.

The video projector that was used on the Betamax tour caught my eye as, surprisingly, it was also being used on Noel's TV show at the time. The engineer knew Noel and I'd become friendly with the different engineers who turned up to operate them. The company, Link Electronics, was based in Andover in Hampshire and their projectors were the General Electric PJ5055. Link hired them out (with engineers) for conferences, films and TV shows. These things could punch an image onto a cinema-sized screen without a problem. As it happened, my mother had taken the decision that she and Dad would move out of Surrey and to somewhere far gentler and (certainly) cheaper: Milford-on-Sea in Hampshire. On the southern tip of the New Forest, the village of Milford was built on a spit which stretches out into the Solent. Life would be easier for the pair of them and without the stresses of business for my father. As it happened, this worked out nicely as Link were recruiting for another projector engineer, so with the connections I made on the Betamax tour, I applied for the job. I was offered an interview and drove down to Andover, met the boss and was given a tour. Within a day or two I had been offered the role and then the hunt began for new digs in or around Andover. I was soon to be nearer my folks and that made us feel a little better.

The Missing Link

I bade a fond farewell to my humping landlady and her new beau, and moved into the top floor of a manor house in Appleshaw, a village a few miles to the west of Andover. The elderly widow who owned this pile was straight out of 'Upstairs Downstairs' (the Upstairs bit) and a geriatric family friend, a retired army Colonel, had a bedroom 2 doors down the corridor from hers. The top floor had three bedrooms, a spacious kitchen, a cosy living room and a freezing bathroom. Nothing up there had seen a lick of paint, a fresh sheet of wallpaper or a square inch of new carpet since Disraeli refused to reinstate the Corn Laws. The lady of the house spelt out the house rules and regulations: "You can only park your car round the back, not at the front. You can enter and leave the house only by the kitchen door and you cannot use the front door under any circumstances, and you are certainly not allowed to entertain any female callers." The retired Colonel, who was party to this regulation showdown, twitched and grunted as only retired Colonels can. Such was the Manor's location that I would often lie in bed at night, kept awake by the live weapons firing on neighbouring Salisbury Plain, or be gently woken in the morning by the sounds of Olympic silver medalist Lucinda Pryor-Palmer exercising her horses in the paddock behind the house.

During my time as a resident of Appleshaw, its population was a mere 380 souls. A matter of a few miles from the Wiltshire border, this delightful little village sits just north of the A303, the celebrated holiday caravan highway which runs a full 94 miles from the M3 to the west, all the way to Honiton in East Devon. Once the locals at The Walnut Tree Inn pub realised I wasn't some chinless wonder from the smoke coming to fill a second home with duplicate chinless wonders, they welcomed me to become part of the community. The pub had a couple of playful forehead-height oak beams which caused more than a few sore heads. A knackered dartboard hung from a wall and a bar billiards table became a firm favourite as I spent many an hour downing frothy pints and making sure that it was expertly propped up. Eight miles down the road is the Army Air Corps base at Middle Wallop where the military trains its helicopter pilots. The pub's landlord was previously an army engineer who serviced and maintained Gazelle helicopters, and as soon as his time in HM Forces was up, the couple had fallen in love with the area and decided to stay, taking over the tenancy of The Walnut Tree. Their lunchtime menu was basic: the usual Cottage or Shepherd's Pie, chunky soup or a ploughman's lunch, with the evening fayre being a bag of ready salted crisps and a pickled egg. However, to balance it out, the beer was excellent and the atmosphere relaxed and enjoyable.

My training at Link Electronics didn't go as I had originally hoped. Their General Electric projectors were made in their factory in Syracuse, New York, and ordinarily Link would fly the new employee over for a week's training. This time they decided to fly the American instructor to the UK and have him teach me in the Andover office. If memory serves me right, I believe the instructor was due to fly onwards to another customer in Europe, so it was cheaper to have him swing by Andover first.

Based on the Walworth Trading Estate, Link had made a name for itself as a manufacturer of television cameras, in fact the only British camera manufacturer still in existence at that time. The BBC had a number of Link's 110 and 125 cameras and a few ITV companies and European broadcasters were also starting to take an interest. The company also made a business equipping outside broadcast vehicles, taking empty pantechnicons with expanding sides and fitting them out to the customer's specifications with sound equipment and multiple camera controls.

I have no idea as to why Link began hiring video projectors, but financially it proved to be a good investment. At the time the PJ5055 was the Rolls Royce (or Lincoln Continental if you prefer) of the video projector world. The beating heart of the machine was a 'light valve': a glass disk rotating through a bath of warm oil. An electron beam 'drew' a moving image onto the oil on the disk and the focussed light from a xenon bulb then threw light through the disk and a picture was shot out of the lens. Clear?

These projectors were highly popular and Link had some lovely customers. The BBC incorporated these projectors into their sets and they appeared on (as previously mentioned) 'The Late Late Breakfast Show' when Noel Edmonds would converse with guests on outside broadcasts and chat to his man-on-the-spot, Mike Smith. They were used on 'Wogan' at the Shepherd's Bush Theatre when Terry used to interview someone on the end of a satellite link, the guest would be projected onto a huge screen centre stage. Up in Tyne Tees, they were used on 'The Tube' and over on Yorkshire TV it was 'First Tuesday' and 'Where There's Life'. Back down to London where Thames TV redesigned the set of 'This Is Your Life' and made the video image an integral part of the show, projecting video clips and messages from assorted guests. It seemed that nearly every television set designer in the UK wanted to use a huge video screen, and as Link were the only people at the time with the right kit, then more engineers and more machines were required.

Although technically-minded, I wasn't 'component-level' technical, if you get my drift. If someone walked me through how a system worked, then I might be able to logically figure out how to fix it should it go wrong, but talk to me about capacitors or diodes and I'd be lost. The projectors had their own characteristics and individual personalities, along with a multitude of tweaks and adjustments. Shadowing the experienced engineers I soon learnt the sequences required to operate these machines and how to correct any problems. I was taught the mathematical formula to calculate the best lens for the desired screen, and from time to time, my mentors would twang the settings of a machine out of kilter whilst I was out of the room, then have me figure out what had been done and set about rectifying the problem(s). Over the coming months I became accomplished at the operation of this expensive and highly temperamental marvel of technology, and problem-solving became second nature. Once I had illustrated that I was competent, I was then let out on my own.

After some time traveling around the UK on a variety of assignments, I was given the chance to go on my first foreign trip. As we were locking up one night, the British-Dutch oil giant Shell rang to say they were holding a sales conference in Lausanne, Switzerland, and that they needed a projector and operator ASAP. Given the time scale, they were told that they'd have to cough up for a private air charter to Geneva and without batting an eyelid, they rubber-stamped a private plane.

A twin engined aircraft was booked from Southampton airport and the aviators were given details of a projector and passenger to work out weight and balance, whilst back in Andover, someone hastily prepared a carnet. For the uninitiated, a carnet was an internationally recognised form of financial bond. If you wanted to take an expensive piece of kit out of the country, you'd hand over a large cash deposit to HM Customs, and assuming that the carnet was correctly stamped on the way out of the UK, again at the point of foreign arrival and again when you returned to UK soil, then you'd get your deposit back. This bloody thing was a bundle of green, white and yellow pages which needed be examined in great detail by everyone in authority and then stamped by everyone else - they were a fu*king pain in the arse, and thanks to Brexit, they're coming back into use.

A colleague drove me and the projector kit to Southampton airport, and with the charter crew, we loaded everything into the twin-prop aircraft. The pilot and co-pilot mounted up, and as four seats had been removed in order to get all my kit in, I sat some way behind them. The plane powered its way up into the afternoon sky, and a couple of hours later we landed at Geneva, parking on the 'private aircraft' side of the airport. Hastily, the kit was unloaded as the pilot hurried off to file his return flight plan. "We want to get out of here before it gets dark", he told me. With a wave, the cabin door was closed and locked, the engines started and the most expensive taxi I'd ever taken buggered back off to Southampton. I sat on my flight cases amid rows of shiny Learjets and waited for ... well as yet no one had told me what for.

This was years before mobile phones so I just sat there as millionaires and their amusements taxied left and right. A curtain-sided 3-ton truck drive arrived and a dishevelled man jumped down from the cab waving a sheet of paper and barking instructions. At that point I didn't speak any French so any conversation with the locals was held in slow and loud English. The driver and I slid the projector and my luggage into the back of the truck and he indicated that I should stay with it for some reason. We arrived at the Customs hut where a Swiss official thrust out his hand requesting "Passport". I handed it over and turned to my hand luggage from where I produced the Doomsday Book (that bloody carnet). He took ahold of that too, and now joined by a colleague, slowly - ever so slowly - began thumbing through the pages. "I want to see ...", he said pointing at various items listed on the pages "this and this ... and this". I opened the fight cases and produced the things he wanted to see. This is what customs people did to those with carnets, they wanted to check individual serial numbers. On handing the items over, he slowly cross-checked serial numbers and descriptions on the carnet. He stamped the carnet in several places, removing the pages that Swiss customs needed to retain and handed everything back to me. He turned and walked away, a dismissive hand waved in my general direction on his departure. My grumpy truck driver waited for me repack the items and then strapped the boxes into the back of his vehicle. Now invited to sit up front, we left the airport and headed over the top of Lac Leman for the hour's run to Lausanne.

The job itself was fairly uneventful, except for a video crew who'd flown in from Heathrow. Shell's conference was possibly a gold medal contestant for the 'Most Boring Of All Time'. The production crew were seated behind long tables at the back of the room, but a cameraman stood in the middle of the seating area with his sound recordist sitting on a chair close by. Part-way through one particularly monotone delivery from a puffed-up oil exec, the soundman gave an enormous single snore and fell off his chair. Priceless. Contagious stifled giggling passed amongst the crew as tears began to stream down our faces.

Car giant BMW flew a large crew out to Singapore to launch a new vehicle destined for the Asian market. When flying commercial, such was the delicate light valve, it had to be removed from the projector housing and travel in its own flight case. Production companies were forced to pay for *two* seats: my bum in one and the light valve in the other. However, on long haul flights my travelling companions became a little jealous as I'd just put the light valve on the cabin floor and I'd have two seats to myself. The job in Singapore involved long hours but the food made up for that. One highlight was a mathematical conundrum involving the 16th floor of the Shangri-La Hotel (our digs), a bowl of fresh fruit and a swimming pool. We knew that 'X' was the room 16 floors up, but what effort was required to propel 'Y' (the fruit) over the patio and for it to land into 'Z' (the swimming pool)? To be fair, a fresh mango hitting flat calm water at terminal velocity at 3am makes quite a lot of noise by itself, though as we were to learn, not quite as much as the hotel's terrified peacocks as they ran around in the dark, shrieking in uncontrolled panic.

It was soon time for me to make my debut at the BBC on 'The Late Late Breakfast Show': an early morning run up the M3 from Andover and in through those famous gates at BBC tv Centre in Wood Lane. Once installed, the projector was positioned backstage and lined up on the rear-projection screen built into the set. I'd done all my technical checks so after lunch the studio went for a rehearsal. Noel arrived and took his place in the doorway of the set waiting for the theme music to start. He looked over in my direction and I grinned. He looked perplexed. The theme music played over the studio floor and he continued to look at me as I continued grinning. Just as his cue arrived and he was to step to into the set, the penny dropped and he realised where he knew me from. Smiling, he raised an arm, waved and walked onto the set. Later, after the second run-through, Noel wandered over to my position and we had brief chat, confirming what I said about him earlier: he was very welcoming and pleased to see me again but now installed as part of the crew on *his* baby at the BBC. 'Breakfast Show' was a huge success, the flagship in the Corporation's Saturday evening programming with a third of the UK's population tuning in. In comparison, if a show these days gets viewing figures of half a million, then it's seen as a hit. I did two series of 'Breakfast Show' and loved every minute of it.

Earlier I mentioned Yorkshire Television's 'Where There's Life', an early evening medical magazine show hosted by Miriam Stoppard and Rob Buckman. My visits to YTV were always fun and the crew in Leeds couldn't have been nicer had they tried. I'd drive up from Andover and spend the night at the Dragonara Hotel, reporting to the studios the next morning. The crew would help me load in, and during the lunch break, would take me over the road to a spit-and-sawdust pub for a pint of Tetley's Ale and a pie. Once back at YTV, the studio technical manager would bring me a roll of cable with a plug on either end: one of which would be connected to a numbered junction box on the wall behind me, and the other to my box of tricks which then went to the projector. My equipment included a colour monitor so I could keep and eye on what was coming down the line and an oscilloscope to check that the signal was technically correct.

TV shows always need an audience so programmes like 'Countdown' and 'Where There's Life' had a plentiful supply from the old folks homes in and around the Leeds area. They'd be bussed in, made to feel welcome and given a seat in the warm studio. I settled into my spot behind the set as the recording started, Stoppard and Buckman doing their best to keep the audience awake with various topics of medical discussion. Every now and again recording would come to a halt for a retake or a change of lighting. It was usual and pick-ups were quick and seamless.

At one point, a murmur grew around the audience followed by a gasp. The place ground to a halt and the floor manager flew around the set towards me. "What the hell are you doing?!" he yelled. I was caught off guard and had no idea what he was on about as I'd been sitting here quietly reading a newspaper. "The picture, man!" he screamed pointing at the projector "Cut it!". Another of the other studio staff was looking for a way to turn the projector off so I stepped in and switched it into standby, "What do you think you're doing for pity's sake?!" he bawled, I was still shocked and without a clue as to what was going on. The old dears in the audience were being placated by the floor manager, being reassured that all was well and that we'd start again in a few moments, but "in the meantime if anyone would like to use the facilities then you'll find them down just the corridor".

By now a small crowd had gathered around me. A very angry man (the director I assumed) stormed towards the group as they launched their enquiry as to what had happened and whose fault it was. I remained deeply perplexed.

A television studio is wired in such a way that sound and vision can be distributed though a matrix system to any part of the building that is similarly connected. So let's say the VT department reserves socket A165 for a particular programme and can send pictures down that line to studio 1, 2 or 3. In any of those studios, if someone connects to the corresponding A165, then they can see and hear what the VT department is sending. Earlier in the day the VT department had assigned my projector to socket

A123 (or whatever it was). With my projector now connected to A123, it showed whatever came down that cable and was projected 8 feet high.

During the recording, some bored technician on the other side of the building had decided to share his private collection of German hardcore porn with a chum elsewhere within Yorkshire TV. Thinking that A123 was unassigned, he connected his VT machine to A123 and gave three dozen OAPs the uncut version of 'Herman The German Plays Captain Wobbly Hides His Helmet'. Once the group of angry studio staff realised that I played no role in this ad hoc smut-show, apologies were made and my area was emptied. I was left as red as a beetroot, my heart thumping like a drum, but did they really think that a reputable contractor would do something like that for kicks?

The Northern Irish boxing sensation Barry McGuigan was to fight Zambian Charm Chiteule at the King's Hall in Belfast, so with a projector kit in the back of the car, I set off for Liverpool docks and the overnight ferry. The fight was a sell-out so the organisers had arranged an overflow auditorium in the city centre's Grand Opera House. My projector was set up in the limehouse above the Upper Circle. Live television images from The King's Hall were to be sent via satellite a matter of three miles down the road to where my projector was rigged. The fact that the signal had to travel around 44,000 miles to get there meant that there was a slight delay, but that wasn't going to interrupt the enjoyment of the hungry boxing audience.

Before any live event it was always advisable to empty one's bladder, so slipping out of the limehouse I made my way to the Upper Circle toilets. With so many beer-fuelled Northern Irishmen passing water I thought it best to keep my English accent hidden and to avoid small talk. The loud conversations at the urinal were all about the fight but the swaying man next to me asked my opinion. Thinking that the best course of action was to remain totally quiet, I then launched into the best Belfast accent I could muster. Spluttering as short a sentence as I could, I was out of there PDQ and safely behind the locked door of the limehouse shortly after. Thankfully, the fight went McGuigan's way and I packed up, left the Theatre and on arrival at my hotel, rolled the projector into my room for the night and left for Liverpool the next morning.

The Ministry of Defence had heard how good these projectors were and booked one for a demonstration at RAF Marham in the flatlands of Norfolk. On arrival at the main gate, the equipment was thoroughly searched and I was thoroughly poked at by men wearing caps and carrying automatic weapons. Once through security I was given directions as to where I was to report. Pulling up outside a dumpy single-story brick affair, next to a sign littered with a mass of military abbreviations, I was met by some of the base staff. They were absolutely charming, nothing was a problem and as their civvy guest, they made sure I had everything I wanted.

RAF Marham was the HQ of the Air Force's Photographic Intelligence Unit, and apparently, the boffins had devised a new photographic process which they were going to demonstrate to Government Ministers and assorted RAF bigwigs. The flip side being that I couldn't stay for the presentation as it was classified. "Your machine doesn't have a recording facility, does it?" one of them asked. "No", I replied. "Ahh, good. Just checking." I was asked to set up the projector, guide one of the RAF personnel through what they needed to know in order to operate it and then kindly invited to bugger off.

With the projector ready to go, a uniformed escort walked me over to another single-story blockhouse where I was to remain for the duration of the secret presentation.

The RAF has the world's largest collection of stereoscopic images, or stereo photographs if you prefer. The process creates the illusion of three-dimensional depth from two-dimensional images. Basically, an angled pair of cameras are placed side-by-side in the belly of an aircraft, and together photograph the same image - be they a landscape, a city centre or a foreign military target. Both photos are then viewed side-by-side through a pair of lenses with the result being a stunning 3D effect. My escort hauled out folder after folder of declassified images to keep me amused for the rest of my incarceration. It turned out to be a fantastic afternoon.

Back in Appleshaw, not having a telephone at the Manor House was a problem. One Sunday afternoon I was dozing in front of the fire when the Colonel came wheezing upstairs to inform me that I had a telephone call. My father had had a third stroke and was in a bad way down in the New Forest. I rang my boss who told me to take as much time off as needed. The next few weeks became a blur as I went to stay with Mum and visited my father a couple of times in the nursing home. Though breathing unaided the doctors seemed pretty convinced he wasn't going to make it so prepared us for the worst.

One morning the house phone rang and Mum remained riveted to the spot. I answered the call and yes, Dad had died a few minutes ago. He was only

61 years old. My memory of the time I spent at Milford with Mum right up to the funeral in Bournemouth has become unclear but it was traumatic and upsetting for everyone. A few days after the funeral, I needed to get back to work but poor Mum went through hell on her own. I'd been given quite a lot of time off already so other family members were needed to take the strain. A few months later, she moved back up to Surrey to be closer to Debbie and Jenny, to where I was to follow (unintentionally) very shortly.

There were developments in Andover and things were changing rapidly. Link's latest TV camera, the 125, wasn't selling as expected. They'd poured a lot of money into its R&D and things had soured. The only department making *any* money was ours, effectively keeping the company afloat. Dave, the boss of the Displays department, left and joined a new and exciting outfit based in Chessington, Surrey, taking two experienced engineers with him. Of course, I wanted to join them but I was told to "wait a while longer but your turn will come". Trying to hang on to their existing projector engineers, Link gave us an incentive of a 30% pay rise. I spent my time teaching the newcomers and our *new* boss was soon announced: another Dave. The *new* Dave had previous projector experience, and although it took some time to get to know him, he turned out to be a really nice and generous chap.

The new outfit everyone was quiet so eager to join was called 'Starvision', owned by a holding company called 'Avesco'. They started off by forming 'Viewplan', an audiovisual facilities company who serviced conferences and trade shows the world over, and now they'd invested in a giant 22-tonne mobile TV screen" the Starvision. This thing was a direct rival to Mitsubishi's 'Diamond Vision' which had previously been seen by millions during Live Aid at Wembley. The Starvision had been developed and built by the English Electric Valve company (EEV) in Colchester, Essex and lived on a 40-foot trailer.

Split into two halves, the idea being that the top half of the screen would flip up and 'sit' on the lower half. Imagine placing a book on a table, spine uppermost. Take half the pages and splay open one half of the book so both outer covers stand at 90 degrees to the table - the outer covers being the screen surface. That was how Starvision opened and the hydraulics required to lift the 11 ton lower section needed to be seriously powerful. This new technology had enormous potential and drew people like me to it like bees round a honey pot.

64

The call from Chessington duly arrived, so tendering my resignation at Link Electronics, I said goodbye to The Walnut Tree Inn and decamped from the Manor House.

The Screening Process

A flat had become available above a framing shop in East Molesey's high street and moved in, starting work with Starvision in Chessington 6 miles away. I soon became captivated by this giant screen. It was simply enormous and the logistics of moving it around were equally as fascinating. Edwin Shirley Trucking, based in East London, had been engaged to haul the screen to anywhere it needed to go - a very long and happy relationship started right there. Edwin Shirley began as a theatre lighting and sound engineer, then opened his rock 'n roll trucking business, expanded into staging (they built the stage for Live Aid) and developed a film studio on Three Mill Island. His trucking company, EST (Edwin Shirley Trucking), was the driving force behind every big band who went out on tour. Brian May of Queen once said "Edwin was at the head of Queen's vehicle convoy for so many years I can't begin to remember how many". There was another phrase doing the rounds. "You haven't really made it until Edwin Shirley is moving your gear around." With declarations like that, who better to be moving our screen?

I learnt how to fold out the trailer supports, wind the legs down with a crank handle whilst making sure the whole thing remained level. Then it was onto the operation of the screen itself, how it unfolded, where to plug the video signal and how to figure out what's gone wrong in order to fix it. The screen ended up on a yearly summer tour of country shows co-funded by Diet Coke and Citroën cars. The screen would be parked up along the edge of the main display ring, our cameras covering the action for those who couldn't quite see what was going on. We hired the screen with or without cameras and we became our own mobile production unit, engaging freelance cameramen when required.

Due to its popularity, it became obvious that we needed another screen, so EEV sold us a second one. The firm had also bought the GE PJ5055 projector that Link operated, and since Starvision was staffed by experienced former Link employees, then it seemed like a good idea to buy a couple. Along with a projector I was whisked over to Germany to work on the 'Monsters Of Rock' tour, the breeding ground of long haired leather-clad Europeans with highly questionable personal hygiene and awful German food. Both me and my projector were positioned high on a scaffold tower in the middle of the crowd, a solitary security guard doing his best to keep long-haired music fans from climbing up and joining me at the the top. I now had to put up with hours of brain-battering metal music, a constant barrage of fireworks thrown by excited fans whilst ensuring a good image on the screen. The Scorpions were the headline act and we did shows in Nuremberg, Heidelberg and Mannheim. It was during one of the earlier shows that on a daily call back to my Chessington base that I was asked to ring someone who'd been trying to get hold of me. I did and was informed that John Lytton (whom I worked with at Playlight) had been killed on his way to work. His funeral was to take place the day after the Mannheim show, and as there was no way I could be replaced, so as soon as that show ended, I packed up as fast as I could and drove overnight for the ferry at Calais. By the time the ferry delivered me to Dover, John's funeral was underway, though I arrived in Surbiton as his mother, his ex-girlfriend and bunch of other friends were toasting him in his living room. John was one of the best and I still think about him today.

The Starvisions were getting some serious miles under their belts and as the bookings came in, new staff were taken on. As winter turned to spring, the summer schedule was announced. The year after Live Aid, Queen were booked to play Wembley Stadium in July 1987 followed by Knebworth in the August, and Starvision was the chosen screen. This was a big deal for us and idea of the event became really exciting. Dave ran us through the schedule and, for once, it didn't sound horrendous.

On Thursday July 10th, together with the screen and a 350 ton mobile crane, our crew of four gathered outside the players tunnel at Wembley. Here I'm talking about the original Wembley (the proper one with the white towers) in which the player's dressing rooms were accessed down a tunnel which allowed easy access for visiting coaches etc. So the crane lifted the screen off its trailers placed it onto 4 huge steel roller-skates and then the whole thing was dragged up through the tunnel and put back on its trailer at the other end.

Needless to say the entire process to get the screen to where it needed to be took ages, so I won't bore you with the details. However, once sitting below the stage on Wembley's running track, the screen had to be craned up onto the scaffolding so the truck and crane positioned themselves where they needed to be as we began securing lifting chains to the screen. If you happen to stumble across the DVD of "Queen, Live Magic", you'll see this entire operation in the extra's section, and if you're *really* quick you'll see me and my colleagues beavering away.

We then climbed the scaffolding and waited at the top for the screen to arrive. Up she came, very *very* slowly as the four of us stood at the top. Via radio messages, the crane driver delivered 22 tons of screen right where the riggers wanted her, and once bolted down onto her steel joists, we unhooked the chains and the crane driver lowered the arm and began packing up. Well, that wasn't so bad, was it? It was 11pm and it had taken a few hours but here she was. All that was needed now was to power her up, unfold the top half, switch her on, check that she was working, then sod off to the hotel for a few hours sleep.

Who said that?

The roof of Wembley stadium was an ancient steel framework covered with corrugated sheeting. With all of us up on the screen, Dave the boss noticed something which we all picked up on: "You know, when the top half opens, I don't think it's going to clear that sheeting." He had a point. A strip of 2 x 4 wood appeared as we began to mimic the arc the top half of the screen would make as it opened. To be honest, there was really only one way we were going to find out if it would make it: open her up and check with the Mark 1 eyeball.

As the hydraulics system pushed 11 tons of steel and electronics towards Wembley's roof, it was a nail-biting affair. With a matter of a few feet to spare, Dave he brought proceedings to a halt by yelling "WOAH!!!" Indeed, someone had got their sums wrong: either the set designer had botched their distances or Wembley had issued them with an out of date building plan. The screen simply could not open, though pleased that it wasn't our fault, here beginneth the tale of how it was fixed …

A number of Queen's management were still up in Newcastle supervising the clear up operation following that night's performance at St James' Park. As Thursday evening turned into Friday morning, their panicked Wembley colleague made an equally panicked phone call to Newcastle: "The screen doesn't fit and it's all gone horribly wrong!" Well, not strictly true as it would have gone in nicely had someone not buggered up their measurements. The reply from Queen's management in Newcastle made it perfectly clear, "If the screen isn't in place and working by Friday night, then the band won't perform and the show will be cancelled."

Our boss, the crane driver and a few riggers from the staging company put their heads together to find a solution. I believe it was the veteran crane driver who resolved the problem. He suggested that with the screen still bolted to its scaffolding joists, they bring it down and place it on the running track. We'd then open the screen, and by lashing the chains to the outside of the frame, the crane would lift the screen in the 'open' position, something that had never been done before.

The driver started the crane, and with our combined sphincters sounding like an out of tune barbershop quartet, he gently started lifting the 22-tonne screen all the way to the top of the tower, where the rigging crew waited to reattach her to the scaffolding. In 1986 a Starvision cost somewhere in the region of £1M which was a fortune back then, so this was all or nothing. With sighs of relief it worked, and apparently the crane driver was rewarded with a small brown envelope. With the screen in place, we'd plugged her up and pumped some video through her. She seemed happy enough. I forget what time we finished but the dawn chorus were clearing their throats, leaving us a couple of hours to get some sleep - we had a show that night.

Throughout the Friday night I was based up at the screen, and as the riggers had installed wooden scaffold planks behind her, at least we had an area to walk about, store spare parts and tool kits etc. However, it was July and the electronics had been working for hours so the generated heat inside this metal box now resembled a Turkish prison. I've often wondered what it must be like for a band to experience the roar coming from a crowd of 80,000 people and now I knew. It was extraordinary and terrifying at the same time. A rush of noise that gave me goosebumps and a chill I'd never experienced before.

After the support bands had done their bit, the crowd waited impatiently for the band they'd all come to see: Queen. From my vantage point above the stage I had one of the best seats in the house. The into playback started, smoke issued from each the side of the stage and the audience went wild.

One of their well-known guitar riffs cut through the air and the decibel level from the 80,000 out front went off the scale. Freddie and the band came out and were met by a wall of sound that rushed towards them. I remember looking at a colleague as we both gawped in utter astonishment, riveted to the spot.

Our boss Dave was towards the rear of the stadium with a walkie-talkie, and whenever there was a problem with the screen, he'd radio it through and we'd fix it. The image on a Starvision screen was produced by blocks of cathode ray tubes (CRTs) mounted in square panels, or 'tiles'. When a tile failed, or was causing problems, it would often just go black, but they often flickered. Dave would guide one go us to the problem tile by playing a giant (reversed) crossword game: "Top section, 3 down from the left and 8 across!" A simple matter of 4 screws, a control cable and the offending tile was whipped out and quickly replaced. We had more than enough spares and the screen was pretty well behaved over the two nights.

Any number which involved crowd participation was a delight to witness. 'Radio Ga Ga' was perfectly executed by the fans who clapped with the accuracy of a metronome, and Freddie's question-and-answer sections also went down well. He'd sing a few notes and the crowd would sing them back. Directly underneath me was a stuffed lighting rig, but I could clearly see Freddie, Brian May and bassist John Deacon. Keyboard player Spike Edney was hidden at the side of the stage and my view of drummer Roger Taylor was blocked by some of the lights. The day before, as I was packing my bag, I'd thrown in a disposable camera. Freddie was dressed in his infamous yellow jacket, and as he splayed his arms, he thrusted his head backwards and my little Instamatic went *click!*

After the Friday show, were were joined by some of the office staff who'd come up to watch the concert. We hit the hotel bar and let rip. The show on the Saturday was a carbon copy and by the time we'd completed the job and the screen was back on its trailer outside the stadium, it was early-morning on Sunday. We'd been on the go for well over 24 hours. For some reason, we'd taken our own cars to Wembley and I remember driving down the North Circular and then the A3 only to see my colleagues pulled over into lay-bys and fast asleep. Eventually reassembled in Chessington, our second wind had kicked in. We locked the screen away, thanked our truck driver, as one by one, we left for our respective homes and some well-deserved sleep.

The company ended up with three screens and shipped one of them to the 1988 Calgary Olympics. It sat at the bottom of the ski jump as Eddie The

Eagle flew off the end of the 90 meter ramp. I didn't go on that job but *did* get to go to Turkey as a travelling election campaign delivery boy. Let me explain: Turgut Özal was standing as President and his party had hired a screen, two engineers, one truck and two Edwin Shirley drivers for a couple of weeks. The screen was driven cross-country by the 2 drivers, and once on-site, we travelled to towns and cities around Turkey broadcasting Özal's live election speeches and pre-prepared videos to the electorate.

The Turkish production company, who'd booked us, was run by two brothers who's Istanbul office was located on the Asian side of the Bosphorus. On a rare day off, the brothers asked me if I would pop over and help out with some editing. Back in the UK I had taught myself to edit video using a basic 2-machine VHS system. It was a clunky hit-and-miss affair but it was capable of the basics. Anyway, one of the brothers picked me up from my hotel in their huge American car. This thing was vast, very bouncy and had typically elegant sweeping tail fins. Once at their office they asked me to take my shoes off, which I did, and someone took them off to be cleaned by the urchin I'd seen sitting on the pavement outside. I was given a seat and a hot sweet coffee as the reason for my honoured visit was revealed: they wanted me to 'edit' naughty American films for the secret world of Turkish black market porn.

They detailed what the Turkish market would and wouldn't accept, showing me what I could leave in and what I had to withdraw (!). I diligently worked my way through a couple of films, for which the brothers were highly appreciative. In the early evening I was driven back over the Bosphorus and to the hotel where, over dinner, I regaled my colleagues with tales of strange 'goings-on' over the water in Asia. Thinking that I'd made a fistful of Turkish Lira on my day off, I was able to disappoint my colleagues by showing them my spoils, when from under the dinner table I produced a clean pair of shoes.

Having a screen at horse race meetings was becoming popular. I was shipped off up north with 'Starvision One', now a screen everyone had their own reasons to loathe: she was the oldest, most bloody-minded and not always technically willing to play ball. From time to time her electronics would falter, leading to bursts of colourful language. The picture would flash, parts of the screen would flicker, and then out of sheer spite, she'd shut down all together. However, even in the 80s, 'turning it off and turning it on again' worked a treat.

Sheltering in the porta-cabin on the front of the trailer, we heard the course announcement of the runners and riders for the next race. Brough Scott,

Channel 4's horse racing guru, along with a 3-man television crew arrived at the bottom of the steps and asked if someone was available for interview. My oppo, being closest to the door, decided he wanted no part of it but told *me* that there was someone outside who wanted a word. I stepped down the ladder and was asked by Mr Scott if I would be "available for interview" as they'd been fascinated by the screen for some time and thought they'd share it with their viewers. "Sure", I said. "Oh and it's live, is that OK?" he added. The cameraman was framing up and the sound guy was pushing a fluffy mic under my chin, so I could hardly refuse.

On hearing that I was going live on 'Channel 4 racing', my oppo rang our office on a giant portable mobile phone of the day and gave them the heads-up. The interview was brief but enjoyable, well up until the final question. I had been asked a range of technical details which I dealt with rather professionally, like "how many pixels made up the screen" and "how heavy was it?". I rattled off the details without missing a beat but Mr Scott then threw me a question to which my answer kind of let the side down: "Is it reliable?" I look round at the old girl, hesitated and replied "Well, she has her moments."

Interview over, Mr Scott thanked me and I climbed back up the steps and into the warmth of the cabin. The phone rang and it was Dave in Chessington. "What did you say that for!?" Yes, I could have said "she's great and never gives us a moments worry!" but I didn't and that as the last time I ever conducted an interview about the screens, live or otherwise. If proof was needed why I have remained firmly *behind* the camera ever since, then that's the evidence that would be produced before the court.

By now the editing bug had bitten me and I loved splicing video together, creating all sorts of fun and interesting clips. The VHS systems had been upgraded to Lowband U-Matic (Google it) and was a definite step-up in the quality stakes. Whilst out with the Starvision I'd sit in the control cabin and cut away to my heart's content. At the end of one of the summer Coke/Citroen tours, I took "Bridge To Your Heart" by Wax and cut a clip together using shots complied over the summer months including the crew and as much fun and frolics as I could find from the tapes on the shelves. Dogan, our favourite freelance cameramen, I believe still has a copy. He married Sally, one of the Diet Coke girls from the tour, we still keep in touch, and with their three children they now live in Stratford Upon Avon.

As Starvision now had three screens, our Chessington depot was too small to house them all, so the office was relocated to Alton in Hampshire and the screens were stored in a yard in Southampton. The drive from East

Molesey to Alton wasn't unpleasant but did add an extra 2 hours to each day. Just before the A31 branches off the A3 at Guildford, there was a second hand car dealership on the left. Each time I drove south and onto the A31, I noticed a black MGB GT winking at me from inside the dealership. One day I pulled over and asked for a test drive. The salesman and I headed up the A3 towards Ripley, and the second I found the overdrive switch on top of the gear stick, I'd fallen head-over-heels for this machine. Once in my office in Alton, I rang my bank to arrange payment and so began a wonderful relationship.

My creative juices were in full flow and more and more I found myself thumbing through job announcements in the trade press. A videotape (VT) editor's job had just become available at an independent facility in Teddington, owned by two former Thames Television engineers. Now, listen up as the following is a lesson in how to dig a hole for yourself…

I rang the facility, found out what they did exactly, quizzed them on the equipment they had and if they might consider me for interview. Now this was the 80s, long before easily accessed online material was available, so as they read out the list of equipment, I wrote it all down. Once we'd arranged an interview time and date, I rang Sony, Panasonic and Abekas and asked them to kindly send me the relevant spec sheets (documents that list the performance and characteristics of the product), and a few nights later, I thumbed though them trying to figure out what it all meant. Some of it was obvious and fairly easy to understand, other bits less so.

Straightening my tie and a final look at my shiny shoes, I presented myself at the front door of a semi-detached house in Teddington. Two former domestic dwellings had been converted into one all-singing, all-dancing edit facility with two suites, a room with 50 VHS machines used to bulk copy films etc., and a Master Control Room, from where sound and vision could be distributed to other parts of the building. A third detached house was owned by a company who specialised in compiling pop promos bound for the wall-mounted screens of glitzy fashion shops of London's Oxford Street and beyond. A mass of plastic tubing between the houses carried audio, video and control cables as one company churned out pop promo compilations for the other. Of course there were lots of other customers who came down looking for editing services such as ITV production houses, corporate video businesses and TV holiday shows.

I was given a tour of the place and each of the rooms were explained in great detail. 'Edit 1' was a mass of screens, flickering computer data and a bank of tape decks. I'd read about the edit controller the previous evening but now looking it squarely in the eye, my initial enthusiasm about this venture was making a break for the door. The equipment we had at Starvision was child's play compared to this. Once the visit was complete, the owners took me for a proper sit-down interview in the pub on the corner of the street. We got on well enough and I told them about my limited knowledge editing but engaged them with informed conversation about shooting in general.

To my utter amazement, I was offered the job. The paperwork and contract would be posted within a few days but had I bitten more off than I could chew? I'd just been offered a job for which my sole responsibility was to operate equipment I'd only read about from spec sheets but never touched in my life. I drove home to change and then head down to Alton. For the rest of the day my head was filled with doubt: should I accept the job or put my hands up and come clean?

A few days later, the screen and I were on another horse racing job at nearby Kempton Park and throughout the day I kept sneaking off to re-read the contract that had arrived the day before. I loved the screens and the jobs we got do, but working outside in wintertime was getting on my wick. Signing both contracts, I posted a copy back to Teddington. I'd made my mind up and that was that. The following morning I asked Kempton's press office if I could use their fax machine. I fed in my letter of resignation and it spat out at the other end, landing on Dave's desk in Alton. At 9.05 the phone rang as Dave 'wanted a chat'. I knew I was leaving a very capable and buoyant ship but I was going to do something a little more creative for a while.

Cutting Crew

Within a matter of hours it was fairly obvious that I hadn't a clue as to what I was doing in 'Edit 1'. The boss sighed and took me through the theory and operation of the computer editing system. Yet another example of someone taking the time to show me how things works and I could then duplicate it for myself and expand my knowledge. To cut a long story short, bits fell into place and eventually I managed to figure this thing out. Within a fortnight I could read and understand the mass of timecodes on the screen, spot and fix irregularities, work out why certain bits of kit weren't functioning and how the effects units should be programmed in order for them to work in sync with the rest of it. I was soon dreaming up new ways to produce really funky effects that weren't listed in the operation manuals.

I cut a show for ITV London charting the history of Pantomime starring Ken Dodd. Of course, we did heaps of pop promo compilations and corporate stuff for companies with pockets deeper than the Mariana Trench. A producer and cameraman 'borrowed' some space from the edit facility and we used to hold drinking sessions in the pub on the corner. I seem to remember that the link between me and the cameraman was the late John Lytton? Anyway, the pair of them had clients who'd fly them business class to the Bahamas just for a 30 second shot of something. This was the era where promoting a good corporate image meant throwing as much money as was necessary at whatever it was you were trying to achieve. Not for me, as the only golden beaches, crystal clear waters and dusky maidens I ever saw, were to be found on the magnetic tapes I was handed.

Dave at Starvision asked me to produce a promotional film for the screens, which I did. He went through the archives in Chessington and I picked up lots of great footage. I wrote a script and asked Philip Elsmore, the veteran Thames TV continuity announcer, to voice it. It was signed off and my private fee was paid, with the edit facility getting their cut. My time at Teddington was most enjoyable as I shared edit duties with a colleague who was pretty much stoned most of the time. However, it all came crashing down around me when I met dear Raymond.

We loved our regular clients but there was one in particular who could be (and was often) a total pain in the hole. Renowned for being disorganised, Raymond had booked an overnight edit and my stoner colleague had been assigned to the job. I was on the day shift and had been editing since 10am, but now it was just after 5, Raymond's booking was due to begin at 6 and I was looking forward to going to the pub. I began cleaning up my edit suite by putting tapes back into boxes, resetting equipment back to zero, clearing coffee cups off the tables and plumping up the cushions on the suite's 'client only' leather sofa. As reality dawned on my stoner colleague that he had Raymond to contend with all night, he rang in sick. Well, you would wouldn't you? Now sitting in reception, Raymond was anxious to get going but my boss took me to one side and asked me if I'd do the night shift as well. M y heart sank into my boots.

Making a round of coffee, I led Raymond up to Edit 1. Altogether he had a box of 10 hour-long tapes and 3 more in a carrier bag (classy). He sunk into the leather sofa and announced "I haven't actually looked at any these so I've no idea what I've got". Oh God. He handed me the first tape which I slotted it into a machine and pressed 'play'. Raymond was expecting to walk out of here with a completed 27 minute show, edited and mixed in the next 15 hours. At 8pm my boss popped his head round the corner, asked if everything was going well and threw me a sandwich that he'd bought for me in the pub. He wished us "good night" and closed the door. Ten minutes later, I'd finished the sandwich.

2am rolled around and I was losing the will to live. At times we increased the speed and spooled through tapes as Raymond was busy writing time codes and making notes on his pad. By 4am I'd had enough. Raymond had booked the edit suite until 9 am and there wasn't a hope in hell he'd get a finished show in the next five hours. His sarcastic side reared up as he began reminding me how much pressure I would be under because we were still skimming through tapes. By 5am the lid of my pressure cooker burst and left for orbit as I gave him both barrels. "We're still spooling through tapes and you expect a finished programme in four hours?!" We exchanged words, and picking up his tapes, he left. I switched everything off, locked up the facility and went home. I knew I'd done wrong but the guy was being a jerk.

My slumber was interrupted by my home phone ringing at 8am. I was hauled into the office and summarily dismissed. To date, that is the only job from which I have been sacked. My 'sick' colleague had now miraculously recovered enough to work the day shift. As I was being shown the door on the way out, he appeared and stopped to talk to me on his way in. "See? I told you Raymond was a twat!" I was furious about the sacking for days, if not weeks. It felt as though my boss had pandered to a selfish and unorganised idiot. A regular client he may well have been, but expecting quite so much without the minimum of preparation was too much.

Westminster Calling

It was 1989 and I was forced to adopt my fallback position and to pick up my lighting skills for commercials and conferences. My wonderful MG was still my mode of transport, though the occasional hired Transit van was required to move the big stuff around. I don't remember much of that year but as 1990 came around, one of my old contacts from Starvision days called with a suggestion that was to kickstart the next 27 years: "There's a TV news outfit up in town and they're looking for someone to shoot and edit for them. Here's their number …" I'd never shot news, so in for a penny, I called them.

At the time, the Guinness Trial was underway at Southwark Crown Court. Basically, four greedy multi-millionaires were accused conspiring to drive up the price of Guinness shares during a 1986 takeover battle for the drinks company, Distillers.

A new and going-places independent facilities company had moved into the basement of the QEII Conference Centre opposite Westminster Abbey, and were looking for someone to help out. Although government-owned, the QEII housed TV studios on its minus 2 level and the BBC, ITN and Sky News moved in. Whenever Westminster's politicians appeared on TV, then all the footage passed through the broadcasting wiring systems down in the basement of the QEII.

Although I believed that I was a confident shooter, news was a different animal all together. On arrival at the QEII I was met at reception and escorted down into the bowels of the building. One of the facility staff showed me the camera kit, I was given a tripod and a rucksack with spare batteries and tapes but told to keep all my taxi receipts in order to be reimbursed. A slip of paper was handed over with the address of the courthouse and I was to get whatever footage I could and be back here in 3 hours. During the short taxi ride to the Southwark Crown Court in SE1, I examined the camera. This was a pro machine and (as I was to learn) cost in excess of £40k, with the lens an additional £22k. I switched it on and played with the buttons, then figured out how to eject the cassette housing and put in a new tape. The microphone inputs worked exactly the same as those on cameras of which I had previous experience, so that was one worry off my mind.

On paying the taxi driver, I saw the gaggle of press waiting by the steps leading up to the courthouse. I found a spot to sit and somewhere I could leave the tripod. There were hoards of camera crews, news photographers, assorted journalists and courier motorbike riders, so space was at a premium. The bikers would grab the latest cassette from their allotted camera crew and speed it over the bridge to the QEII, and into the sweaty palms of whichever TV channel was paying them.

The court was a busy place with briefs in flowing gowns gliding back and forth, with junior clerks staggering under the weight of files in cardboard boxes. A constant stream of people came and went through the doors as each and every one was pursued by the pushing and shoving press pack. I followed suit.

"Who's that?" I'd ask one of the veterans. "Oh that's so-and-so, he's the brief for such-and-such." On the paper insert of the cassette box, I noted times and names. When the other crews became excited, picked up their cameras and started shooting, I did the same. One of the accused, flanked by his demure and loving wife and a seriously expensive brief, delivered one of those heartfelt pleas asking that he be understood and that the case be dropped. We all knew that these bastards were as guilty as hell. As I didn't have a soundman, I couldn't get good audio but I'd push and shove, trying to get to the front of the pack each time one of the accused gave whatever impassioned speech his brief had written five minutes ago. My time was soon up, so flagging down a black cab I hoofed it back to the QEII.

Handing the tapes to the editor, I relaxed with a cup of tea. "Well" he said a few minutes later, "it's not the best footage I've seen, but it'll do". It was true, the footage was crap but it was my first time and they could tell. Launched by an ex-ITN cameraman, this small company was fast making a name for itself as an affordable facility that hired out camera crews and edit suites. TV cost a lot of money to make back then, so rather than try to bankrupt everyone, this new facility offered clients special half-day and hourly rates. Two of their freelancers could it all: they could shoot, they could do sound, they could do lighting and they could edit. The company made an absolute killing.

I was taken into the edit suite and my mistakes pointed out to me. I grimaced at what I saw on screen but accepted my shortcomings, turned and walked out. Well, I gave it a good go but that was that. "Can you come back tomorrow and do the same, only better?" the boss said. Of course I could.

The boss was, and still is, a lovely bloke and I keep in touch with him even to this day. The Guinness case continued and I was filming on behalf of

RTE (Irish State television) and select footage was played down a satellite link to Dublin late every afternoon. Needless to say, back at Southwark Crown Court, the judge found the four multi-millionaires guilty, though none of them received a truly worthy sentence. Well, with that amount of money behind you, you'd expect 'light duties' behind bars, would you? Early release and fines they could easily afford with the change in their pockets.

When I returned to the studio I couldn't help but notice the controller in the edit suite - it was the very same I'd mastered in Teddington. I convinced the boss to let me show him what I could do and he agreed. Another multi-skilled operator was born.

I now had a freelance job at the Westminster facility for as long as I wanted. Taking a copy of my passport, they applied for a press card on my behalf. Should there ever be the need for pre-approval to the many Ministry offices which surrounded Westminster, or even access to the pavement opposite the black front door of No 10, then I was now in the system. The majority of freelancers at the facility were made up of ex-ITN cameramen and sound operators, all products of a recent cull, or as bean counters called it, a 'redundancy drive'. Close to retirement age but still highly active, they were only too happy to show me the ropes. Each lunchtime they'd treat me to wonderful stories of when they worked in Vietnam, deepest Africa or the sweaty jungles of Asia. I listened, learnt and loved every minute when I joined them on assignment across the capital.

My transition into editing TV news was quick - it had to be if I stood any chance of earning a living. I had to learn the industry format, its terminology and the way things were done. Of course I made a few early rookie mistakes but soon picked up the labour saving tricks editors used to simplify their work and the techniques with the journalist's narration and flow of the piece. Next I was to learn how the MCRR (Master Control Room) worked: to send sound and vision to other parts of the facility and up to the BT Tower in Cleveland Street. At the time, the tower was the kingpin of distribution when to sending television signals around the UK and beyond.

When out on a shoot I'd take a pair of 300w Redhead lights, they were small but punchy and ideal for interior jobs. Drawing on my experience with lighting I soon had them placed correctly. Unlike a commercial or a film, for which you waited months to see the finished article, here I could shoot an interview and see what it looked like minutes later. I was now shooting *and* editing my own pieces so I now had an all-round understanding of how news went together. Any camera operator who edits their own footage becomes a walking storyboard as they know exactly what images they're going to need to illustrate a report.

Let's say you've interviewed the Police Commissioner at New Scotland Yard, then you're going to need a selection of extra shots to illustrate the story: you'll need a wide shot of the building, a shot of its name, any flags (if fluttering nicely in the breeze), shots of the windows, the main door and maybe shots of people going in and out. Of course after the interview there's normally time for some 'setup' shots with the the journalist and the Commissioner: over the shoulder shots and time permitting, a reverse shot over the Commissioner's shoulder as the journalist asks the same questions or nods like an idiot.

So that I had good all-round knowledge, I was taught how to operate an SQN: a 4-channel portable battery powered sound mixer that sits in a pouch hanging from the sound operator's shoulder. Depending on which microphones were being used, certain switches and screws need to be twiddled and adjusted on the SQN. I hated this bloody thing and I'm still not entirely sure I ever mastered it. Still, I had to learn how to use it, and with the umbilical cord joining me to the cameraman, I spent a few months running behind trying to keep a hold of the sound mixer, spare batteries, tapes, boxes of clip on microphones and the boom pole.

Sky Movies was swiftly becoming a mover and shaker, but long before it grew to what it is today, prior to a film's release they'd book our facility to attend press junkets and shoot interviews with the film's stars. As the sparrows of London were squeezing out their first fart of the day, a collective noun of yawning TV press and assorted entertainment journalists sat in the corridor of a posh West End hotel. I forget which film was being premiered that evening, but we waited our turn to interview the stars and their director. Today's junkets are very well organised with a dedicated crew and where the lighting is pre-set, but back in the early 90s crews changed rooms for every interview and had 20 minutes to set up, while the 'star' had a break in an adjoining room. To be honest, it was all a bit knackering.

Our slot came around and we were ushered into one of the beautiful furnished rooms hired by the film's PR company. Normally they were sumptuous and I'd help the cameraman set the lights and dress the set, and once he was happy I'd sit on the floor with my SQN mixer and a big fluffy mic on the end of a pole (you never got to pin clip microphones onto to film stars). Once ready, the PR people wheeled in the star, and today in walked Glenn Close. My God she was beautiful. A vision of smiling loveliness, she sat down, and once settled, I gently moved the fluffy mic closer to her. The cameraman looked through his eye piece, disappeared round the back of Ms Close to adjust to one of the lights and then it happened: she looked down at me, smiled again and counted to ten, giving me a few words for microphone level. "How's that? Any good?" she said. It was at this point that I knew this was the woman I wanted to marry. By the time the interview was done, in my head I had organised the wedding, the honeymoon, where we were going to live (and it wasn't East Molesey) and how many children we were going to have.

Another early morning start had us cabbing it to Leicester Square for Channel 4's "Big Breakfast" and an interview with Arnold Schwarzenegger. Austria's second most famous export was in town to launch the London branch of his Planet Hollywood burger restaurant, which also happened to be piggy-backing the release of his (surprise, surprise) new movie, Terminator 2. We were to setup in the restaurant and wait to be called. At the time "Big Breakfast" was pulling in huge audience figures and the film's PR department saw this interview as an ideal opportunity to promote their product. Ideally, they hoped that Arnold might 'click' with the presenter, so the night before had arranged a dinner for the pair of them. The "Breakfast" producer hurried in. "It didn't go well", she hissed under her breath, "They hated each other, absolutely *hated* each other!". Apparently, as the evening wore on at the posh London eatery, a mutual dislike materialised as they traded snide comments over their lobster goujons and courgette fries.

It was now the morning after and the chaos pixies of the film's PR department became agitated as the minute hand clicked closer to interview time. In came our presenter who was shown through to where we had set up. She was a pretty blonde, a bit ditzy with an air of disorganisation - her name was Paula Yates. She and the producer fussed around for a while and then the temperature in the room plummeted. Despite the numerous 'no smoking' signs, Arnie strode in puffing on a cigar. Fu*k it, it was his restaurant and he'd do what he liked. The late great Clive James once described Arnie's physique as a 'condom stuffed with walnuts'. He wasn't far wrong.

The interview got underway but last night's animosity was still evident. To every question Paula asked of Arnie, he turned it around intent on promoting 'brand Arnie', whether some TV company liked it or not. He wasn't charming nor was he a gentleman. He took it out on some poor girl and left me with the impression of nothing more than an overpaid bully.

In 1992 "Spilt Second" was due for release, so our chums at Sky Movies sent us on a junket with leading men Rutger Hauer and Alastair Duncan. I made up one half of the two-man team and we toddled off to another London hotel. Once crammed into a small room with far fewer luxuries than we had with the future Mrs McAlister (who, for some reason, wasn't returning my calls), the mixture of hot lights and a lack of suitable ventilation saw Hauer and Duncan sweating like glassblowers. However Rutger Hauer was hysterical and instead of giving us the plot and inside story behind their new film, the pair giggled like school children, wiping rivulets of water from their eyes.

Another thespian with a sense of humour was Helena Bonham Carter. Recently arrived off an overnight flight from LA, she was clearly knackered and suffering the effects of a skinful of free alcohol for the past 10 hours. She'd returned to the UK to promote 'Howard's End', and the premier was later that night. As the interview came to an end, she sank back into her chair, took a mouthful of water, looked down at me and said *"Christ, I really don't want to go to this fu*king thing tonight, will you come with me?"* Sweet of her but as I was already promised to Glenn. I find letting people down so very difficult.

I shot an interview with the veteran director Lewis Gilbert ('Alfie', 'Carve Her Name With Pride' and 3 Bond films) and his latest film 'Stepping Out' had its premier that night. In 1991 Gilbert was already 71 years old and still going strong, but to listen to this man talk was pure gold. Sadly, I had no interest in his new offering starring Liza Minelli, but when he reminisced about Bond etc., I was well away.

Of course, it wasn't all Hollywood A-listers and posh hotels, far from it. I fell in with a bunch of chaps who spent their Sundays filming Touring Cars for BBC's flagship sports programme Grandstand, and I fancied a drop of that. My baptism was at Brands Hatch, and once I'd proven myself as a solid camera operator, I was soon became a regular fixture of the multi-camera team. Setting off early on a Sunday morning, we'd all meet up at whichever circuit was hosting the next race, pick up radio headsets, check that all cameras were working and then drive off around the access road to our allotted camera positions. The director would be bawling instructions as to which camera was to follow which car, and where the good battles for positions were. He could see most of the entire circuit as he was standing on the roof of race control, but also had a first class talent when calling the right shots.

Once the race was over, we'd assemble back at race control, hand in our tapes and get back on the road for the drive home. The following Saturday the race would be broadcast on Grandstand as Murray Walker commentated as only he could. These Sundays were great fun and one weekend I remember taking sister Debbie's husband Steve to a meeting at Brands Hatch. After the camera team briefing, we drove unchallenged round the access road, parked up behind some fencing and simply walked onto the race circuit. No one batted an eyelid - we were carrying camera kit so we looked legit. The racing was *right there*, with only a thin metal barrier between us and saloon cars were smashing into each other. Health and safety? My arse. If any dislodged bodywork comes flying in your direction, then duck and just hope it misses you.

Back in Westminster, the independent facility was servicing every channel from Scottish (STV), Grampian, Tyne Tees, Granada, Yorkshire, Central, HTV Wales & West, Southern and Anglia. The long standing account with RTE encouraged the Irish channel to rent an office in the QEII Centre and become daily clients with reduced rates.

At three-ish one afternoon I settled into my edit suite and prepared to cut a usual 90 second evening news report for STV and their regular correspondent walked in with a new colleague. He introduced me to this fella and could I "look after him?" After some initial guidance, the full-time correspondent left, leaving me and the newbie to carry on with the edit. I helped him with his voiceover delivery and we did a few retakes to smarten it up. Together we went through the shots we thought were right and chose the soundbites from the interviews. Slowly it came together but he seemed pleasant enough and certainly eager. Clearly he'd stepped smartly out of Uni and straight into a plum job with STV and fast-tracked to Westminster. Sadly, in later years he was to become a little too full of himself as from out of this shiny new pupa grew Michael Gove. I wonder whatever happened to him?

About this time I was introduced to a group whose members included a well-known rock guitarist, two acclaimed photographers from the musical press, one of the authors of Kiki Dee's hit "I've Got the Music In Me" (and Moody Blues tour keyboard player) and 'Ade the Trade', a convicted drug dealer. We'd all get together in the evenings until the wee small hours and I'd often find myself driving home from Kensal Green at 4am. They were a fun bunch and happy to have me along. 'Ade the Trade' had struck upon the idea of making a documentary about Screaming Lord Sutch and would I shoot it? If there was an opportunity to make a few quid, well yes of course I would.

There was a by-election in The Ribble Valley (north of Blackburn) and The Monster Raving Loony Party was once again fielding Sutch as their candidate. He'd agreed to take part in this project, and with my car packed with camera kit, I headed north. We arrived on the last day of campaigning, and with voting starting the following morning at 8am, Sutch needed to get out on to the streets.

David Sutch's role in British politics shouldn't be underestimated: in the 1960s he stood as a candidate for his National Teenage Party, promoting their key policy to lower the voting age from 21 to 18 - in 1969, the voting age was lowered to 18. They also realised that the young of the day weren't being catered for over the airwaves so campaigned for commercial radio licenses and a broader choice of music - in 1972 the first commercial radio licences were issued. In their 1983 manifesto, they pledged to "issue pets with passports so that they could travel abroad without lengthy stays in quarantine" - such passports were introduced in 2001. So, there you go, four examples of a politician doing something constructive, other than lining their pockets.

Sutch and a fan.

Sutch was a political celebrity and the general public flocked to see him. Dressed in his colourful animal print jacket and trousers, a chest full of rosettes, a top hat and megaphone, he'd mock-terrorise the locals telling them not to believe the lies coming out of Westminster and that they should vote for him instead. A passer-by would shout some friendly abuse at him and he'd race after them, his leopard print jacket flowing behind him, berating them through his megaphone. He was a ball of energy and I was exhausted just trying to keep up with him. Around the town he'd engage anyone and everyone in friendly banter, sign autographs and kiss babies (and adults for that matter).

The next day was quiet for all concerned but around 10pm we ended up at the count along with a host of national broadcasters. Sutch was in good form, saying hello, waving and smiling wherever he went. At one point Tony Mottram, the renowned rock photographer, took a shot of me and Sutch (see p83) which is now framed and has been proudly displayed wherever I have lived since 1991.

At 2am I handed all the footage to Ade, and with Tony the photographer in the passenger seat, we drove out of The Ribble Valley and back down to London. I kept in touch with Ade over the years as he was an absolute character. Many years later he moved to Brighton and worked as a taxi driver. In 2019 he fell ill so I said I'd pop down to see him. In the February of 2020 he died of an illness unconnected to Covid. I wish I'd kept my end of the bargain as I now regret not popping down see him while I had the chance. Still, I was very pleased to have known him and he certainly made life more interesting.

Anyway back to 1991, and within a year the QEII asked all its tenants to kindly vacate the building. Everyone upped sticks and everyone moved to their new home, and one to where they have remained ever since: No 4 Millbank. It was slightly closer to The House of Commons than the QEII, but much nicer with the addition of a shop and a large (though expensive) restaurant, The Atrium. Our Irish chums at RTE rented an office next to us and the relationship continued. Such was the available space in the new office that desks were installed and rented to those out-of-London ITV regions who needed somewhere to work when in town. Two dedicated edit suites were built, there was a medium-sized studio where we could just about operate three cameras (four at a squeeze), and a brand new kit room was built to store the camera, sound and lighting kits. The firm leased three Renault Espaces which could easily be converted into mobile editing vehicles and 'House of Commons TV' was launched.

Birmingham's Central Television made a popular weekly programme called 'The Cook Report'. It remained on air for 12 years and was the highest rated current affairs programme on British TV, with audiences peaking at over 12M. Former BBC newsman Roger Cook devised a show where he travel the world investigating 'serious criminal activity, injustice and official incompetence'. It was both a ground-breaking and highly popular show, but as Cook confronted more and more *ne'er-do-wells*, he and his crew suffered more and more physical abuse. The boss wandered over to my edit suite and asked for a word: Cook's producer had been on the phone and they were thinking of hiring a cameraman from here to act as 'insurance'. Basically, the Cook team would plough in and square up to the target but wanted a second camera to hold back and film whatever happened next, be it nothing or a good kicking. Was I up for it?

I filmed a number of 'Cook Reports' and I found Roger to be a charming bloke, and on such long filming days he made sure that we all had a good lunch inside us. When the main team wasn't available, I was called on to shoot feature footage. There was one episode that took a while to complete and that was "Pretty Polly". Sadly, I unable to find it on YouTube or on IMDB, although they list most of the programmes from 1991, a few are without a title so I expect that "Pretty Polly" might be one of them.

This particular episode concerned some highly dodgy operators who were illegally importing parrots from Africa, bringing them into the UK via Southend airport. Their African contact was hatching baby parrots in sheds abroad, then sliding the tiny birds into cardboard tubes and shipping them to the UK. Great armfuls of these tubes were stacked into a container, sealed and flown to Southend in a cargo plane under the cover of some *right-on-the-limit* import licence. Anyway these birds arrived in the UK, it wasn't all strictly legit and the Cook team knew it, so expose them they would.

Once through customs and away from the airport, the gang would sort through the tubes, dead birds wold be destroyed in a furnace and the lucky handful who *did* survive this terrible ordeal (despite weight loss) were placed in a coop where they would hopefully return to full health. What made it even worse was that this dodgy arrangement called for an official visit by a registered vet. A quick inspection of the housing and food situation, official papers were stamped and all was well. Somehow, the gang were circumnavigating the system by telling porky pies somewhere along the line, either that or the vet was taking a backhander.

No longer the 'insurance' cameraman, I drove to a residential address near Southend and met up with the producer. The Cook team were expert at keeping a very low profile and their mastery at cajoling the public into helping them film was second to none. Sitting in my car, the producer watched and listened what was going on in and around the housing estate. He pointed out the gang's house, told me to stay put as he got out. Crossing the road he walked up to a neighbour's house and rang the doorbell. He spent a while talking to the chap who opened the door and returned to the car. The neighbour was up for helping us out.

Within 30 minutes the producer and I were standing in the neighbour's garden and looking over the fence into the gang's centre of operation. Thankfully, none of then were at home, so perching on a box that the neighbour had supplied, I started filming next door's garden. There was a small shed which we figured housed the parrots and a three-foot high furnace which had badly charred the lawn beneath it.

My producer became a little agitated as this sort of footage wasn't going to win any awards. What we were doing wasn't illegal as we'd been given permission by the neighbour to be in his garden and we weren't trespassing into next door. Yet. "We need to see what's in that shed", said the producer, "would you be so kind …?" he said making a sort of jumping over gesture towards the fence. I didn't need asking twice. So long as the producer kept an eye on the house next door and checked for any movement, then I was happy to pop over and have a nose-about. I slid down the other side of the fence and into next door's garden. The producer handed me my camera and I made my way over to the shed. The door was locked and there didn't seem to be a sound coming from inside, so the birds must have been moved on.

I filmed around the shed looking for clues: a few feathers, birdseed or anything that said 'parrot'. Round the back I found scattered fluffy feathers and a pile of poo but as I filmed the incinerator I heard the producer say "Take a look inside!" That's the trouble with producers, they don't think a cameraman ever uses their own initiative. To be fair, this was the first time we'd worked together but I replied "Ya think?!" I pointed to the house and then at my eyes, hoping he hadn't forgotten that he was my lookout as I opened the lid of the incinerator. Amongst the ash was a mixture of beaks and claws. Finally we had our evidence, although it was *kind of* illegally obtained.

"Quick! Someone's in the hallway!" hissed the producer. I replaced the incinerator lid, ran over to the fence and almost threw the camera at him. He hooked an arm through the camera's shoulder strap as I jumped up and hauled myself over the fence in somewhat of an undignified manner. We sat on the neighbour's lawn with our backs against the fence, my heart trying to beat its way out of my chest. We gave it a few minutes and retired to the neighbour's living room. Thanking him profusely, we left and made our way back to my car, I tried as best as I could to conceal the huge camera under my jacket.

The next time we met was a week or so later in an Essex pub, where having seen seen what I'd shot in Southend, the team gave me the thumbs up. There was an animal trade fair up the road where the gang were peddling both their legit business *and* their less-than-legit parrot trading. Roger and his team were set to confront the gang outside and I was to hang back and film the encounter.

The Cook team had done an extraordinary job in scoping the place out, but rather than use the normal visitor's entrance to the event, they'd contacted the farmer who owned the field and asked if we could use a side gate. This gate would also be our quick getaway if needed. With the Cook team leading in their car, and with me in mine, we entered the field and made our way towards the marquees and the exhibitors parking. As we bounced over the uneven grass, the producer's flat palm pressed up against the rear window of their car. This was the sign for me to stop as they were to carry on. Parking up 20 yards further, we all waited. The producer got out of the car and went into the marquee to spot the target. He was soon out, and once at his car, bent down to brief the crew inside. The target had been eyeballed and the crew set off in 'confrontational' mode as I slipped out of my car with the camera rolling.

It was quite a sight to see and I applaud them for exposing quite so many crooks over the years. I filmed every step they made but kept the shot fairly wide so should anything kick-off, we could identify assailants and use it as evidence should charges be pressed. It was clear that Roger had found his man as a microphone was up in this guy's face and the target had obviously been taken by complete surprise. Although I couldn't hear what was being said, Roger wasn't taking any shit and was quizzing this guy about the rules that had broken, listing the evidence they had on him and the rest of his gang. Our target then pushed Roger, who didn't budge. Then he pushed him again and again and again.

A crowd of estuary onlookers had slowly surrounded the crew but the team managed to extricate themselves and get back to their car. I leant against the side of mine and continued filming, convinced that the crew were going to be creamed and their camera smashed. Thankfully, once back inside their car, they reversed at speed across the field which was the point that the angry crowd saw me. I put my camera on the passenger seat and turned the ignition key as a mass of tattooed and overweight Essex men wheezed their way across the grass. The main crew had already left so I threw my camera onto the back seat and got out of there myself. A few miles down the road, sure that we weren't being followed, both cars pulled over. A quick de-brief later, I handed over my tape, we said our goodbyes and I headed home to Westminster. I've only been to Essex twice in my life, and both times were for Roger Cook. Happy days.

One other job that I should mention was with Ed Boyle, a journalist with a wonderfully dry sense of humour. He had a slot on LWT's Sunday lunchtime news magazine show where he'd take a sideways look at the weeks events in Parliament. He'd have half a dozen or so inserts per show, and they were normally fluffs made by MPs or things they wish they'd never said. Every Friday at 12 he'd book an edit suite and together we'd spool through hours of video to find those comic gaffes made by the politicians he was going to lambast in 48 hours time.

These edit sessions became regular events and Ed made a point of asking for me. To the bookings folk it was obvious that Ed liked my company but he also came armed with two glasses and a bottle of wine from the Atrium restaurant downstairs. Whilst everyone else was busy with their heads in political hoo-ha, the sound of riotous laughter was coming from my edit suite. The boss, complete with a headmasterly scowl, made repeated trips to the suite to tell us to "shhhhhh keep it down!" I'd watch the show go out live on the Sunday and was impressed at Ed's comic timing and how well the clips he'd selected hit the mark.

The facility now had three multi-skilled operators who could do everything with their eyes shut: shoot, light, operate sound *and* edit. More and more the industry was on the lookout for multi-skillers and our facility lead the way. We became known as 'one-man-bands' and ITV regional news departments would book us for a 15 minute slot to join their journalist on either St Stephen's or College Greens (one of the two lawns in front of the The Houses of Parliament/Palace of Westminster). It would be a quick piece to camera (PTC) or an interview with a regional MP, though sometimes a longer shooting session would be requested, followed by an edit. We loved what we did and made sure everyone got the same level of service. Our clients were wonderful people and despite rumours about stroppy and precocious TV journalists, I don't think I ever came across one. Oh, now hold the phone, there was one ...

A novice female journalist had been given a reporter's job with a foreign network doing a report on London's transport system. She wanted to do her piece to camera in front of a bus garage somewhere in South East London. It was fairly noisy so we advised her that it might be better to find somewhere not quite so populated with diesel engines. "Yes, thank you for your opinions but we're running out of time, so this is where we'll shoot it, OK?" Even the producer looked a little shocked at her youthful hostility.

Bill the sound operator fixed a mic to her lapel, getting it as close to her mouth as possible and used a fluffy mic on a boom pole as backup. She began to run through her PTC working out the sequence and what she was going to say. I looked over at Bill who was transfixed by the VU meters of his sound mixer whilst he moved the pole around trying to find the sweet spot for the fluffy. "The tie mic's even worse." I gestured to the producer and pointed towards Bill who took his headphones off and handed them over. She put them on as Bill illustrated the noise problem by switching between the tie mic and the fluffy on the pole. Without uttering a word, the producer removed the headphones and strode over to our starlette, strongly advising her against recording in this position. By the look of thunder that came our way, we knew the battle was lost. The recording went ahead, and back in the edit suite the novice journalist watched her precious PTC and became visibly upset. She'd barked at her crew, didn't listen to their advice and now we couldn't use the PTC as she was drowned out by revving engines. Now 30 years later, she's reading the news on ITN. There's no justice in this world sometimes.

When Three Tribes Go To War

The last few years had been great fun but I fancied a change (as they say) to 'broaden my horizons'. Some of the older lags who'd served their time in this business viewed us youngsters as *flash-in-the-pan* kind of things, though secretly we were the future of television news, and quietly, they knew it too. Our one-man-bands were scurrying around the lawns of Westminster, working side-by-side the three-man crews from the BBC, ITN and Sky. I should point out that there never any hostility as they believed that multi-skillers were underpaid and overworked, which wasn't strictly true. No matter, as written across their faces was a trace of doubt which obviously read '*that one-man-banding better not be the future of my job*'. Of course it was, but not just yet.

My beat around Westminster had me bumping into loads of familiar faces from the mass of broadcasters all chasing one story or another. On passing one of the sound ops from Sky News, he happened to mentioned that their Osterley HQ was looking for VT editors, "They could use someone like you." He furnished me with a phone number, and from a quiet edit suite at No 4 Millbank, I rang and spoke to a chap called Charles. He seemed pleasant enough so I gave him a quick roundup as to what I had done and what I was currently doing, the kit I could operate, and in return he told me what the job at Sky involved.

Sky's newsroom was organised chaos, people running everywhere. Down one wall were 6 edit suites full of beavering editors and flustered journalists. The sprawling duck egg coloured newsroom was a mass of untidy desks populated by scruffy people furiously typing or engaged in animated phone conversations - often both at the same time. The newsreaders sat in a studio partitioned from the newsroom by huge panes of soundproofed glass. The whole place was highly charged and way different from the Westminster cocoon I'd come from. I don't actually remember where the interview took place, but Charles had done his homework and had been asking questions around Westminster and seemed to know more about me than I'd initially shared. He showed me around and pointed out a few key members of the editing staff.

We got on well, and as I left, he said he'd be in touch. When you interview for a job you really *really* want, normally you don't get it. Well, contrary to that belief I got this one and handed in my notice at Westminster. My colleagues threw snide remarks my way like "They'll work you to death down there!", though with hindsight I think they were rather sad to see me go. Two years previously, the boss had seen my potential, had given me a massive leg up and I'd proven myself to all concerned. In fact, over 30 years later my old boss and I are still in touch.

The commute from Surrey each day was becoming tiring, as more often than not we finished late. I was regularly sprinting across Westminster Bridge, taking the steps outside Waterloo station three at a time in order to catch the last train home. It was an irritation to say the least, so as I arrived onto the concourse for the last time, I realised that Monday morning's 25 minute drive from East Molesey to Isleworth would be a very welcome change of scenery.

At that time Sky News worked a seven-day fortnight: in every 14 days you worked seven, and 12 hours shifts. For example, in week one you worked Monday, Tuesday, Friday, Saturday and Sunday and in week two you worked Wednesday and Thursday. Once a fortnight like that was out of the way, you went back to the week one pattern but this time on night shift. The 12 hour day shift started at 6am or 10am and for the 12-hour nightshift, 6pm or 10pm. This overlapping worked well, though the 10pm to 10am shift was a bugger as the morning traffic was in full flow. Again, after a fortnight of nights, back to days.

Each shift had a leader to whom you reported on arrival. Once assigned a suite, you'd sit in it like some kind of Dutch whore, installed in a dimly-lit soundproofed room as the shift leader sent reporters and producers your way to be serviced. Once a reporter was back after a location shoot, they'd arrive script in hand, and the pair of you would craft the news package ready for the next hour. Being a 24-hour rolling news organisation meant you didn't just edit for one bulletin, you edited (or updated existing packages) every fricking hour. Very quickly I had to learn how the library system worked, how to correctly fill in the daybook and how to use the whiteboard which listed tape numbers and story topics. All editors needed to know which master tape was last used by such-and-such a reporter and where the hell it was in the system. The work was often furious, and to begin with, all this filling-in nonsense didn't make much sense: forget to leave a paper trail for the next editor in line and you'd soon find yourself out of the 'flavour of the month' contest. However, after my fortnight I had a better grip on it and a fuller understanding of why things ended to be done the way they were.

Sky was owned by the Dirty Digger, Rupert Murdoch, so naturally the place was crawling with Australians. Every one of them had worked at Channel-this-that-or-the-other down under and most of them were good eggs. Many of them were over here for a few years' experience and passing through, but the majority had every intention of settling for good in the UK. The other editors were Brits and I don't remember there being any animosity between the nations except the usual 'whinging pom' jokes from the Aussies and our taunts about 'coming from the world's largest open prison'.

The best way to get to know your fellow editors was during a nightshift, the quietest slot being between 1am to 3am. Very little editing was done between these hours. Yesterday's reports remained untouched and ran all night, so there was plenty of time to chat and see who was who. The Breakfast bulletin started at 6am so fresh reports came at you from around 3am in such a rush that it was all hands to the pumps. Thankfully, the remaining hours of the night shift didn't drag on as we always had lots to do. At 6 the theme music announced the start of the Breakfast show, a bright and shiny incoming day shift arrived smelling of shower gel and cornflakes, as the night people began their sluggish journeys home.

'Drop The Dead Donkey' was popular on our TV screens at that time and we were amazed at how real-life at Sky was often mirrored on that show, to the point that we were convinced the writers had a mole at Osterley. They captured life in a 24hr news channel perfectly as we had newsreaders just like Henry Davenport and Sally Smedley, and a whole newsroom full of overly-confident Damien Days and babe-trawling Dave Charnleys. Gerry was the unseen outside broadcast cameraman who often came off worse when working with Damien Day, and the head of cameras at Sky News was also called Gerry. If you ever get a chance to watch the show (it's on YouTube), then do so.

If you've edited video yourself, then I very much doubt you'll have edited video as you will at a 24hr news channel. Unlike current affairs or feature pieces, news doesn't require artsy transitions (fading in and out) as it's all cut, cut, cut. At times we were given no more than 30 minutes to cut a 90-second news piece from scratch or to re-cut an existing piece that needed fresher pictures or a new voiceover.

All editors had to be spot on - choosing the best images to illustrate what was being said and be accurate and bloody, bloody fast. An outsider would be lost watching news VT editors at work as an editor's mind is always thinking one or two cuts ahead. At times, our fingers danced over the controller's buttons like a concert pianist knocking out 'Flight of the Bumblebee' - and I'm not making this up. The speed we worked at was extraordinary, constantly against the clock and always with the threat of the edit suite phone ringing with the usual bleating request "is it ready yet?"

Only the editor knew what was happening and how long it would take to finish. I could stand behind another editor, though unable to figure out what they were doing. Every last movement and decision remained in the head of the editor tapping commands into their controller. We all enjoyed beating the clock, getting the piece to air with seconds to spare and every editor will tell you that television is made in the edit. You could employ a BAFTA-winning camera operator to shoot hours and hours of beautiful footage, but without a competent editor who knows about construction and storytelling, you're left with a roll of raw footage.

There was an Australian lad who rang his mother in Sydney to tell her that the Queen Mother had died. In reality she was still very much alive, but here's what happened: all TV and radio outlets rehearse for when certain Royals or States-persons pop their clogs, and right now during a nightshift, Sky were rehearsing for when the old Queen Mum finally goes. The Aussie had just woken up from a 10 minute post-joint snooze in his edit suite, and looking at his screen, he saw a news presenter dressed in black announcing the tragic news, accompanied by library footage of the old dear waving and smiling. Quick as you like, he was on the phone to tell his mum in Oz. She then told her local radio station which, of course, went on to tell someone at a TV station. Anyway, you get the idea of how this snowballed. He lost his job with immediate effect, became the laughing stock of the industry, was interviewed on Channel 4's 'The Big Breakfast' and then disappeared into obscurity. That was until 2019 when I spotted him in my local pub in Dorking. His face dropped when I told him who I was. "Do you want to tell everyone my claim to fame?" he asked. "Nah," I said, "it was funnier back in the 90s".

There were some bleaker moments too, like the time on an overnight shift when a small passenger coach loaded with school kids driven by their teacher, was wiped out on a northern motorway. Plunged into thick fog just as a school trip was coming to an end, the teacher driving the kids ploughed straight into the back of a 40 footer which had stopped in the emergency lane but had switched off its lights. Via a courier, a copy the fire brigade's tape arrived and our shift leader looked around see who was best equipped to deal with these images. I was called into his edit suite and the door was shut. "Look, this is not going be very pleasant so do what you can and cut out all the grim stuff, ok?" He was right, it was awful. This was what the firemen saw on arrival at the scene. A few colleagues came into my edit suite out of morbid curiosity but left within seconds and dissuaded anyone else in the newsroom with the same intention to think again.

It was now 1993 and I'd been editing in Osterley for about a year. I'd had a few outside broadcasts and even a few shifts up at Sky's Millbank studio where I took the opportunity to pop in to see the boys and girls downstairs at my old facility. They were doing well but now Yorkshire Television had become involved, ploughing a ton of cash into the business. In the next few years Yorkshire TV were to take over completely, forcing my old boss to wave goodbye to his baby.

The one thing everyone wanted at Sky was a trip away, somewhere other than Osterley. In the autumn months it could be a party conference in one of the Bs: Brighton, Blackpool or Bournemouth, and at any other time of the year, it could be a G5 (6, 7 or 8 whatever) summit meeting. Of course, there was the 'big one' that was at the top of everyone's list: Bosnia. The civil war had been raging for nearly 2 years, and to begin with, it didn't get as much headline coverage as it deserved. Seen as a local spat that the UN assumed would sort itself out, it had now developed into a truly despicable uncivil war, the worst we'd seen on European soil since the end of hostilities in 1945. The news producers, camera, edit and satellite teams who were sent to Bosnia were the best - and no doubt about it, they had to be. Level-headed, vastly experienced and know how to problem-solve a long way from home and with minimal equipment and I was (childishly) in awe of them.

During one shift, our department head Charles, popped into my edit suite and closed the door. Would I be prepared to go to the Balkans for a month? I felt honoured to be asked but it left me with a chilly sensation trickling down my spine. Charles had employed me with forethought, using analytical tactics if you will. At Sky, camera crews shot, sound ops did sound and editors edited, that's how it was and that's the way they liked it. Each did their own job and no one strayed into the other's territory, but because I had arrived at Sky as a fully-formed and capable multi-skiller, Charles knew there might come a time he could put me to good use out in the field. Despite the daunting choice ahead of me, Charles had made it perfectly clear that if decided that I didn't want to go then there wouldn't be any repercussions and I had every right to say "No". He gave me 24 hours to think about it and mentioned that if I accepted, then it might be an idea to talk it through with my loved ones etc.

I didn't dare mention this to my mother. No way. In fact, I'm sure the only people I told were my sister Debbie and a mate of mine, Peter Homewood, who was shortly to become the Rev Homewood. The Bell Pub in East Molesey was a two-minute walk from my flat where Peter and I (along with a group of assorted others) would while away the hours. Pete looked at life with a level of intrigue, a great deal of humour and was someone I feel I could talk to about anything. When all was said and done, he suggested that it was up to me, as he'd rather I came home safe and sound.

With my mind made up, I informed Charles that I'd go. On hearing that I was next on the list, news spread throughout my colleagues and bubbles of animosity began surfacing and words were exchanged. Understandably, a number of them had been at Sky longer than I, and as far as they were concerned, I certainly didn't qualify for such a plum assignment even after a year. Charles was no fool and it was his decision who went and his alone. He'd spoken to shift leaders and asked for their honest opinions. The camera department also had something to say about it. Apparently Charles validated his decision of a multi-skiller by asking the head of the camera department if there was anyone on his team who could edit as professionally as one of the editors on the other side of the newsroom. "No", came the reply. I was given a list of vaccinations and made various appointments for other bits and pieces.

My local GP in Molesey was ex-RAF and was delighted to learn that one of his flock was heading to war-torn Bosnia. He gave me my jabs over the course of a week and wished me well. It was January 1993 and cold, really cold. The Bosnian team I was joining would be heading out shortly so preparations were well underway. I needed to buy (and supply receipts for) a large rucksack, a sturdy pair of boots, a woolly (or thermal) hat, thermal gloves, several pairs of thick socks, a thermal jacket and salopettes (not necessarily matching as we *weren't* going skiing), a sleeping bag and as much thermal underwear as I could manage. A flak jacket and helmet would be supplied once out there. My editing equipment consisted of two edit machines in chunky flight cases, a pair of monitors (small TVs), an audio desk, a voice-over microphone, assorted mains cables and several boxes of virgin cassette tapes. Everything went into flight cases but I was warned that the excess we were to be charged by the airlines would be into the hundreds (thousands today) so I was issued with an access all areas company Amex.

I arrived at Heathrow, solo, and checked in with a little over 300kg of excess luggage. Once everything was piled onto a trolley, it was a balancing act but as for going for a pee, well that was out of the question. You couldn't leave £90,000 worth of kit unattended on a trolley outside the Gents. Best to get checked in, relive yourself of all that kit and *then* you could relive yourself. For the first leg of the trip, my hosts were Lufthansa, but before they'd entertain giving me a boarding card they wanted a little over £800 for excess baggage. With that now paid for, all my edit equipment went crashing down the conveyor, and minutes later the check-in clerk and I were still wincing at the noises coming from deep within the luggage system.

The flight from London to Split, via Frankfurt and Zagreb, afforded me blue sky above, a thin carpet of cloud below, and the occasional glimpse of a snow-dusted Europe. By the time I touched down in Split, it was early evening, the day having simply disappeared swallowed up by three flights. To my surprise, everything I had checked-in at Heathrow was accounted for and slowly came round on the squeaky conveyor belt. I found a trolley, stacked the kit and simply walked out of the terminal building with not one eyebrow being raised. Split airport in 1993 was a single story, sad-looking building full of armed, smoking and lethargic Police officers, shady foreign types and hyperactive taxi drivers. Sky had hired a team of local producers/fixers and one had been dispatched to collect me from the airport. I had his name written on a piece of paper but, for the life of me, I couldn't pronounce it. With a collection of black flight cases and an over-filled green rucksack, I stood out like a sore thumb.

Hotel Split was the *de facto* collection point for all journalists heading into or out of Bosnia Herzegovina. The Reuters news agency ran its operation from the hotel with Mike Sposito, a long-haired Canadian in charge. Born in Manitoba, Mike, a former cameraman (now Reuters Rome bureau chief) was one of the nicest and funniest guys you could ever hope to meet. Shortly before his untimely death in 2014, he was quoted as saying "Remember, if something happens to me I want you to see to my burial in Port Stanley," adding, "Liver to be buried separately with full military honours." I met my other Sky team members and went to visit the UN office on the ground floor where my photo was taken and my UN Press Pass issued. It was then dinner and a nightcap before bedding down for an early start the following morning.

Still yawning, we assembled in front of Hotel Split and began loading all our paraphernalia into a soft-skinned people transporter. Until we got within range of the fighting, we didn't need anything bulletproofed. With our Hungarian translator Arpad behind the wheel, we set off south along the coast road, eventually turning left and heading up and over the lemon-coloured mountains for Kiseljak (pron: Kiss-el-yak) which was, for now, a safe multi-ethnic town 20 miles north-west of Sarajevo. Today you could probably drive the cross-country trip to the very heart of Bosnia Herzegovina in around four hours, but in the winter of 1993 and in the middle of a very uncivil war, we arrived in the early evening, suitably exhausted.

Kiseljak was a smallish town which played host to a garrison of Canadian UN troops and a few shops and restaurants. Once our vehicle was unloaded and we'd had a quick look round our night's stopover, we set off out for dinner. We met the outgoing Sky crew in a dark, cramped restaurant 10 minutes walk away. Squeezing in around the table, we said hello to those we knew and introduced ourselves those we didn't. In the morning they were due to handover flak jackets, helmets, a petrol generator, and of course the prized armoured Land Rover. By tomorrow night those lucky sods would be in Hotel Split, and as this was the last fresh meal we, the incoming team, were likely to have for a month. From the following morning, until the point that we returned to civilisation, we were to be on an exclusive diet of what the military term as MREs: 'Meals Ready to Eat'.

These highly calorific pouches of dried food are designed to give the soldier their required daily nutrients when out on manoeuvres or in combat. Empty the contents of the sachet into your billy can (we were issued those too), add water, heat and swallow for everything you need to keep you going - with the added surprise of instant constipation. UN troops around the world existed on their own versions of this dried cack whenever away from the comforts of a field kitchen, and the UK media bought boxes and boxes of the stuff from the Ministry of Defence.

For that one night in Kiseljak we slept in a rented house whose walls were covered in pine panels in the style of a Tyrollean ski lodge and peppered with faded panoramic photographs of the Austrian mountains. I could swear that I heard yodelling coming from somewhere. The next few hours were to be the last few hours of 'lasts' - last proper food, last proper bed, last shower and last proper toilet. From now on we were to sleep in our clothes, flannel wash very quickly and crap over a precipice. The next morning we loaded the vehicles as a never-ending stream of cardboard boxes full of delicious MREs passed from person to person. A mass of rucksacks followed, then spare body armour and equipment. So as to distribute the weight evenly and get something heavy over the rear axle of the armoured Land Rover, my edit suite went next, followed by the cameraman's flight cases, the sound man's kit and anything left over went in the soft-skinned van.

We were to head in the direction of Gorazde, a town in Eastern Bosnia currently surrounded by a heavily armed Serb Army, effectively turning it into an enclave. The Bosnian Army had been forced out of the town and those citizens who had stayed were now captive. A few months prior, Steve Connors a British photographer working for Time Magazine, discovered a huge military secret thanks to the Bosnian Army: the inhabitants of

Gorazde had developed an effective food supply chain which passed right under the noses of the surrounding Serb military. Each night, guides and their ponies would set out with hundreds of Gorazde's townsfolk on a 40km walk which took them up and over the snow-covered mountains. They passed within 200 meters of Serb troops and the route finally emptied out at a Bosnian Army supply camp on a mountain called Grebak. Accountants, decorators, mechanics, teachers and the retired made the trip dressed in whatever clothing they could find.

Loading the armoured Land Rover with my edit suite,
a generator, fuel and boxes of yummy NATO rations.

Once at the camp, they'd sleep for few hours, stock up on meagre supplies such as rice, fatty meat, bread and whatever else was available, and at nightfall the guides would lead them along the frozen 40 km route and back into Gorazde. However, others decided that they could no longer continue living in the town, so after a reviving nap would simply walk out the other side of the camp to find safety amongst their Bosnian brethren elsewhere. Apart from the uncertainty of the trip itself, and so long as you weren't spotted or shot by the Serbs, there was something the Bosnians called 'The White Death'. Exhausted after hours of trudging through snow, many would sit and rest for a while. Inevitably they'd fall asleep in the icy conditions, never to wake up.

We, on the other hand, were kitted out in modern thermal micro-layered clothing and purpose-made boots, but these poor individuals had nothing more than work trousers, donkey-jackets, woolly hats, thin gloves and walking shoes.

Steve Connors had shared this gem of a story with a chosen handful of Western agencies and a single broadcaster, Sky. We were to meet up and travel in a convoy with a number of others: the Associated Press, The New York Times and a collection of press photographers and journalists from various agencies such as Newsweek and Time magazine.

With a groaning chorus from suspension springs under tension, we were ready to wave goodbye to Kiseljak and we mounted up, ready for the onward journey. The Sky News armoured Land Rover had space for two in the front, taken by Zoran our Serb translation/producer in the driving seat and journalist Aernout van Lynden in the passenger seat.

Our camera crew, Dave and Scott, travelled in the back sitting on metal benches. The London-based Producer Catherine was offered a seat in the people mover which Arpad was driving, and the satellite crew, John and Yuri, had their own two-seater vehicle that they'd brought down from Budapest. That left three of us without a seat: me, and a couple of photographers: a Brit called Gary and an American. The only transport with any space still available was the open back of an armoured Land Rover belonging to the Associated Press. So dressed in thick winter clothing finished off with flack jackets and helmets, the 3 of us made ourselves as comfortable as we could sitting exposed to the freezing elements on icy metal flooring.

Associated Press' open-backed armoured vehicle.

The first couple of hours were bearable as we still had the feeling that this was all a big adventure, but by midday it began to suck big-time. Hour after hour we bumped across the snow-covered countryside as the route was now nothing more that a collection of deep-frozen tyre tracks that swerved here and there, forcing us to stop every few kilometres to deal with the multitude of problems: holes, snow, ice and hidden ditches.

"Please make it stop!" became our battle cry as we got in and out every time to help dig or push. With every bump in the road, hip bones collided against the bodywork and further damage was caused from wheel arches or someone's boot. If it was ever possible to ride a Clydesdale along a rollercoaster, then this was it and we'd got our money's worth. One of my travelling companions produced a hip flask of brandy, which at least numbed some of the pain. From behind the bullet-proof windscreen of the armoured vehicle behind stared miserable faces belonging to those who, although nice and warm, were utterly joyless and sober as the three of us were becoming gently lit on brandy.

We overnighted at Hotel Treskavica in Trnovo (pron: Turn-o-vo), a town 20 miles or so south of Sarajevo. The surrounding mountains were once full of carefree skiers belting down black runs, but those were distant memories as these peaks were now home to trenches full of trigger-happy soldiers. So that the enemy could keep an eye on who was using the roads, with high explosive artillery rounds, they'd sliced all the trees that flanked the mountain routes in half. Hundreds of trees had been blown down and we felt more than a little exposed on these roads, especially when the lead convoy vehicle stopped to check their map.

To be fair Hotel Treskavica was a dump. It had once been a beautiful and popular hotel welcoming skiers during the winter and hikers in the summer, but here it was now bombed, pockmarked and scared for life. Those windows that hadn't been blown out had their glass removed and replaced by wooden slats which served to block a sniper's view of anyone in the rooms or on the stairwells.

For now it served as a temporary army base in which the wounded were tended and from where fresh troops were dispatched. With John and Yuri (the satellite boys) we walked the corridors heaving with armed soldiers. The 3 of us were assigned a room in which was already a soldier, rather worse for wear and pissed (yes, some Bosnians Muslims do drink). There was a basic cooker sitting on the floor between two beds and a tube that took the smoke and fumes out through a hole in the wooden slats. The ensuite toilet was blocked to the point that I wretched whenever I went near it. The hotel had been hit several times by mortar rounds and great lumps of its structure were missing as scorch marks bled across the exterior.

I was not alone in being thrilled to get out of there. One night was bad enough. The following morning, the soldier in whose room we'd crashed, now sober, came down to wave us off. He was a pleasant enough chap and the previous night we shared our MREs with him, and using hand gestures, we'd managed basic conversation. Gentle muscular reminders of yesterday's battering I'd received on the way up here convinced me that I'd had my fill of 3rd class travel so forced my way into the van for the 15 mile trip to Grebak. It was the longest and slowest 15 miles I'd ever experienced with yet more ice, fords, holes, snow, more holes, snow chains, more ice ...

Sky had sent a crew of nine into Bosnia, and on arrival at Grebak, four of the team would be leaving for Gorazde: cameraman Dave, soundman Scott, journalist Aernout van Lynden and the producer/translator Zoran Kusovac. With them went John Burns of the NY Times and those feature photographers who had traveled up with us. That team were to spend the next two weeks filming reports within Gorazde, and all their kit, and that of the other photographers, was loaded onto ponies for the 40km nighttime walk. It was winter, heavy snow everywhere, and with the wind chill factor, temperatures regularly tumbled to -15c.

So that then left five remaining members of the Sky team who were to stay behind at the Bosnian supply camp on the Grebak mountain: Catherine the London-based producer, Arpad our translator, John and Yuri the satellite engineers and me the VT Editor. Steve Connors, the story's originator, would also be remaining at Grebak. We'd been traveling for seven hours, and with the sun now on its way down, the vehicles were parked up and the team remaining at Grebak took charge of the keys.

Those heading for Gorazde made ready by repacking rucksacks and helping the guides with which pieces of kit needed to be loaded onto the ponies. Sky's walking team wasn't made up of trained athletes, nor were they fit and healthy military types, but two lads from London, a chain-smoking Dutch/British journalist and a slightly overweight Serbian producer. With everything packed and strapped down, backslaps, handshakes and messages of encouragement were exchanged as the guides lead their heavily-laden ponies into the setting sun as our anxious team made their way along a crunchy winter walkway and slowly out of sight.

Dave, Zoran and I adjusting crampons while
Aernout does what journalists do best.

Accommodation at Grebak was alongside the Bosnian troops who'd very kindly erected a tent for us with all mod-cons. The base of our bed was made up of fat, stubby logs onto which they'd laid planks of wood. An empty 45-gallon oil drum became our cooker/heater with a metal tube poking through a hole in the canvas and acted as an extractor. In order to work, my editing kit was now on a wooden picnic table which had been pilfered from the mountain's former picnic area. We spent the next few days entertaining ourselves, getting to know our hosts and waiting for news from the team in Gorazde. We taught a few basic English words to the Bosnian soldiers, and discovered that most of them were Manchester United fans.

Arpad, Steve, Catherine and I lay across our communal bed swigging tins of beer and playing cards for matchsticks. At Heathrow's Duty-Free I'd bought a giant bag of fun-size Mars Bars, excellent fuel for cold weather and even better as stake money. The occasional 'whoosh' went over our heads as Serb-fired mortars attempted to locate the supply camp. In the soldier's tent we listened to crackly BBC World Service bulletins on a radio powered by a car battery. The Bosnian troops brought us fresh wood for our oil drum cooker and I prepared endless MRE meals using its lid as a hob.

John and Yuri, the satellite team, slept in their van which was located on the other side of the camp and which took 10 minutes to reach. Satellites need a clear line of sight to operate so those poor lads lived in a small vehicle which was out in the elements, regularly battered by stiff Balkan winds and engulfed by numerous snowstorms. On the other hand, we were cocooned in wood-fired heated tent set amongst a forest of trees with protective branches.

Every morning Steve Connors would get up before sunrise and walk along the route leading towards Gorazde, looking for the first overnight arrivals, and I'd often go with him. Other than our boots making that satisfying crunch on fresh snow, there wasn't another sound to be heard: no birdsong and no noise of civilisation of any kind. We'd chat and have a quiet laugh over a joke or something. After an hour or so we'd hear muffled conversations as around the next corner came the first group of refugees. Led by a guide, these were the fittest and also the happiest of the nighttime walkers. "*Dober dan*" we'd say in our basic Bosnian, smiling and waving. Steve banged off some photographs as I looked on, taking the occasional one myself with my Instamatic. In dribs and drabs they came, some with walking sticks made from branches found along the way, others carrying rucksacks or canvas bags slung over their shoulders.

Back at the camp, another of the overnight guides would find their way to our tented palace and ask for our translator, Arpad. We'd received word from Gorazde as our producer Zoran, had sent a message saying that "a cassette would be arriving tomorrow morning".

Sure enough, a couple of times a week, a guide would arrive at the tent and hand over a package containing videotapes and sheets of scribbled notes from our team 40kms away. We'd always offer these guides something hot to eat or drink in exchange, but they normally refused. They were a proud and hardy bunch. I'd start our petrol generator and Catherine and I would spool our way through the cassettes, have a look at what we'd been sent and decipher the handwritten notes that Aernout had jotted down.

Our 'des-res' accommodation-cum-edit suite on Grebak.
Left, the author at work and right, his view of Central Bosnia.

Now left to my own devices, I'd edit the package starting by listening to Aeronaut's voiceover. I'd match up the relevant footage, make notes of time codes when I found useful stuff and scribbled notes next to his instructions. Dave and Scott had captured some extraordinary scenes, and now matched with a wonderfully descriptive voiceover and Zoran's translation of the interviews, the best stuff I'd ever edited began to take shape. I don't mean to sound all showbizzy and histrionic, but here I was sitting in a tent up a mountain in the middle of Bosnia watching footage from a war that no one gave a stuff about - and it fell to me to put it all together and make a good job of it. The footage that was landing in my lap was a gift and only a complete idiot could bugger it up. Each roll of tape that found it's way to me could only be described as a free pass to make some exceptional television reports. Sky had a deal with American broadcaster CBS, so at a stoke our viewership had increased by millions.

Our employers had invested heavily in this trip, so unlike your average 90 second news report, *our* news packages weren't under the cosh of time restraints. Taking the subject matter into consideration and the quality of what was being delivered, we were regularly given a free-rein of three to four minutes per report. I could let the packages breathe, allowing the viewer to soak up what was happening on screen. Compared to the usual instantly forgettable shitty TV reports of scandal or celebrity news (tomorrows chip paper if you will), this was exceptional viewing and its effects have been with me ever since. Here was a nation being ripped apart: its men, women and children dying needlessly every single day in a war that the UN should have done something about well before now.

The cassettes coming back were packed with images of long drawn-out faces, normal everyday civilians physically and emotionally drained from the constant threat of starvation and death. There were scenes of malnourished children whose mental states had now turned them into scavengers. These victims were now being controlled by a twisted political leader who wanted to put the lot of them into hastily-built concentration camps. Don't forget, this was happening a mere two hours flying time from Heathrow, though UN continued to drag its heels in a vain attempt to find a diplomatic solution. Was this how the 1990s were to be remembered?

Once Catherine and Arpad had watched the finished report, and after the odd final adjustment, I'd eject the tape and walk it down my side of the mountain and up to the satellite boys who'd be dusting off the dish on the other side. We'd make contact with Osterley via the SatPhone, check that they could see our signal and then play the tape to them.

We sent them stories of hospitals full of injured children peppered by shrapnel, adults who'd lost limbs and doctors losing all hope, weeping as they were close to running out of basic supplies such as clean needles, surgical knives and oxygen. On a wet Wednesday afternoon in March, a UN convoy of Canadian troops forced its way through Serb lines, and on witnessing the current state that the town's population, began throwing them their *own* MREs in a vain attempt to sustain them a while longer. The Canadian Major, along with his troops, was bewildered by what he saw. Almost lost for words he said, "I've never seen anything like this before. I have children of my own that age. That's an eye-opener." His troops stood around, mouths gawping, shaking their heads in disbelief.

In proper TV news reports, good journalists won't describe what the viewers are watching, but give supplementary information which can be taken on board while the pictures float by. Aernout van Lynden is an excellent exponent of the art and his use of language, phraseology and description was a gift to an editor such as me. His delivery wasn't hurried, it allowed for breathing space and the viewer could watch a sequence unfold without having someone talk over it. Thankfully I was in the driving seat (if you will), so if I thought a particular sequence deserved some extra space to make a point, then I made sure it got it. After all, the team hadn't come all this way for some twat in a tent to slash this extraordinary footage down to 90 seconds and be done with it.

On days when we had little to do we'd make social visits to the soldier's digs, which was a construction made from logs with woollen blankets hanging from its angled ceiling by way of insulation. Men and women slept in a long line across a log/plank arrangement and they'd made the place very feel homely and comfortable. Of course, a constant fug of coffee fumes and cigarette smoke hung at nose-height, but the real draw was their radio. They'd sit and listen to war updates and to how it was all progressing. Of course, it all depends which side you were on as propaganda is propaganda, but to know what was *really* going on, we'd tune in to the BBC World Service. Arpad would translate for the troops.

On World Service radio, the distinctive and instantly familiar signature tune, '*Lilliburlero*', first came into existence at the BBC in November 1955 and remained for the best part of 70 years. "This is London" crackled out of the radio. The Bosnian company commander was the only one who spoke a few words of English, he was well educated and everyone got on well with him. A synopsis of the current situation in Bosnia was read out followed by a story which had a familiar ring to it. Strangely, it resembled something *very* close to a story we'd been working on. The next thing we

John, Yuri and Steve on the ledge
overlooking the supply camp.

heard coming from the BBC was Aernout's voice. Unbeknownst to us, our reports were receiving substantial interest from both national and international broadcasters. The BBC were seriously miffed that a four year old TV channel had scooped them to a major humanitarian story. So, asking Sky if they could use the audio from its TV reports, they were now broadcasting them over the BBC World Service. 1300 miles away, three of us sat in a snow-covered log cabin stunned as we listened to our work coming back at us from the little radio's speaker. The next time we called the office from the SatPhone we asked what was going on.

24 hour news is a ravenous beast which requires a steady supply of vittles in the form of news reports. It devours them like Augustus Gloop and the Gorazde story was gaining pace. Representatives from the UN were being interviewed on the subject, British MPs were making statements in the House and CBS in New York was under siege, well kind of. Thanks to this partnership with our American colleagues, CBS were broadcasting our Gorazde reports across North America. The public reaction to what was happening caused consternation and the New York offices of CBS were overrun by deliveries of food parcels, medicines, winter clothing, packet and tinned food, toys and messages of love from Americans.

The team in Gorazde continued sending tapes as we continued to feed the news monster. Life in our mountain retreat carried on and the temperature inside our tent was perfect until someone opened the flap allowing guffs of Balkan chill to spoil it all. None of us had brought an extensive wardrobe and doing laundry caused much merriment with underwear, socks and thermal vests hanging off the clothes line, solid to the touch within minutes and capable of snapping in half. I learnt a valuable trick when living in those conditions: when changing clothing the next day, take your boots off and get into bed fully dressed. Stuff tomorrow's clothes down to the bottom of the sleeping bag, and the next morning whilst still within the bag, remove yesterday's clothes and put the new ones on. Hey presto, nice and warm. However, in order to carry out tasks such as flannel washing was another thing entirely but just ask for a bit of privacy and get on with it.

As I said earlier, Charles had decided to employ me partly due to my multiskilling abilities and today I was able to validate his decision. With the crew in Gorazde working long days and sleeping rough on frozen concrete floors, they had the only camera. There had been some discussion about doing a report from the supply camp but we lacked the one piece of kit needed - a camera. One evening, John and Yuri joined us for supper and as we sat supping beer and chatting, a lightbulb moment came along. "Oh, we have a camera in the van" said John. Of course it's quite normal for satellite crews to travel with their own camera but these cameras were used for 'live' transmissions so didn't have a recorder strapped to the back end.

The ideas pot was stirring nicely and we decided that if Catherine could present and I was to operate the camera, then we could indeed send live pictures and sound from the Grebak supply camp back to Sky. The satellite van was 100-or-so feet above the camp, and as the camera didn't come with batteries it had to be powered from the van. Being the expert tekkies that they were, John and Yuri took the van's 12v battery out, made a rudimentary connector which gave the camera the right amount of juice and put it in a plastic shopping bag. Audio and video cables were in abundance, so with now Arpad carrying the shopping bag/battery combo, we had a range of 100 feet. Using an earpiece from their sound kit, the boys worked out a way to get the studio sound into Catherine's ear. As the hours went by, this 'Macgyver' operation was looking increasingly feasible.

Sky was sold on a live link-up from the Grebak camp but there were stipulations as pointed out by Arpad: the Serbs still had no idea on the exact location of this supply camp, though they knew something was out there just not quite *where*. If we happened to show the camp in a wide shot, there might be a chance that the Serbs could figure out the location by looking at the outline of the surrounding mountain range. So, keep the shots tight and we should get away with it as the last thing we wanted to do was to put the Bosnian Army, the supply camp or the Gorazde refugees in any danger. However *had* the Serbs attacked, we would have perished along with everyone else.

With Catherine on the end of a microphone and me cradling the camera, we carefully worked our way down the steep incline from the satellite van to the tented refugee camp, Arpad and his shopping bag followed behind. When everything was connected, one of the lads in the van radioed down that we were now up on the satellite, Catherine looked down the lens, smiled and nodded as she could hear the Sky gallery in her earpiece. It was obvious that she was talking to someone she knew, so gave them a weather report from Bosnia and confirmed that, as a crew, we were all well. As the news presenter introduced the piece about Bosnia, she stopped talking and composed herself. "That's right", she began answering a question that had been thrown to her, "this camp is the halfway point for those stocking up on supplies or making their way out of Gorazde all together …" we were now live on air, off and running.

The author failing miserably with even the simplest of poses.

The sheer volume of refugees was astonishing but every last one was fed and watered, with some returning to Gorazde at sundown.

We were on air for a fair few minutes as Catherine illustrated key points about the camp, but all the time I was keeping the surrounding mountains out of shot and Arpad struggled with the car battery in an effort to retain a coil of loose cable between us. The newsreader in Osterley brought the item to a close as Catherine looked straight down the lens. Pausing for a second, she waited until a voice in her ear told her we were off air then she relaxed. We all relaxed. Packing up, we thanked John and Yuri and retired to our tent to celebrate with another slap-up meal of dehydrated cack with a dollop of mystery sludge.

As time went by, the UN were pressurised into taking action as something clearly had to be done. The longer they pondered, the longer the poor people of Gorazde suffered unnecessary misery. Just before bed each night, I'd stand on the edge of the precipice and take my pre-bed widdle over the precipice. Above me, the coal-black sky was punctured by millions of stars which silently twinkled and blinked. It was a stunning sight, ice cold and completely still. One night I heard the unmistakable but distant sound of propeller aircraft, as from their German airbase in Ramstein, American Hercules transport planes under the UN flag were now flying high over Gorazde, as much needed supplies spilt from their cargo doors, gracefully floating to earth under big fluffy parachutes. If the reports we had made had gone as much as 0.01% in swaying the UN into making a decision to help those suffering in Gorazde, then I'd be a happy man, though the horrors of Srebrenica were still two years away.

During one early morning delivery of footage, a message arrived saying that our team were coming out, so we were to expect them in a couple of days.

On D-Day, a 6am alarm call brought us all to life and we raided our MREs to make hot food and drink for the arrivals. Guides appeared first along with the fittest refugees then the Sky crew and the photographers a little later. Shattered after a 40 km overnight walk in freezing temperatures they were dead on their aching feet, so we fed them and gave them our communal wooden bed for a few hours of sleep. The ponies were unloaded as camera and sound kit was returned. Apparently on the way back from Gorazde in the dead of night, one of the ponies had stumbled and disappeared over the edge of a ravine taking a substantial amount of photography kit with it. Of course the affected photographers were mortified though it was left to Zoran to reimburse the animal's owner in hard cash. On handing a dodgy looking handwritten receipt to the Sky accountants, he wasn't sure if they thought he was taking the piss: '1x pony 200 DEM' (Deutsche Mark).

After a few hours of much needed kip, the Gorazde team gathered around the monitor as I showed them the results of their distant handiwork, to which I think they approved. They now set about shooting one last report from the supply camp itself as again, Aernout's signature narration was married to exceptional footage. The team went back along the trail early the next morning to film the first overnight arrivals. It snowed heavily all night and into the next morning, videotape showed nothing but abject misery written across faces which served as a lasting and pitiful reminder of what, as humans, we are capable of doing to one another. However, before we were to leave Grebak, one last twist in the story was about to materialise.

Some of our military hosts on Grebak. The Company Commander (right) perished whilst rescuing civilians during a Serb attack further down the valley.

The Bosnian military included two brothers: Nedzad and his elder brother Ziser (pron: Zit-ser). Nedzad had been detailed to bring us wood for our oil drum fire every day and just 'stick around' should we need anything. We couldn't pronounce his name properly so just called him 'Nele', he didn't mind and just kept smiling. His elder brother Ziser hatched a plan with the company commander. So that his younger brother could get out and hopefully survive this awful war, could the Sky team help by taking him with them? The other soldiers at Grebak offered no resistance, as had they found themselves in the same position, they'd have probably done the same. The commander said he could organise the correct paperwork to get Nele away from the camp and also part-way out of the conflict zone.

Now, getting Nele (in his 20s and over 6 feet tall), away from Grebak now became Catherine's pet project. She had a huge heart and was committed to getting this sorted, so using Arpad as a linguistic go-between, she took the bull by the horns and decided that she'd sponsor Nele and get him to the UK. We all thought she was bonkers but we packed up all our kit, cleared the tent of any trace of us being there, loaded the vehicles and said long but heartfelt goodbyes to our hosts. With all the necessary paperwork now in his top pocket, Nele embraced his colleagues and then spent a last few quiet minutes with his brother.

For the return trip to Kiseljak I pushed my way into in the passenger van, winning a seat and arguing that as I'd initially travelled to Grebak in the back of an open armoured Land Rover and I wasn't doing that again for love nor money.

Kiseljak was sight for sore eyes, especially our faux Tyrollean ski lodge with its temperamental shower and electrics. So that we all had a fair crack of the whip, everyone was allowed to take "no more than 2 minutes in the shower", and once fully restored and smelling much sweeter, we went out in search of food. The one place that was open offered us a basic meal of mystery meat and rice, polished off with a bunch of mangy bananas. Faster than a pistol draw at a poker game, they were gone. The bill was settled and we wandered out in to the night and off towards our sleeping bags.

Early next morning, with contented snoring coming from behind closed doors, I crept downstairs to the kitchen and rustled up some fresh coffee. Nele was up and sitting at the table. Grebak had been his home for the past year so he felt very much out of place here in Kiseljak. Unfolded on the table was a NATO map which had been supplied to the press but, of course, *not* been shared with the warring factions. We sat and studied it and Nele was fascinated by what he saw. He could clearly see where the front lines were, who was in what territory, who had advanced and who had retreated. It was clear that whatever he was saying in Bosnian was along the lines of "If only we'd had this map at Grebak, can you imagine…?" What little of the language I *could* speak amounted to counting to 10, asking for two beers and directions to the town hall. None of which were going to be of any use at this hour, nor in this situation.

Slowly, the rest of the team surfaced, breakfasted, showered and packed. As there wasn't an incoming crew, we were unhurried. However, we still had to get young fella-me-lad over two borders, so ideas were thrown into the pot. Today, I was due to head off with Aernout, Zoran, Dave and Scott to Belgrade, so taking Nele and two photographers with us for a while, we squeezed ourselves into the back of the armoured Land Rover. Nele hardly said a word, being unable to speak English. I remember getting through the Bosnian checkpoint at lunchtime without any hassle as his paperwork was in order, and as far as the border guards were concerned, we were giving one of theirs a lift as he was 'on leave'.

We headed towards the next border crossing, knowing that Nele was never going to be allowed over the lines, what with being a Bosnian, wearing a uniform and with no formal ID. One of our taller photographers started rifling through his rucksack and produced a pair of trousers. Someone else stuffed a sweatshirt and sweater under Nele's nose and a woolly hat appeared from another benefactor. Nele hurriedly divested himself of his military attire as a chain of people handed items along to those nearest the door. Seen from the following vehicle, piece by piece Nele's military uniform was thrown out. For his military issue boots, well he'd have to tuck his feet under his seat until someone could get him fitted out with something less conspicuous.

Nele's hour of need was not over just yet as he was missing the essential UN Press Pass. One of the photographers had an expired pass deep inside a camera bag, so that was hung around Nele's neck with the photo side facing his chest. Before we arrived at the Croatian border, we mimed 'go to sleep' and with a huge grin on his face, Nele understood what we meant. The Land Rover came to a halt at the checkpoint and Zoran began talking to the soldiers. He answered any questions they had, as in the back we all pretended to be napping. Even with my eyes closed I could the feel the air pressure and ambient temperature change as the rear door was opened and an inquisitive torch flashed over us.

The military gave a cursory glance at our passes, but still under threat of being found out someone in the van swore very loudly in English, as you would if interrupted from a much needed sleep. This convinced the soldier that we really were who we said we were and I heard the door slamming shut. Zoran pulled away and 30 seconds later much laughing erupted. Nele, now an international illegal, had made it across the border.

We said goodbye to Nele, the two photographers and everyone else in the other vehicles who were headed for Split, and we set off north-east, towards Belgrade. At Kiseljak, the Sky Land Rover had been reunited with its trailer, upon which now was all my edit kit, the generator and anything else oversized. It was now five of us for the next few days: me, Zoran, Aernout, Dave and Scott. After many uncomfortable hours bouncing around in the dim surroundings of the armoured Land Rover, we arrived in Pale (pron: Parlay).

A municipality of Sarajevo, also an entity of Bosnia Herzegovina, Pale was Serb territory nonetheless. For some reason, Aernout and Zoran needed to swing by to sort out some business, so parking up in a car park in the middle of town, they left the three of us in the back. Sitting in the gloom of the Land Rover we chatted as another box of MREs was ripped open and plundered for its boiled sweets. Someone's foot held the heavy rear door ajar giving us a welcome drop of cold, fresh circulating air. Then it all went off. Zoran and Aernout (both smokers and somewhat unfit) arrived in a wheezing tizzy, fumbling for keys and swearing loudly. Slamming the armoured doors shut, Zoran started the vehicle, crunched the gears and the straining engine hauled the 2.5 ton steel vehicle and trailer out of the mud and the hell out of Pale. It was never explained to us as to what that was all about, but a gun had been pulled. Anyway, next stop Belgrade.

We drove for hours across muddy roads until we finally hit glorious flat tarmac. Not forever glorious, but until it ran out and the pot holes started, my *gluteus maximus* certainly felt the difference. As we headed deeper into Serbia, I remembered that no one liked the Serbs one bit. Put it this way, since before the Cold War whichever side Russia or China supported was generally seen as a rotten egg. To level the playing field, I ought to say that the Croats and the Bosniaks had also been naughty boys and girls, but at least they weren't starving civilians and interring them in concentration camps.

Arriving at The Intercontinental in Belgrade, we were exhausted, hungry and ready to go home. All the edit kit was dragged off the trailer and taken up to my room, after which I showered and changed, then downstairs for drinks and dinner. The next day I edited some other pieces with Aernout and Zoran while Dave and Scott went out on the piss.

With the edit suite packed the following morning, we loaded everything onto the trailer and our merry band headed further north for the Hungarian border and onwards to Budapest. We arrived well after night fall, Dave, Scott and I hitting the nightlife until the early hours. With delicate hangovers, we made our way downstairs and into the Land Rover. Zoran would drop us off at the airport, then he'd turn round and return the Land Rover and trailer to Belgrade, ready for the next crew.

Meanwhile back in Split, Catherine (and with Arpad's help) had all the paperwork which registered Nele as a sponsored alien travelling to the UK. As of now she was fully responsible for him: he was to live with her and she had to support him in every way. This was either a very brave or very stupid thing to do.

We landed at Heathrow and I rang my mother from a payphone. "So, how was Bosnia?" she said. She knew all along. I arrived back at Sky a few days after the Split crew and Charles was delighted with what we'd achieved. On a given afternoon, when the entire team could make it, the management invited us to the board room for drinkie-poos. As my team members disappeared on a fortnight's leave, I was back in the edit suite for three days assembling all the news reports I'd cut on Grebak into a non-stop 30-minute short-form documentary. I barely spoke to anyone as all I wanted to do was sleep.

A few weeks after leaving Grebak, the Serbs discovered the supply camp and attacked, killing as many as they could find. As they pressed home their advance, the Bosnian Army stragglers retreated down the valley and into the next village. A large number of those we lived with and got to know were either killed or injured, and I don't even want to think what happened to the women. The company commander who helped facilitate Nele's release was mown down as he attempted to get an elderly couple out of their bullet-ridden home. As to whether Catherine's idea was sound, well the proof of the pudding is that 29 years later Nele is still the UK. Now married to a Bosnian woman and living in London, they have a couple of children and he works as a manager on a building site. We still keep in touch by text message every now and again, and in 2018 he sent me a holiday photo from Sarajevo of him and brother Ziser, who thankfully survived the Serb attack on Grebak, and the war.

Brothers in arms on Grebak: Ziser (left) and Nele.

Below, reunited 2018 in Sarajevo.

Back For More

The door of my edit suite slowly opened as a familiar face appeared. "Hi," said Charles, "I can see you're busy but you wouldn't fancy going back would you?" I'd been home for a couple of months, during which time I'd had my fortnight's leave, visited Mum quite a bit and made a fair few trips to The Bell in Molesey. Spring was certainly in the air, I was seeing a young lady and all was good.

Throughout this time, Sky News had retained a constant presence and their next assignment was well into the planning stages. Of course I agreed to go back but this time the outgoing team would be made up of five: a much smaller team now with four of us from Osterley and another translator from Hungary. The sound recordist had never been to Bosnia and Charles asked me to keep an eye on him. Kevin was the reporter, B was the cameraman, R the sound recordist and Imre, our Hungarian producer/translator was to meet us in Split.

I was soon back on familiar territory - the departures hall at Heathrow, forking out another £800 for excess baggage. This time we were to travel to Vitez in Central Bosnia, where thankfully, there was a heavily armoured British contingent of UN soldiers: BRITBAT (British Battalion). No more tents this time around, though it would have been acceptable what with temperatures now in the high 20s. For the next month we were to rent accommodation from the locals, and this coincided with my added role as crew banker. Before the war, the common currency in the region was the Dinar, but it now it had been devalued and hyperinflation was rife. In order to mitigate some of the problems, the German Deutsch Mark had been in circulation for a few years and had become the folding note of choice. Sky's accounts department had me sign a receipt for thousands of them, and I mean *thousands*. I had wads of cash about my person: in my carry-on bag, in my jacket pockets, down my undies, everywhere. I couldn't take a shit at Heathrow without stacking piles of bloody Deutsch Marks on the toilet floor first of all. I was through security without an issue but spent the remaining pre-boarding time constantly tapping parts of my body to check that all my wads were where they should be. I must have looked a sight giving myself endless pat-downs as I headed for the gate.

Once at Hotel Split, we met up with our translator Imre, and of course in the Reuters office, the inimitable Mike Sposito. It was late April, warm enough to sit by the pool though we quickly became fascinated by a Japanese television crew who were scurrying about on their 3rd floor balcony, setting up their camera and assorted bits and bobs. If you were prepared to take a lengthy cross-country drive form Split, then after a few hours you'd find yourself in the middle of a full-on raging war complete with bullets, missiles and copious amounts of misery. With everything prepared and now dressed in flak jackets and helmets, the Japanese pair stood with their backs against the hotel wall and bowed to the camera. What followed (we assumed) was a detailed rundown of the day's action from the various front lines which criss-crossed the theatre of war. Down at pool level, Mike Sposito (who loved referencing Vietnam at every conceivable opportunity) mimed cradling an automatic weapon and yelling "Charlie's in the bush!". He'd then scamper across the patio, dodging imaginary incoming fire and taking cover behind the concrete uprights. We never quite worked out if their the Japanese bosses had *told* them to stay where they were, or independently, the pair of intrepid journalists had decided that Bosnia was far too dangerous and that they'd prefer to report on the war from the safety of their hotel balcony. As a modern reference, if you get the chance to watch the 2016 Ricky Gervais film 'Special Correspondents', then you'll know exactly what I'm on about.

Tensions remained high in the region and the next day we were due to travel up-country, so another quick visit to the UN office at the hotel to renew our passes. As a final treat, dinner was to be taken on the beach at a restaurant whose table and chair legs were plunged into the sand. Diners sat facing the setting sun as it gently extinguished itself in the Adriatic. The meal was wonderful: seafood, fresh bread and excellent wine. We were lost in the scenery as the water lapping around our legs helped delay all thoughts of the MRE hell that was coming our way as of tomorrow morning.

Sky's armoured Land Rover had made its way to Split, and now Imre was behind the wheel, Kevin beside him upfront and the three creatives suffered in the heat in the rear compartment, along with all the kit and supplies. Our first port of call was to be Gornji Vakuf (pron: Gorny Vak-Oof), so once again, we headed south along the coast road, past last night's beach restaurant and to a junction where Imre turned left and we headed up into the lemon-coloured mountains. I seem to remember that Gornji housed a British UN supply depot and that was where we were to meet other news organisations. The military had their own transport vehicles and a pair of Warriors (tracked armoured vehicle) that would act as our convoy guardians, one at the front and one at the back. Sure enough, at Gornji we met the BBC, ITN and an assortment of freelance photographers and journalists. The military had warned the press that to attempt the drive from Gornji Vakuf to Vitez *without* UN assistance was 'unwise', but since our brave lads were heading back to Vitez, anyone who wanted to join the convoy would be made welcome.

The relationship between the military and the press has not always been a bed of roses, they remained constantly wary of us keeping one eye open just in case some Fleet Street scumbag started digging for dirt. I am proud to say that I have never acted in such a manner with the military and will disassociate myself with anyone who does. The press vehicles lined up, and now a good dozen waiting, the convoy set out for Vitez. The morning's temperature climbed and the air in the rear of our Land Rover turned a little funky. However, crack the rear door open, and for a brief moment, the air was slightly fresher.

Through the small square of bullet resistant glass mounted in the rear door we could see flashes of scenery as we drove into the Lašva valley (pron: Lash-var). Abundant green fields were cradled between the slopes of gentle mountains. This was farming country and some of the older men-folk were out tending their crops. They gathered around rusty 1st generation tractors, smoking Balkan cigarettes and watched as our noisy convoy rattled by.

We reached Vitez by mid-afternoon and were to base ourselves half a kilometre from the town centre in a rental house. Out first house was down a twisty country lane nicknamed 'TV Alley', named as such due to the sheer volume of TV companies who'd rented the top floors of family homes. Before we arrived in our house, the older married couple (the owners) and the mother-in-law lived downstairs, but their son, his wife, their child lived on the first floor. Both the father and his son served in the local militia, so at night they donned tatty uniforms, shouldered their rusty AK47s and reported for night stags in the trench at the end of the road. When we arrived, and in need of cash, the son, his wife and their baby moved back downstairs with Mum, Dad and Grandma.

The family looked after us with extraordinary care and attention despite having very little themselves. I spent the first week getting to know them, though for the life of me I cannot remember their names. What little food they had, they shared. Whenever we offered items from our MREs they thanked us but refused. I think it was a Muslim thing as the mystery meat inside our packages could have been anything, and of course we respected that. As the editor I stayed in the village all day, every day. Kevin, Imre, B and R would go out and visit the local area to film news reports so I would stay at - or near - our digs waiting to edit with Kevin when the crew returned mid-afternoon. A few houses along were the BBC, and in their garden they had a satellite dish so that would be our transmission route back to Sky. We could also do the odd 'live' from the BBC's garden so everything we wanted was catered for, meaning that we didn't have to drag tons of crap around with us.

TV Alley ran along the perimeter fence of the British base, and at the end of the lane was a T-junction: Vitez town centre to the left and Travnik to the right. Directly opposite this junction was a small brown house with a picket fence that had been rented from a local man. This was PINFO, 'Press Information'. Inside, the British military held daily media briefings and answered any questions that the visiting press might have. Each evening, surrounded by the media, the British commander (or his no 2) would sit in a dimly lit room and deliver updates on action from the fighting zones, detailing losses or gains in territory, artillery bombardments, random shootings, skirmishes and casualty numbers. The British military were tasked with patrolling the region in their fleet of Warriors, and every now and again would take members of the media with them.

The weather continued to improve and the BBC took to hosting BBQ evenings in their spacious garden. It was at one of these shindigs that I met BBC Cameraman Nigel. Armed with a thatch of red hair and a fabulous sense of humour, he was a good man to have around. We'd bump into each other again over the years and I am still in touch with him to this day. These evenings were marred by one thing: the sniper up in the hillside overlooking the British base. He had a clear line of sight into both the base *and* the BBC garden in TV Alley. It had been decided that those who were attending the BBQ should drive their armoured vehicle (no matter how short the trip) and park them in a line in the garden, then we could block the sniper's line of sight and enjoy our BBQ uninterrupted.

With the food slowly cooking and the beer quickly flowing, apart from the odd shot ringing out in the distance, for all we were concerned, you could have been in a Kentish garden. So long as you brought something to add to the party, then you were most welcome to join in.

With somewhat of a fanfare during a morning briefing we learnt that our happy band was to be increased by one: the 'official war artist'. He was collected from Split by HM Troops and delivered to Vitez where he promptly suffered a panic attack and was removed from the area the following day. A senior BBC producer also went down with a case of the jitters, and he too was evacuated. Anxiety and I have a long and checkered history so I could sympathise with those poor sods.

Although this particular assignment didn't equal the difficulties or extremes of the Gorazde, it was a humanitarian story nonetheless. Every day the boys came back from their filming sortie with something to show for it: they'd been pinned down by snipers, run through trenches with UN troops and side-stepped a few close calls. Many of our reports concerned local government or spats between feuding warlords or the forced migration of the innocent as they escaped the bloodshed. I spent my days either compiling footage from the day before or wandering up and down TV Alley visiting other broadcasters or our hosts downstairs.

On one such outing I'd met up with a bunch of freelance photographers who'd clubbed together and rented the first floor of a house at the end of TV Alley overlooking the village trench. Invited round for an aperitif, I duly RSVP'd. The sun had set and we started to enjoy a lovely balmy evening, and although we couldn't *see* the soldiers in the trench, we knew they were there. The beer and laughter flowed and one of our group produced a huge bar of chocolate and a battery-operated CD player with portable speakers. With mouths full of chocolate, we started thumbing through his CD collection and discussing the merits of each artist we selected. "Well we can easily sort all this out", said one of the photographers, "Who likes Tina Turner?" A show of hands later and 'Steamy Windows' got the session up and running.

"Oh I like this bit", said one of the photographers turning the speakers up to the max, as a second later there was an ear-splitting crack and blinding flash of light from the field next to us, the type of noise that causes you to soil yourself. As one of the photographers hit the balcony decking, he ripped the speaker lead out of the CD player, silencing Tina mid-chorus. Once the noise had died down and the initial shock had worn off, a faint voice came from out of the darkness, "He no like Tina Turner!" It was one of the soldiers in the trench and this caused much merriment. Offering them beer, one of their ranks came out of the dark and stood under the balcony, indicating with his fingers how many were in the trench. We lowered beer and chocolate to our comrade and plugged Tina in for another crack at 'Steamy Windows'.

As Sky had been entertained by many of the other broadcasters, we had to keep the flag flying by hosting a party of our own. We organised a fair amount of booze and paid our downstairs hosts to prepare some local delicacies. Naturally, we invited them to join in but they preferred to keep themselves to themselves. Our guests arrived, the music started, the food was polished off while the booze and conversation flowed. The evening eventually fizzled out in the early hours when everyone went on their merry way.

The following morning I was awakened by a heated conversation in the garden directly below my balcony. I pulled on my jeans and a t-shirt, and with my head sticking out of the balcony door, I saw a young British freelance photographer, lying on the grass, covered with a blanket and surrounded by our host family. Clearly, this lad was in great pain, so not medically trained I didn't see how my intervention would help. A white UN Land Rover belonging to the Brits drew up in front of the house, two officers got out and one of the host family ushered them into the garden. They examined the poor lad who was now delirious and the Brits radioed for backup. An army ambulance arrived within minutes and the medical attendants gently slid the injured lad into the blood wagon and off they went.

Word came through that he'd broken his leg and he'd done rather a good job of it too. The British army surgeons operated, screwed everything back into place and he was now likely to be a resident of the military hospital unit for at least a week. It was going to take a while for the insurance to be sorted and a medical evacuation to the UK arranged. "Insurance?" he said, "I don't have any insurance!"

Let's backpedal: some time ago, this headstrong chap had decided that more than anything, he wanted to be a war photographer. With his photo kit and a backpack he got himself to Split, wangled a UN Press Pass, hitched a ride into Vitez and was now running around the place taking photos of anything that went 'bang'. He then tried selling his pictures to other agency photographers. During our soirée, he'd got well and truly hammered and passed out on a balcony, though I'm not sure if was mine or someone else's. At daybreak he woke, couldn't figure out where the hell he was and simply stepped off the balcony. He fell 11 feet and it was the way in which he landed that did the damage. His parents had to pay a handsome MoD bill to ship him home, and I don't suppose they let him out on his own again for a very long time.

A well known and highly respected children's charity was operating in the area distributing food, medicines and clothing to only the most deserving of cases. They drove a distinctive yellow Transit van with British plates and appeared to be omnipresent. However, as time went by, the authorities began monitoring their activities. UN patrols were logging dates and times, making notes of which checkpoints the van went through and the time periods between each entry and exit. Suspicion led to an investigation and the van was eventually stopped by British UN troops who ripped it apart. Lo and behold, on closer inspection, it was found that panels in the metal floor of the van were sporting fresh welds around the edges.

Once the van had been transported into the British base, the army engineers put their angle grinders to work, and as the panels were removed they revealed neat rows of AK47s along with boxes of ammunition. The penalty for gunrunning in a war zone could be measured in decades behind bars, but thankfully this crime had been discovered by the Brits and *not* by one of the many warring factions. The charity was banned from the conflict with immediate effect and its personnel removed from the country in advance of any official announcement.

As mentioned previously, the road between Gornji Vakuf and Vitez wasn't at all safe. Along the way there'd been reports of an armed group of thugs who prayed on single vehicles. Their camp wasn't far from a trout farm, from where they stole their food, so they became known as 'The Fish Head Gang'. Italian television had sent a three-man team into the area, but rather than wait for the next available UN convoy, the Italians decided to go it alone with the inevitable result. The Fish Heads fell upon their vehicle, ordered the Italians out at gunpoint, robbed and executed them in cold blood. That awful incident sent shivers through everyone in Vitez.

PINFO was throwing a party where everyone was invited, and as this event was being paid for by the MoD, anyone would have to be nuts to miss out. I had some recycling to finish up so I told my crew that I'd be along a little later. So as the sun set, Kevin, Imre, B and R walked the length of TV Alley towards the little brown house at the end of the T-junction.

Once I'd finished, I switched everything off and left the first floor apartment, but for some reason I decided to drive, so pocketed the keys to our Mitsubishi Pajero. I had no idea why but I supposed I'd be at the party quicker if I did. When driving at night, civilian vehicles were advised not to use headlights or indicators and should tape up the dashboard. It was a clear night and the moon was bright enough to easily navigate down the single track road.

I was no more than a matter of 30 yards from our PINFO and 31 yards from my first drink when the horizon in front of me lit up with a mass of streaking red lights, they disappeared into the bushes to my right. I couldn't quite make sense of it to begin with and was temporarily blinded, but then shocked back into reality by an ear-splitting noise. I brought the Pajero to a halt and sat thinking: what *was* that? It took a second or so to realise the position I was in: a soft-skinned vehicle full of fuel and I *think* that someone was shooing at me with tracer rounds. One of those fu*kers in the hills to my left had seen me and was getting in some target practice.

I switched off the engine, jumped out of the Pajero and ran around the front and sat in the dirt with my back against the front near-side wheel. With the engine block between me and the sniper I felt a tad safer, but a soft-skinned vehicle couldn't stop bullets. Hang on, was I imagining this? Had I got it all wrong? The sky above my head lit up for a second time with another generous spray of bright red lights. They whipped over the top of the car and thumped into the grass verge in front of me, fizzing and spitting until extinguished. A split second later, the unmistakable cracking sound of a weapon firing confirmed my suspicion. No, I hadn't imagined it, this *was* tracer fire and I *was* the intended target.

Now increasingly concerned, I reckoned that my luck had indeed run out and I clearly remember the onset of panic. As it increases, it debilitates the senses as the mind throws up multitudes of 'what if' scenarios. They assault the brain, magically conjuring up wild and wonderful examples of how it's all going to end with the body going into the 'fight to flight' mode. What had started as a 'what *if*' situation had rapidly turned into 'what *now*'. I began to pull myself together and I realised that logical thinking was my friend and it was to be the only way I was going to get out of this.

A third spray of red came shooting over my head, quickly followed by more cracks from the weapon. Still, the tracer fire went slamming into the undergrowth rather than into the vehicle. The magnesium-tipped bullets bounced and fizzled into the hedgerow, some taking a few seconds to die out completely. The firing was erratic so I assumed that the sniper wasn't in proper control of his weapon. We'd been advised that these sods were often shit-faced on Slivovitz (triple distilled plum brandy) and would happily take potshots at anything they saw, had they single or double vision. There was one thought that went through my head, but it went as quickly as it arrived: I began to imagine tomorrow's dawn, the marmalade sky, the sound of birdsong and the rising morning heat. If I didn't do something PDQ then I was likely to miss all of that. I started thinking of my family … no, I had to stop that too. PINFO was some way off to my left and I could clearly hear the sound of *bon homie* coming from inside. That was now my goal.

Shielded by the Pajero's engine block, I got myself into a crouched position and paused. A forth spray of tracer fire set over my head and i tot he shrubbery, my heart was beating out of my chest. I counted down from three, and at zero I ran like a thing possessed towards the safety of the military. I couldn't tell you if the sniper let rip with a fifth clip as the sound of blood pumping through my ears was deafening. I reached the small fence surrounding the house, leapt over it, bounded up the steps and crashed in through the front door. My arrival brought the place to a standstill as it must have looked pretty comical when a wide-eyed, shaking individual came flying in through the door and was now flat against a wall, trying to get as much air into his lungs as possible.

The major who ran the place made his way over to me, "We heard some shooting. Was he having a go at you?" All I could do was nod as he led me to a chair where I was given a very stiff drink. Once I was sufficiently anaesthetised, the major called up a couple of NCOs and told them to escort me back to the Pajero. The two soldiers led me to the door with one barking instructions, "Right, stay between us and if he starts shooting, lie down. Got it?"

The threesome walked out into the night, my escort scanning the moon-lit scenery with weapons at shoulder height. The sniper had neither run out of ammo, too pissed and given up or he'd spotted this little group. "He'll not give us any trouble" said my 2-man private army. PINFO had called the duty night officer at the base and asked him to "warm up a Warrior" and if necessary, "lob a couple of rounds up into the hills if that twat had any further ideas". We made it to the Pajero and I thanked the two lads, who then watched me turn the vehicle around and drive off home. In 1898 Winston Churchill wrote: "Nothing in life is so exhilarating as to be shot at without result." I concur.

A few days later we moved from our little house in TV Alley. Imre, our translator/producer, told the family downstairs that we were off but that the nice young man with the cash (me) would settle the bill.

I knocked on the internal connecting door and was invited in, the patriarch directing me towards a cushion on the sofa next to his son. Now dressed in military uniform ready for his nightshift in the trench, the son smiled and shook my hand. Concluding this transaction whilst flying solo, was more than a tad nerve-wracking, especially when I hardly spoke a word of the language. A tray of shot glasses appeared along with a bottle of homemade Slivovitz. Commercially produced bottles of this stuff is supposedly around 56% proof, but this was the homemade variety, and even tramps would think twice about drinking it. I've never tasted anything quite like it, and when my brain returned to clear thinking I reckoned that NASA had known about this secret liquid since the late 1950s.

In the room were 6 adults, two children and me. A round of this heavy clear liquid was served to the adults and a toast was made "živjeli!" (Pron: Jivoli "cheers"), down it went in one. The first glass was quickly followed by a second, then a third. My arms and legs began feeling rather loose and strangely I was now fully conversant in Bosnian. I could understand everything they were saying and they just laughed at every utterance I made. The father went to a skirting board, prised it open and produced an English phrasebook. For a while he entertained us with heavily-accented English words and phrases while everyone just laughed. More Slivovitz was poured and it was soon time to settle the bill. A piece of paper was pushed under my nose with a figure written on it. Now, was this today's date or a bill using a really bad Deutsch Mark exchange rate? I reached into a pouch under my shirt, produced a wad of notes and began counting aloud in English, while the family followed suit in Bosnian. I was in such a good mood that I gave them a tip, just a little bonus for looking after us so well: for putting up with our noise, for making the snacks for our party, being so welcoming, and hey, just for being poor in a war zone. I counted my remaining float the next day and I think the tip was bigger than the overall rental bill itself. Still, I'd make sure it was all accounted for by concocting a bunch of dodgy receipts before we returned to the UK.

On to our second house, it was almost next door to PINFO and our new landlady was called Vesna. She made sure we were well looked after too. A lovely woman who made such a fuss of us, but for the life of me I can't remember what had happened to her husband. He was either serving in the Bosnian army or had been KIA. Whatever, she was a delight and her house was well away from that bloody sniper in the hills.

One hundred yards behind the house was a quarry in which stood a Swedish relic from the 1930s and still in working order: a 40mm Bofors gun. Sitting on a trailer, this anti-aircraft gun was occasionally used to pound the Serbs up in the hills. Every now and again rounds were shoved up its back end, and with a heart-stopping 'whump', would be launched into the wide blue yonder. Once the firing was over, the gun was driven away and hidden from view until it was required again. Of course, this was a country at war so no one was going to publish a firing schedule, but it took everyone by complete surprise every time someone pulled the firing cord.

News of other shocking events filtered through to us: civilian charities were driving across Europe and through front lines to bring urgent and necessary donations to the neediest in the region. With the blessing of the UN, 100s of these aid lorry made the trip every month as foreign help began to arrive into Bosnia. Of course, this was yet another opportunity for egotistical local war lords to spoil the party. The UN had manned checkpoints along the way, their staff dressed from head to toe in white. Pulling the vehicles over, they'd note the name of the charity, the cargo being carried and the vehicle's destination. The aid drivers were then briefed as to the latest info as to 'hot' regions or areas to avoid. Sadly, a number of criminal gangs decided that they wanted a piece of the action, so built their own checkpoints and furnished their 'staff' with identical clothing. Once at the so-called checkpoint, the trucks would be redirected to a quiet, secure area off the main road where the drivers were ordered out of their cabs and then shot in the back of their heads. The trucks were then looted for their merchandise. Food, clothing and medicines that were destined for the needy were sold for huge profits on the black market. Honestly, those bastards stopped at nothing.

Vesna had a 12yr old daughter whom she wanted out of the region and as far away from Vitez as possible, so could we help? We were the lucky ones as we could come and go at will but nearly every local you came onto contact with had suffered some appalling personal tragedy along the way, or were about to. A plan was hatched to get the girl to her aunt in Split, soon everything had been discussed and agreed as memories of getting Nele out go Grebak returned. We were about to do the same thing again, only this time with a civilian - and a minor. The front line to the north had moved, so if we wanted, we could use a safer alternative route out of the Lašva valley and back towards Croatia.

Together with a Reuters producer (a Croatian whose name escapes me) and the girl, the three of us were to drive cross-country in a soft-skinned Land Rover and deliver the young lass to Vesna's sister at an address somewhere on the outskirts of Split. With the Reuters producer behind the wheel, and as he spoke the lingo, he dealt with the checkpoints along the way. I sat in the passenger seat doing the 'foreign journalist' bit while the girl was in the back hidden by boxes of MREs and empty flight cases. I should add that between checkpoints she was upfront with us until we needed to go into stealth mode and hide her in the back again.

Having successfully negotiated the last checkpoint, we got her out of the back and told her that we were now in Croatia and that she was safe. By mid-afternoon we were trundling through residential streets on the outskirts of town, asking locals for directions. On finding the house, and with the girl tucked in behind us, the producer knocked on the door which was answered by a woman. My colleague began quizzing her and, yes, this was the right place and yes, this woman was indeed Vesna's sister. We stepped aside to show her what we had brought her and the young girl burst into tears and ran into the arms of her sobbing aunt. Tears began to ran down my face and that of the Reuters producer. We said our 'goodbyes', got back into the Land Rover began the return cross country trip.

Our time in Vitez came to a close, but to this day, I cannot tell you that our first host family survived the war or that Vesna was ever reunited with her daughter. Along with Imre, our translator/producer, the pair of us dressed in flak jackets and helmets as we mimed to Incognito's cover of 'Don't You Worry 'bout A Thing'. Why? Well it was for an outtakes clip I made whilst we were in Vitez. Every broadcaster wanted a copy of it and it's still fondly remembered to this day.

A few years later, while covering the Albanian elections, Imre died of a heart attack. Arpad, our translator from the Grebak trip, had to organise the repatriation of Imre's body from Tirana to Budapest. In 2020 I posted the Vitez video online and was stunned to receive a message from Imre's son who said it was wonderful to see his Dad again, doing what he loved. Imre was indeed a charming man with a great sense of humour.

On arriving back in Osterley, no champagne reception or nibbles in the boardroom this time. I returned the flight-cased edit suite to Charles and took a fortnight's holiday, spending most of it inventing dodgy receipts to make up my shortfall in Deutsch Marks. I submitted a load, but at the end of the day I was way off and the accounts department taking a huge chunk out of my next paycheque to cover it.

Imre and I giving it the beans in that now infamous underground hit from Vitez.

Madiba

The following January Mum died and only 70 years old. I had been at her house the night before and the last thing I had said to her as I hugged her goodbye was "I love you." How many people get the chance to say that to a loved one before they leave us? She'd not been well for years but seemed happy enough now living in her little semidetached house in Esher's West End. She had Theo her Cavalier King Charles, and spent her time bumbling about the house and keeping herself busy. I am unable to recall exactly why I went back to Mum's the next morning, but I arrived to find both my sisters' cars out in front. Debbie and Jenny broke the news to me that Mum had died and had only just been taken away by the undertaker. I think one of them had been trying to get in touch with her, and getting no reply and had called a Policeman friend to pop by. He'd had a good look around and hopped over the garden fence, but when he looked through the kitchen window he saw Mum lying on the hallway floor. He smashed a kitchen window, opened the door and rushed over to her but she was already gone so there was nothing more he could do. The chosen undertaker was based just along from me in Molesey high street and it was strange to think that for the next two weeks she would be resting no more than 100 yards from where I lived. I think Debbie dealt with finding little Theo a new home.

My old mate Peter Homewood was now The Reverend Peter Homewood and was installed at his own parish in Ruislip, Middlesex. He'd met Mum on a few occasions so I asked Debbie and Jenny if they minded if he conducted the funeral service. They agreed. I must admit that the when person officiating at a funeral *knew* the customer in the box, it does make things a lot more personal. I rang Charles at Sky and told him what had happened and he told me not to bother coming back for at least a fortnight.

The day of the funeral arrived and I drove to Randall's Park Crematorium in Leatherhead and met up with Peter. We wandered through the grounds and sat under a tree for a smoke. Peter was typically sympathetic and understanding, keeping my spirits up with some excellent words of support. I'm sure this is half the reason he went into the church in the first place. I've never been religious, but if people find strength and peace by following whatever it is, then good for them. The service, the day and the emotions came and went and my memory of it all has pretty much been erased. I was shocked to hear that my mate Peter died in October 2015. He was a good friend to me for a long time and we'd been in touch occasionally over the years - it was always good to hear his voice.

In the 1st week of May 1994 Charles offered me another foreign trip and this one was a real doozie: the South African Elections. Sky had a small permanent team in Johannesburg, but with such a huge global event looming, reinforcements from the UK were called for. I was part of the fresh troops who boarded an overnight 747 from Heathrow. The sunshine that met us the following morning at Jan Smuts International airport (now O. R. Tambo International Airport) was glorious. I was more than a little excited to be here.

The team was ferried into Jo'burg and to the studios of SABC (South African Broadcasting) where, in one for their larger studios, they'd installed 30 or so temporary offices in which visiting TV and radio stations could work. For now I was to edit inside one of these flimsy units, cutting hourly reports in the run-up to election day.

Eugène Terre'Blanche was an Afrikaner white supremacist, founder of the Afrikaner Weerstandsbeweging (Afrikaner Resistance Movement - ARM). A nasty piece of work, and with his cohorts, set out to cause as much trouble as possible. Every morning black commuters from the townships would jump into fleets of passenger vans which would deliver them to a Jo'burg central station. They'd scatter from this central point to their places of work, and in the evenings, these same passenger vans would return them to the townships. On one of these routine mornings, an ARM foot soldier parked a 4x4, complete with box trailer, at this central drop-off point, locked the driver's door and simply walked away. Unbeknownst, the trailer had been packed with homemade explosives, and when the station had reached peak commuter capacity, the second hand ticked round and the whole thing exploded.

The noise was heard for miles around. I was in the Reuters office at the time and we all congregated at the windows as a huge plume of grey smoke headed skywards from between the buildings up on the hill. Needless to say, when the footage arrived back from our crew most of it had to be junked as I couldn't use it due to its graphic nature. One of the most striking images was of a VW Beetle that had been parked on the street one minute but was now cradled in the branches of a tree. The supremacists went on to bomb Jan Smuts airport too, which brought the suspended ceiling down and caused 100s of flights to be diverted.

A few days before the election, the Sky editorial team flew me to Cape Town as that's where I was to edit on election day. Again SABC had converted a studio into a temporary workspace for foreign broadcasters, so I set up and tested my kit, then went for a wander to see if I could find anyone I knew. Nigel, the big South African BBC cameraman with whom I worked with in Vitez was in town so that was a major bonus. Within 24 hours everyone in the Cape Town studio knew each other and with the big day in sight, an international/inter-broadcaster cricket match had been organised and was held in the passageway between the offices. Someone produced a bat and someone else fashioned a set of stumps from a cardboard box and a ball was made of rolled up gaffa tape. One of the ITN boys who was press-ganged into playing, no matter how reluctant he appeared. We all knew that Trevor MacDonald was a huge cricket fan and he graciously bowled an over and even had a go at batting.

Voting was held over four days and I was stunned by the extraordinary helicopter footage of people in far-away villages as they formed never-ending snaking lines waiting their turn to vote. Many unable to read or write but all eager to put an inked thumb-print on the ballot paper. Many of the older generation were utterly confused about what was happening as they'd never been given the opportunity to exercise their democratic rights before. I forget how many reports I cut using such pictures but most of them showed ecstatic faces of those who'd just voted for the first time and now, having left an indelible print next to their chosen candidate, were breaking out into celebratory dance.

Archbishop Tutu did a 30 minute stand-up routine in Cape Town as the mixed populace in the square below waited for the delayed new President to fly in from Pretoria. I enjoyed my time in South Africa, a country that had now turned the corner with total change as the eyes of the planet watched on. Sadly my trip came to a premature end thanks to a spiteful local producer who thought it would be a jolly jape to pull my chair out from underneath me as I went to sit down. My coccyx connected with the edge of a low wall, and after two sleepless night in agony, I was flown home. Thank you very much.

The Management

Back in the UK, the industry was abuzz with rumours of a brand new television agency who were now busy recruiting. The world-renowned American-owned print and photo agency The Associated Press (AP), was launching into television news and looking for staff. My interest was sparked when they said they were looking for a couple of Production Directors: TV all-rounders to keep an eye on quality control and teach novices the basics of news gathering. AP had already poached a senior news journalist from Sky and he was due to make the jump in a month or so. The two us got on well so one day I dropped into conversation the fact that I'd applied for one of the Production Director's positions. He said he'd put in a good word for me and lo and behold, I was invited for interview.

Around this time, my landlord at Molesey took the rash decision to put my rent up by 100%. I was astounded. The greedy sod. It doubled overnight so I rang around looking for alternative digs and my old mate the Rev Peter in Ruislip offered me his spare room until I got myself sorted. En route, I thought it time to lighten the load and get rid of a ton of old clutter. It dawned on me a few weeks later that amongst the crap that I'd thrown out up at the tip was the lighting plan from "The Meaning of Life" and the photos of Queen from Wembley. Honestly, #whatanarse.

I moved to Ruislip and took the tube from Ruislip to Chancery Lane for my interview. As both stations are on the Central Line, it was a direct trip door-to-door. Apparently, I suitably impressed the board at AP as a week later I was offered the position.

Back at Sky I kept my mouth shut until all paperwork had been received and a confirmed start date had been arranged. However, a clue to my departure came from an announcement in the trade press, but thankfully without a photo. My editing colleagues at Osterley reacted to the news of my appointment with a substantial amount of resentment. Many of them had applied for the same position, but not being multi-skilled meant that they weren't considered. With the stress of it all, one of the shift-leaders who'd applied lost all his hair. Still, what's done is done. I was away from the fun factory and sorry to be saying goodbye to Charles and the others.

I was now management, and for the first time in my working life, wearing a suit and tie five days a week. With my first month's paycheque, I moved out of Ruislip and into an apartment in Bow, East London. The job was great fun and with the second Production Director, Mark, we set about designing a training programme for the 35 producer/journalists arriving in

6 weeks time. I'm not sure my input was that great at this juncture as Mark had done this type of thing before, though I *would* shine when it came to the actual training sessions.

The AP building was in Norwich Street EC1, a few paces from Chancery Lane tube and even fewer paces to The Castle pub, of which the landlord was to make a considerable fortune. AP was spending millions converting the 6th floor of their London HQ into a newsroom, a Master Control Room (to receive and broadcast footage from and to the rest of the planet), edit suites and more importantly, a desk for the two Production Directors. Mark and I decided that after launch, when things were up and running, we should adopt a seven-day fortnight working routine *à la* Sky News. This was accepted by the higher-ups, however that was some way off as the builders were still banging and crashing their way through the sixth floor. There was still a mass of knitted cabling to be concealed and the occasional head of department could be seen wandering about the place with a sheet of A1 trying to envisage where desks and chairs would be going.

Global offices throughout AP's existing bureaux were also going through remodelling, busy recruiting local multi-skilled camera operators/VT editors, producers and journalists. While the grown-ups and HR looked after that, Mark and I split the world in two: I would look after Europe (as far as Romania), Africa, North and South America and Mark would have everything in Europe (east of Romania), the Indian subcontinent, Asia and Australasia. What made AP different was the belief in its quality: their journalism would be better, delivery to clients was to be faster and the technical quality of the product, second to none. Mark and I were the frontline scrutineers, but first we had to train a bunch of newbies in the art of editing television news.

The company hired two large function rooms at The Charing Cross Hotel, and over the next fortnight we turned 35 adults from wide-eyed newcomers into proficient editors. Let's cut to the chase: many of them shouldn't have been there. They were probably excellent journalists, but editors? Nah, forget it. Once again multi-skilling was flavour of the month and when these positions had been announced, AP had made it quite clear that journalists and producers would be expected to edit their own news footage. So, turn them into editors we would, though one American in particular needed tipping out of the 2nd-floor window even before the end of the first day.

This was the last hurrah of the analogue era of tape-to-tape editing with expensive, heavy and capricious machinery. We split the group of 35 down the middle(ish) and took them through a structured introduction. At least 70% of them came from television news so were familiar with the editing format having watched others perform it. Now it was up to them, as their instructors (Mark and I) started by removing the lids from the edit machines. I would understand if you thought that odd, but ordinarily, once someone pushes a cassette into a machine, pictures would appear on screen and you would start editing. However, what we were keen to show them was what happens *when* a cassette tape was fed into a machine.

Each group gathered round and stared intently into the guts of the mechanism. They became fascinated watching the intricate and delicate set of spring-mounted arms, levers and cogs, spin and swoop in an orchestrated mechanical ballet. The tape was finally extracted from the cassette housing and laced around the playback head. What utterly beautiful technology it was. The message here being "Now you see how delicate this equipment is, think twice before you start bashing it around." Over the years I'd seen enough herberts treating machinery with a heavy hand, so was keen to avoid it at AP.

At the beginning of the training fortnight we presented all our new editors with a copy of an instruction manual that Mark and I had carefully written and illustrated. "Don't forget to take these with you as and when you travel abroad - you're going to need them." By the end of that fortnight, the one who needed tipping out of the window was proving to be a Royal pain in the arse.

As luck would have it, sometime later, this individual was sent on assignment to the Far East, and as Mark wasn't on duty, I was the one who copped the satellite phone call in the wee small hours. Her edit machines weren't working so she rang the London news desk looking for help. The Duty News Organiser (DNO) patched her cry for assistance through to my home number. Bleary-eyed, I picked up the receiver to learn that it was my favourite American on the other end. My teeth began to itch. "The machine's display is flashing an error code and I don't know what it means!" she whimpered.

Unlike 21st century computer editing programmes that display a message telling you why it's all gone wrong, the old-style analogue edit machines used to display an error code - in red. For example *ER-01*.

There were about 25 known errors in these machines, but cross-referencing the ER code displayed on the readout with the list in our training manual would give:

a) the answer to the problem.
b) how to fix it.

"Right, this is an easy one" I began. "Look it up in the manual you were given during your training course in London." Silence. "I don't have it with me, I left it in my desk." Now, many of you will think that what I did next was vindictive and spiteful - and you'd be right. "Well more fool you", I said and put the phone down. That whining American had it coming. I made a cup of tea, drank it, waited a few more minutes and rang the DNO, in Norwich Street asking to be reconnected to "*that woman* on the satellite phone". Once patched through, she sounded pissed off (I wonder why) but I talked this harassed creature through the problem and had it fixed within minutes, returning to bed very much in 'smug mode'.

Let me just remind you: we weren't dealing with children but seasoned journalists who *knew* what they had signed up for. Each one of them had received more than adequate professional training and both Mark and I were at pains to stress to every single one of our fledgelings how important it was to travel with the manual. After all, that's what we wrote it for. Mind you, her card was marked from the off and if she decided to leave London without the one thing that was designed to help her in times of trouble, then that was her lookout.

The Washington D.C. bureau was our North American hub and the apple of AP's eye. It fell in my footprint so a flying visit was arranged. Along with a few others, we flew out for three days to meet the locals. Being management meant we took advantage of a return business class ticket and a grown-ups expense account. Whilst in D.C. I was also to give a quick training session to camera/edit personnel from the West Coast and a number from APs Latin American bureaux. Taking a handful of training manuals, I handed them out to my new scholars and we went through everything they needed to know. Thankfully they'd all had prior shooting and editing experience so it wasn't too painful to get them up and running and doing things '*the AP way*'.

The D.C. bureau was on K Street, no more than 5 minutes away from "The Crow Bar", a fantastically dingy joint with a muscular security unit on the front door. One by one, my jeans-clad Latinos and assorted Americans went sailing through the front door but me, dressed in a suit and the oldest, was carded. Yes, my bladder on a stick moment had arrived as I had to produce my ID. Internally mortified, my students thought it hysterical. After such a brief visit I was sorry to say goodbye to Washington D.C. and also my business class reclining bed on the world's favourite airline.

Because of my multi-skilled background, there were times when I was asked to step in and shoot. Andy was an ex-Reuters man, now a senior manager at AP. I'd traveled with him to D.C. and he'd figured me out pretty early, seeing an opportunity to use me in the field as and when necessary. He was a very likeable chap and we enjoyed each other's company. Slightly older than me, he'd worked his way up through the management ladder at Reuters, jumping ship and now at the competition.

"Here's the deal" he began, "a job up in Suffolk needs your talents. It's a nice early start, and I know how much you love those. The US Dept of Defence has invited AP to film the air-to-air refuelling of a B2 Stealth bomber over the North Sea. Fancy it?" I was off home and back in the office with an overnight bag before he'd had time to draw breath.

After a night in a cheap hotel in the flatlands, I reported to the main gate and to the PR officer. Not being an American citizen didn't seem to bother them as I was an accredited employee of a respected American-owned news agency. I was to board a KC-135 flying petrol station, take off and wait a couple of hours until we reached the refuelling point where we would meet up with a B2 Stealth Bomber that had just crossed the Atlantic. The 135 would top up the B2 for its onward journey to an undisclosed destination and we'd return to Suffolk.

I powered up the camera and ran through last-minute checks, opening the cassette tray and sliding in a brand new tape …. clunk. Something was up. Clunk. The camera made that noise again. Clunk. I knew my way around these things by heart so I switched it off, opened a side panel, and thinking it was a loose connection, jiggled the circuit boards. I tried it again. Clunk. It clearly wasn't working as it didn't seem to be accepting the tape and now my Airforce escort was impatiently tapping his foot. Clunk. I began stripping the camera down, taking the circuit boards out, blowing on the gold plated contacts and reseating the boards inside the camera. "Hang on", I said and tried it once more. Clunk.

Loathed as I am to break bad news, I turned to my escort and said "Look, I'm sorry but the camera's not playing ball so there's no point in me going. I can't fix it here and time is against us." My escort radioed the PR officer, thanked me for my quick decision-making and marched off. Before the 135 had even started an engine, I was shown off the base and back out into the wilds of Suffolk. Needless to say, the office wasn't happy, but if I couldn't fix it on-site then what was I do to do? As it happens, the USAF videos all such operations themselves so sent us a copy of their tape. For the curious, the camera was sent away and fixed. Apparently, a logic microchip had blown so no matter how much jiggling I did, it wasn't going to fix anything.

New people came on board and Mark and I supervised yet more rounds of training. One day a tall, smiling journalist appeared, his name was Simon Cumbers. An Irishman with a soft lilting accent, a constant wide grin written across his face and a fabulous sense of humour. He'd played around with cameras a bit but wanted to learn everything there was about shooting TV news. I admit that we all thought that this was a flash-in-the-pan moment but Simon obviously had something about him. He was a sponge who listened to everything he was told. He asked relevant questions and, to be honest, was an absolute natural. After his time at AP he went freelance, bought himself a camera kit and started working with the BBC. In 2004 both he and BBC correspondent Frank Gardner were ambushed by Al-Qaeda gunmen in a neighbourhood of Riyadh. Simon was killed on the spot though Frank survived and is still working at the BBC. Another good one gone.

Whenever anyone mentions 'paparazzi' and then accuses me of being one, I'll defend myself to the hilt. I have never and *would* never align myself to such a pack of immoral arse-wipes. Princess Diana was going through a tough patch and our newspapers did little else but concern themselves with her every move: out driving, walking, exercising, you name it. No London-based camera ops were available but AP wanted footage of Diana arriving and leaving her Chelsea gym the following morning, so would I cover it? Did I have a choice? Had I said "no" on moral grounds, then it wouldn't have gone down at all well, but I hated this type of journalism and I always will. Already feeing uncomfortable, I was given the keys to a crew car, into which I slid a large set of step ladders and told to arrive at the gym before 5am.

The drive from east to west London through such dark streets at 4.15 was a doddle and I slid into the genteel backstreets of Chelsea well in advance of Diana's ETA. Parking close to the gym's entrance, I was further rewarded with the sight of a greasy spoon over the road - and it was open. As 5am approached, I sat with a mug of tea cupped in my hands, and from what I could see, no other press had crawled out of the woodwork. No bother, I rang the night shift DNO and told them I was on-site.

I took a wander over the road, and still no other press were in evidence so I returned to the caff for a second cup of tea. At just before 5.30 a two-door Mercedes drove past me and in through the gym's gates - it was Diana. Well, maybe the press pack will turn up for her departure? I thumbed through the morning's red tops full of their dire ramblings and stuck my head out of the door on occasions but *still* no ladders up against the wall, and *still* no press hanging off them.

At 6.30 a pair of headlights swung out of the gym as Diana's Merc turned right and sped off towards Kensington Palace. I paid for my teas, took one final wander over the road and *still* no press. I'd got away with it so called the office to tell them that Diana was a 'no show'. After all, there was no one around to prove me wrong so I was in the clear. I arrived back at the office as the dark rings around the eyes of the night shift gave way to the chirpy day shift. Informing the incomers of my early start, I'd stick around until midday and take the rest of the day off. There was no argument, my moral compass remained intact and pointing in the right direction.

Bonjour Matelot

I was enjoying my time at AP, but the more I was asked to go out on the road, the less paperwork I wanted to do. Another call from Andy and yet another military press facility: "Got a three day job for you in the Adriatic", he began. Now, whenever someone offers you an assignment quoting a timeframe, take its reliability with a pinch of salt. "Fly down to Italy, spend three days onboard a UK aircraft carrier … you know, our brave lads and all that … and back home by the weekend. How does that sound?". The lift appeared at the 6th floor as I was ripping the tie from around my neck. Usual routine, home, pack, back to the office, pick up my kit and off we go.

'Operation Deny Flight' was a NATO mission that began in April 1993 as the enforcement of a military no-fly zone over Bosnia Herzegovina. Land-based military jets from the US, UK, France and Italy patrolled the Balkan skies acting as a deterrent to the warring factions below. Their role ensured that the Balkans states kept their strike hardware firmly on the ground, parking brake on and ignition keys locked away. At the same time, the US, UK and France took turns patrolling the Adriatic with their carriers, launching aircraft in support of the no-fly scenario. After its tour of duty in theatre, an American carrier was leaving and our very own HMS Invincible was its replacement. My job was to film the British matelots at work and document how the ship operated under NATO control.

Flying from Heathrow to Rome, I changed for Bari and a connecting taxi which delivered me to a stool in the hotel bar by 8pm. From my vantage point I quickly spotted the other journalists who were busy making deep holes in their own expense accounts, so I headed for the English-speaking crowd, hoping to make some friends.

On my way to breakfast the next morning, the hotel's main doors were wide open and some lovely warm Italian sunshine wafted in. Once checked out, I sat on an elegant sofa surrounded by my kit as I waited for my Royal Naval (RN) contact to arrive. A military Land Rover appeared at the front door and a stereotypical naval officer in summer kit (cap, white shirt, long shorts, long socks and shiny shoes) dismounted. I stood up, gestured toward him and he strode over, shook my hand and introduced himself. He could have easily have stepped out of the 1953 film 'The Cruel Sea' and it was good to see the British stiff upper lip so far from home. Loading my camera kit and bags into the Land Rover, I jumped aboard. As the naval rating behind the wheel pulled away from the hotel, the officer ran me through a few procedures along with a rundown of what to expect.

5 miles away, at Bari airport, we pulled up in front of a set of wire mesh gates, but now we were on the *other* side of the general area and somewhere the Italian and visiting military could do things out of view of *il pubblico generale*. Since taking over their role in the Adriatic, the RN had embarked on a daily programme in which a Sea King helicopter flew a return trip from Invincible to Bari carrying mail, supplies and personnel, and today I was the chosen cargo for the return trip. After dismounting the Land Rover, the officer handed me a dry suit. This bulky orange and black ill-fitting body condom would keep me alive should the helicopter need to ditch in open water. I was to step into it fully dressed, still wearing my footwear. Despite is cavernous interior, the stale body odour from its previous occupants made my toes curl. It was now 10am, and as the sun began climbing into a cloudless sky, I began basting inside this thick rubber suit. The officer, resplendent in his aerated summer kit, kept checking his watch but still no sign of the chopper. I could feel my clothes beginning to stick to my body, with the added complication that I now needed the toilet.

The faint *wokka wokka* sound of blades slicing through the air announced the arrival of a whirlybird. Sea Kings are impressive machines and mine soon settled in the hover right in front of us, gently lowering itself down to make contact with the concrete. The RN officer tapped my shoulder and gave the 'watch him' sign with his fingers, pointing at the helicopter's wichman. A few naval personnel dressed in civvies and carrying luggage jumped out of the helicopter and ran towards the Land Rover. The Sea King's winchman pointed at me so I picked up my camera, tripod and rucksack, the officer waved me off and I walked towards the helicopter.

Loading my kit in through the cargo door, I was shown a foothold and a handle with which I hauled myself up and inside. I was instructed to buckle myself into a cargo-net seat and the winchman stored my kit aft, then handed me some foam ear defenders. I looked towards the pilots as one of them looked round at me and waved. I waved back, as did the officer standing by the Land Rover, so I waved at him too. In fact, everyone was waving at someone and the situation became a tad comical. With the winchman standing in the doorway, he looked below and behind the aircraft, said something into his headset microphone and the noise and vibration of the machine increased. We became unstuck from Italian soil and clawed our way into the sky.

Sliding the huge cargo door shut, the winchman approached me and started shouting. I removed one foam ear plug as he asked if I was OK and if I had any questions. I shouted back "how long is the trip out to Invincible?" He replied that it would be about 45 minutes and would I like to shoot the carrier from the air before landing? I gave him a thumb's up and he handed me a carton of orange juice and a banana. What kind of message was this? Oh right … the in-flight meal.

The constant shaking and the monotonous drone in my head seemed to go on far too long as we juddered our way over the Adriatic. Just as boredom was setting in, the winchman tapped me on the shoulder and gave me the international charades sign for 'filming', then pointed at his watch, splayed five fingers and pointed to my camera in the aft storage area. I powered up the camera and checked that it was working and on my way forward I stopped briefly to swap my ear defenders for a headset. Putting the camera on my shoulder and started filming cockpit activity: a mass of dials, switches, navigation instruments and assorted bits and pieces. One pilot extended an arm, pointed out to sea and his voice in my headset announced: "Just coming up on Invincible now".

A steel grey hulk appeared out of the sun's glare, leaving a long salty wash behind it. "We'll do a couple of runs for you" the pilot said. Behind me, the winchman was now passing a belt around my waist and ushered me to the cargo door. He clipped a safety line to the back the belt and threw open the door pointing to where I should sit. At a hundred or so feet above Invincible with my legs dangling in fresh air, I framed my shot onto this monstrous floating airport. We flew up and down the deck, from the stern to the bow then the same in reverse. Below us, a flight deck full of busy individuals, each one going about their duties. Other Sea Kings were on their pads and being fussed over by their flight crews. I looked aft and saw an exclusive little group of aircraft in their own VIP area, these were the toys I *really* wanted to play with: the Shars - the Sea Harrier jump jets.

As the Sea King settled on its pad, a line of deck staff in yellow day-glo jackets pointed me towards an open door in the 'island', the metal building sticking out of a carrier's deck. I stepped inside and the helicopter's *wokka wokka* noise was replaced with a low hum. Invincible's Press Attaché was there to greet me, asking that I divest myself of the rubber boil-in-the-bag outfit. He helped carry my kit and overnight bag down ladders, along a vascular system of passageways and to my cabin. He informed me that the

BBC and ITN were already aboard, and sure enough, in my cabin I met my roommate, a BBC cameraman. The Press attaché said that there'd be a briefing for all the press in 30 mins in the Wardroom. As visiting civilians we were to enjoy officer status with which we could use the officer's showers, eat in the Wardroom and make full use of its bar, wherein a gentlemanly gin and tonic was only 75p. Unlike the BBC or ITN, I wasn't editing my footage onboard, so for the next two days I was to be escorted onto the flight deck and to put my cassette with that day's footage *directly* into the outstretched hand of a Sea King pilot.

AP had organised a freelance Italian producer to hang around at Bari airport each evening from where they'd collect the tape from the RN and take it to the local studios of Italian State broadcaster RAI and play everything over the satellite to London. I had to be frugal with how much footage I shot each day as the satellite booking only lasted 15 minutes and an extension would cost a fortune. 15 minutes of footage, to be clear, is quite a bit when the finished package is only 2-3 minutes.

Officer's quarters on a carrier are directly *under* the flight deck. Harrier pilots need to be close to their machines and each aircraft worked a rota of three pilots. We found our way to the Wardroom where the Press Attaché introduced us to a few of his colleagues. He then gave us a timetable of events followed by a few house rules. The trickiest thing was learning how to navigate oneself around this vast behemoth as it cruised the Adriatic. "If you find yourselves unaccompanied, and if you get lost, don't be shy, just ask a member the ship's company." Although we weren't given *total* free-range, we were authorised to travel freely between our cabins, to the Wardroom or to a viewing platform on the second level of the island, but *not* to the bridge, the war room or the flight deck.

My first night at sea was a broken affair, in fact my first night anywhere unfamiliar normally is. Before dawn, noises above my head had woken me. and I lay there trying to figure out what on earth they could be: prolonged scraping sounds, followed by a growl which turned into a roar which only lasted for a couple of seconds and then it died away.

The next morning I wanted answers so I set my alarm for 5am. I dressed, crept out of the cabin and navigated my way up to the authorised viewing area. The noises from the previous morning now had visual explanations as a group of aircraft technicians worked around the Harriers, dragging chains across the deck and fixing them to points underneath the aircraft. One technician jumped into the driving seat, and as the engine started, the system warm and ready to go, he pointed the nozzles downwards and slowly increased the throttle to full. As the Pegasus engine reached its maximum, the surface if the deck surface under the nozzles turned white-hot, lasting for a second or so and then and as the engine was throttled back, the colour of the deck turned to orange and back to black. I repeated the exercise the following morning.

The next 48 hours saw us out on the flight deck filming aircraft movements, day and night Harrier sorties, a trip to the dramatic and hush-hush war room, ship-to-ship and ship-to-shore helicopter shuttle duties, armaments wheeled about the flight deck, and my personal favourite, a RAS - 'Replenishment At Sea'. An auxiliary ship from the merchant navy came alongside, a shot rang out and a line was sent from Invincible towards the visitor. This line was connected to a rope and the rope to steel line, which in turn, was attached to a thick rubber fuel pipe with a metal fitting on the end. As the refuelling detail hauled the pipe over, the metal fitting on the end locked into Invincible's fuel intake with a satisfying 'clunk' and the pumping began. OK, that's the simplified version but you get the idea. The strip of water between the two ships turned into choppy froth as each captain kept a wary eye on matching the other's speed and ensuring a correct and safe distance was maintained between them. Over the next hour or so, other supplies came across the divide in a sling until another 'clunk' signalled the metal fitting separating from Invincible. The refuel had come to an end and she was back to full operational status.

Once alone and out in open waters, the press were granted an interview with Captain Hastilow, the man in charge of this giant floating hotel-cum-airport. One of my esteemed colleagues in the press made the fatal error of referring to HMS Invincible as a 'boat', at which point Captain Hastilow offered to put him ashore the moment he used that word again.

The Wardroom bar was well stocked and very cheap. After dinner, we'd mingle with Harrier and Sea King pilots, along with Weapons, Warfare, Mechanical and other assorted officers. What struck me was not only the diminutive proportions of the Harrier pilots but also their premiership level of arrogance. Contrary to popular belief, a fighter pilot is not selected for his or her qualifications, but a key measurement taken from the hip bone to the knee. If this measurement is too long, then they don't get to fly frontline mud-movers or fighters. The reason being if they ever need to eject and they're too long in that department, then as the Martin Baker ejector seat rockets them out of the cockpit, then the lower edge of the instrument panel will remove their legs at the knees. Aircraft manufacturers don't make individual cockpits to fit individual pilots, so the pilots have to fit the ready-made cockpits. Being a Harrier pilot was one of the coolest jobs out there, though they had no qualms in telling you that they were the best of the best, until of course you met a Tornado jockey, which I did years later.

After 3 days I was looking forward to being whisked off the deck and flying home to London. The Press Attaché popped his head round the door of my cabin, informing me of a call on the satellite phone. I followed him along the now familiar passageways and was ushered inside the Comms office as someone pointed at the handset resting on a table. It was the office back in London: "The MoD have extended the visit and everyone else is being asked to stay, is that OK with you?" Bollocks.

Despondent, I wandered back to my cabin where I bumped into my BBC colleague who told me that they were staying too, so we were all fu*ked a while longer. It was now that my own personal emergency surfaced and I needed to do something about it. I went on the hunt for our Press Attaché as I was down to the last of my clean clothes. To give them credit, within the hour they'd come to my rescue and found me some spare kit. I was decked out in officer's black trousers, a white shirt, naval sweater and some brand new underwear - the latter of which I was invited to keep. With my dirty laundry in a carrier bag, I was escorted to the Chinese laundry. Yes, it's true. Half a dozen Hong Kong Chinese were housed in a cramped steamy sweatshop up in the bow area. They washed and ironed all day, every day, but these poor individuals weren't allowed to step ashore again until the ship docked in a sovereign port. The next afternoon a brown paper parcel tied up with hairy string was left on my bunk. They did a cracking job on that little lot and my undies had creases you could cut yourself on. As I was almost out of video tapes, AP's Rome office organised a delivery of fresh stock which came in on an afternoon Sea King drop.

One morning the Press Attaché hijacked us during breakfast to announce that today was a half day, of sorts. The ship's company was on duty this morning but later most of them were to surface for exercise and relaxation on the flight deck. However, around 1230 there was a little surprise which we were invited to film, so could we gather in the Wardroom at midday? Harrier pilots needed to keep sharp with some live weapons practice, and as this part of the Adriatic had been sealed off to all fishing, ferry and container shipping, Invincible now ruled the waves … well until the exercise was over. A Sea King was to fly ½ a mile away and drop an inflatable target into the sea. Meanwhile, a Harrier loaded with a 1000lb bomb was to climb to an undisclosed height, then swoop down and release its payload. The ship's company would line up along the port side to whoop and holler as the bomb ripped into the target, destroying it with an almighty bang.

Half and hour later, and now up on the viewing platform, the FDO (flight deck officer) waved a Sea King off from the deck and out to sea. It dropped the target, returned to the ship where it hovered some distance away as the Harrier prepared to depart. With a roar, it raced off down the centre line and up the ski ramp. Tucking its undercarriage away, it climbed for the heavens as the Sea King returned to the deck and shut down.

The ship's company lined up along the port side, and up on the viewing platform the Press Attaché held an index finger in the air as if asking for silence on hearing the first bird song of spring. We all heard the scream of a jet engine as the Harrier headed for the drink at great speed. With my camera locked on the floating target out at sea, all eyes looked skywards. The pitch and the noise of the jet increased rapidly and then, all of a sudden, the pitch went down a note or two "He's released the bomb!" said the Press Attaché. I checked my shot just and saw nothing more than a feeble splash as the 1000lb bomb missed its target. Everyone was willing the bomb to explode, but nothing. Sod all.

With a shrug the Press Attaché led us below decks for lunch in the Wardroom. As we tucked into our meal he explained that if an exercise bomb failed to go off, then 30 minutes after it was supposed to explode, then the retarder would automatically take over. The ship was now some way away and with the bomb now at the bottom of the sea (and assuming that its internal pressure meter was working) it should detonate out of harm's way. Just as dessert was being served, a dull thud was felt throughout the ship. That afternoon we joined the ship's company on deck and I took a stroll up to the top of the Harrier ski jump.

Over the coming days I kept in touch with London by Invincible's satellite phone, shot loads of footage and was always on time for my 5pm escort across the flight deck to deliver my tape. By now we were now pretty much part of the ship's company and spent some fun evenings in the Wardroom. Once they realised we weren't the gutter press digging for stories to embarrass the MoD, they relaxed and enjoyed having us around. We'd been at sea for about 10 days and fresh faces who also shared a love of dark humour were made to feel very welcome. I struck up an instant friendship with Invincible's photographic unit. They'd done some really funky stuff themselves from helicopters whilst being buzzed by Harriers, but then they showed me what the Harrier pilots had done themselves whilst flying in formation over Bosnia. Flying a small single-seater fighter whilst operating a camera at the same time was impressive and some of their photos were wonderful. I bought a couple and the photo unit gave me some Flying Tigers squadron flashes - the cloth badges that are sewn onto flying suits.

One glorious morning we were called to a lower aft deck which opened out with a view over the ship's wash. Captain Hastilow arrived flanked by a number of senior officers, the entire group looking rather glum. He made a short announcement and asked us if we would comply with his wishes. The five of us looked at each other and instantly agreed to play ball. It went like this: just after breakfast as the ship's offices were filling up with personnel, a junior rating had been found hanging from a water pipe. The young lad had been the victim of bullying and simply couldn't take it any more. Captain Hastilow asked us not to report this event as the navy was still in the process of contacting the lad's parents back home. Personally, I saw no reason why this *should* be reported as it has nothing to do with us.

A coffin had been arranged via Invincible's onshore team and a Sea King was sent to Bari to collect it. The arriving helicopter landed on deck and I watched as its cargo door slid open and two ratings in white bibs ran over to haul out the bubble-wrapped box. What was strange was that the other deckhands just turned their backs on it, as if simply looking at the coffin would put a hex on their current mission - a bad luck omen so to speak.

Two bloody weeks I was stuck on that ship.
Two.
Bloody.
Weeks.

I filmed more Harriers, more helicopters, more exercises, more trips to the 'War Room' to watch radar screens and drank more subsidised booze. Then one final trip in that smelly orange condom and Alitalia returned me to Blighty. My footage had been very well received back at HQ and some of the management team and the MD took me to The Castle for some light refreshment, along with some of my colleagues who finally poured me into a black cab around midnight.

As for HMS Invincible, in 2003 she appeared on BBC's Top Gear when a Jaguar XJS was catapulted off her ski ramp but in 2011 she left Portsmouth for the final time under tow, dragged to Turkey, broken up for scrap and turned into motorway crash barriers and dog food cans. God bless her.

Part Two

Tunnel of Love

The Production Director role at AP was a busy but enjoyable existence. If we weren't instructing new recruits then we were keeping an eye on incoming footage or solving technical issues. We could be shipping replacement equipment to bureaux the other side of the world or sorting out the computerised playout machine in MCR (Master Control Room). As I mentioned, occasionally I was being taken out of the loop to fill-in for London-based camera ops who were off in sunnier climes. Each time I was hauled away Mark, my opposite number, had to take up the slack. I soon became a little disenchanted, as initially, I had joined to be a quality control expert and trainer and not a shooter out in the field. Still, that's what happens when you're multi-skilled as your employer will exploit your talents whenever and wherever possible, and you can't blame them for that.

I was dating one of the journalists at the time, an American woman, and handed in my notice and went back to being freelancer. I either wanted to do one job or the other, but not both. AP had been very good to me, and I to them, but decided to return to freelancing nonetheless. I renewed my association with my mates at No 4 Millbank, and the American and I rented the top floor apartment at 57 Ponsonby Place on the corner of Millbank. A handy location as it was a stone's throw from my chums and a stumble from the Morpeth Arms pub. From our living room windows we could clearly see MI6 on the other side of the Thames, and in the summer months, spy on their verandah drinks parties.

My old Westminster boss and I started 'Crew Cuts', a company which offered location shooting and mobile editing. I funded a Citroen people carrier which we converted into a mobile edit vehicle - dark blue with AC and seriously comfortable seats. It worked its way into being a good little business and I managed to keep a few freelance shifts at AP. The American announced that she was popping back to the States to see her family, so I remained in London to prepare for the upcoming political conference season. Ten days later, on a Sunday morning, my business partner drove our mobile edit suite up to Blackpool and I was to follow by train later that day. I sat on the sofa with a coffee watching the news and heard a key in the front door. The American stepped through carrying a large suitcase and a face like thunder: "I'm leaving you", she announced.

Apparently, she'd met up with an old flame while she was home, and after some horizontal floor exercises, they decided that they wanted to be together. She unpacked her Matryoshka suitcases and began stuffing her belongings inside. I showered, dressed and finished packing my bag for my own trip. The previous night I'd hosted a party in our flat and one of the girls from AP had left her business card as she wanted to meet up with the American. Anyway, the business card was found and the immediate conclusion was drawn that I was having an affair with the card's owner, which of course I wasn't.

After midday and several really difficult conversations, my minicab driver broke the atmosphere by ringing the front doorbell. I had to leave for Blackpool despite a feeling of shell-shock. The American told me that she'd leave her keys in the letterbox downstairs when she finally left in 2 days so off I went, bemused as to what had happened since I'd woken up that morning. She did indeed fly back to the US two days later, never bothered answering any of my emails which politely asked for her part of the rent … she then married her beau.

Anyway, the girl who left the business card? Well, we hooked up and if I were to be asked if I had any regrets, then letting *that* one go would be one of them. I was still in Ponsonby Place and paying for it by myself when my old boss suggested that if I needed help with the rent then Will (an Australian cameraman/editor) was looking for somewhere to live. I'd known Will for ages and we got on well, so I told him how much the monthly bills were going to cost, he agreed and moved in straight away.

Meanwhile, the Associated Press called and asked me to drop over as there was something they wanted to talk about. I'd recently been to Paris to cover the death of former President, François Mitterrand, when APs Paris bureau chief Bill, hatched a plan to bring me over to France on a full-time basis. I'd known Bill for a while as he'd been based in London for a year or so, and what with him having a French mother and American father, was best placed to run the new office in Paris. Andy welcomed me in to the office and got straight down to business. "Bill's asked if you'd like to go over to Paris as a Cameraman/Producer?" he began. "So, what do you reckon?" London and Paris had been discussing how they were going to fill this role and my name had been put forward.

Reg, one of the upper management who had been one of my original inquisitors 18 months ago, came into the office and perched on the edge of the desk. "Well, the only reservation I have", he began "is that you don't speak French." I thought about this for a second and parried with "Tell me, does the new Beijing chief speak Mandarin?" He didn't so the three of us decided that language wasn't an obstacle and that I could overcome it so set about talking contracts, start dates and salary.

My business partner wasn't exactly thrilled at me breaking up our new venture, but he bought me out nonetheless and I readied myself to leave London. Will was happy in the Ponsonby apartment, so signing the lease over to him, I packed my belongings and put my life into storage. Through an Anglo-French rental company in Paris, I found a bedsit, paid a deposit and had been told that the keys would be waiting for me with the building's concierge. Bill had come over on the Shuttle with an empty Renault Espace, so we loaded my suitcases and other personal effects aboard and I waved goodbye to London.

We made it to my new abode by nightfall, and ringing the doorbell, Bill exchanged a few words and I was handed my keys. In a couple of trips we'd moved all my crap up three flights of stairs and into a squalid little bedsit. It had a bathroom the size of a broom cupboard and a mezzanine single bed. "See you in the morning!", said Bill as he disappeared down the staircase and back to the car.

The following morning I woke to some very strange sounds. My bedsit overlooked a courtyard, people shouted from one apartment to another, wishing neighbours 'good morning' or asking to borrow a cup of flour (for all I could imagine). My bedsit was empty of groceries, so I needed to mount a scavenging operation. Of course I didn't speak a word of French so it was going to be accomplished by a mixture of pointing and sign language.

My digs were located in Rue du Sergent Hoff, in the dreadfully posh 17th arrondissement. I'd scored big time with this place as work was a matter of a brisk 20 minute walk away: a right turn towards Avenue des Ternes, then left and carry on straight until 162 Rue du Faubourg Saint-Honoré in the 8th arrondissement. I knew the office well as I'd visited a few times in my capacity as an AP Production Director and a freelancer. The first chore was to apply for my Carte de Sejour (a residency card) which, so I'd been told, was a mere formality. However, getting anything approved or stamped by any governmental department in France is like pulling teeth: if you don't hand over all the *right* paperwork to the *right* official at the *right* time then you'll find yourself at the back of the queue - and for months at a time.

With my passport, a completed application, a letter of introduction from AP (with official stamp), and all the other silly things they needed to have a look at, I made my way through the metro system and to the Prefecture de Police on Île de la Cité, two minutes walk from Notre Dame.

I wandered the passageways like a bewildered tourist, asking the occasional grumpy French cop to point me in the right direction. Although I was in the right building, and I'd had been given an office number, I'd not been given the right floor. Eventually, after what felt lie an age, I found the one I was after and gingerly knocked on the wooden panel. Upon opening, the female fonctionnaire (civil servant) behind the desk indicated the chair in front of her and asked my name. I passed over my file of paperwork, and in return, she handed me a form. In bad English she asked me to "go away and answer questions".

Now back in the corridor, down one wall was a row of metal chairs populated by a few shy black immigrants, silently looking at their shoes. I sat and looked at the form in my hand. It was a duplicate of what I had in my folder but, as I was to learn, by completing it with today's date on it was preferred by the paper-loving, anally retentive immigration department. To complete the form I was going to need a pen but the French State had already thought of that. Short chains had been screwed into the wall behind me, each sporting a well-worn biro at the end, and just so you were nice and comfortable filling in your form, they'd also bolted the chairs to the floor. Ergonomics in total agony.

With the new form completed, I went back to the office and the unhurried civil servant slowly read through my duplicated answers before manually adding them to her computer. I was told to report back to this office in two weeks. And just so I knew exactly what was going on, I was in France now and fully expected to speak French - "no Eengleesh", she said. However, this civil servant went the extra kilometre by picking up her desk calendar, pointed at the date and put three fingers up to tell me at what time. I felt like telling her I'd be here at two but as this was my first brush with officialdom, I thought better of it.

The next ID I required was a Press Card, and being a foreigner, everything went through the Ministry of Foreign Affairs. Another characterless office in the centre of town, more bloody forms and yet another introductory letter from AP with an official stamp. To cut short another long and tiresome story of French administration, my Carte de Sejour was issued and I was summoned to my Press Card interview. I'd only been in the city for 1 month and the only French I knew was 'hello', 'croissant' and 'beer'. Again, sod all use in my present situation as I sat in a dull, smokey room in front of five lethargic inquisitors. These veteran press men had seen it all, and the one at the far end was chewing on a pipe and thumbing through a copy of 'L'Equipe', the French sporting newspaper.

I handed the head man my CV, my passport, my London Press Card and AP's stamped letter of introduction. He glanced at them and passed them to the next man who passed them … everyone had a gander at my credentials until they arrived with the pipe-chewer. Without even looking up, he gave a cursory wave of his hand and my papers made their way back down the line. Copies were made and everything, except the letter, was handed back. Three weeks later my press pass arrived and I now had a residency card and official journalistic status - and it had only taken seven weeks. I wasn't used to such official foot-dragging but it was to become part of my life for the best part of 2 decades.

My previous sojourns to Paris had fascinated me: I loved the city, the culture, the attitude, the food and the women. On Boxing Day 1994, AP flew me out following the hijacking of Air France flight 8969. On Christmas Eve, four armed men had boarded an Orly-bound Airbus A300 at Houari Boumediene Airport in Algiers.

The four idealists had hijacked the plane and announced that they would fly it to Paris where, above the Eiffel Tower, they'd blow it up. By Boxing Day the French government had had enough of the hijackers as they'd already executed three passengers. The plane took off and made a refuelling stop in Marseilles, at which point members of the GIGN (the elite police tactical group) stormed the plane, killed the four hijackers and brought the conflict to an end. Nine members of the GIGN were injured in the process. AP Paris' staff cameraman, Yves, had flown to Marseille on the 24th but didn't manage to get anything usable as the cops had swept the airport and removed any press they found hiding in amongst the cupboards, toilets and potted plants. You can, if you so wish, see the GIGN's action in Marseille shot by French TV on YouTube.

I found myself at Orly's prestigious Pavillon d'Honneur, the out-of-the-way private terminal for visiting heads of state. The press were formed into two lines leaving a walkway down the middle. We were there for hours, but just as the sun went down, a passenger plane drew up outside. From within spilt the surviving hostages, the Air France crew and the GIGN's walking wounded. They all traipsed into the Pavillon d'Honneur, walking right past our lenses and out the other side.

The relatives of some of the former hostages had been allowed into the building, and the scenes of them greeting their loved ones was very moving. Like the British SAS, and most of the world's special forces, the GIGN has a strict policy that they are '*not allowed to be publicly photographed*', well all that went out the window for some reason. Walking or limping, helping injured colleagues or supporting at least one of them in floods of tears, unmasked they walked right past the press and out to a waiting coach which took them to a military base somewhere, their weapons having been left in Marseilles for post-op analysis. Given the threat level, it was fairly obvious that the French government wanted to crow about their success so had orchestrated this parade in front of the world's media just in time for a real Christmas good-vibe story.

As mentioned before, the year prior to moving to France I'd been over to cover the death of former President François Mitterrand. He and his wife had a little *pied à terre* just off the Champs-Élysées and it was here where he'd succumbed to his cancer. Pressed up against crowd control barriers, I filmed his coffin as it slowly made its way out of the front door and into a waiting hearse. Paris Match, the weekly news magazine, had a reputation for publishing close-to-the-edge photographs to accompany its articles. Some of them were incredibly graphic, especially from war zones. Within days, the latest issue was on the newsstands and it included a photo of their former President, dressed in a dark suit laid out on his deathbed. The furore that erupted over this image sent the government into a tailspin, and with such a high level of police security on the door logging visitors in and out, how could this have happened?

In order to find the guilty party and how Paris Match had acquired this image, police investigators returned to the apartment and recreated the scene, minus the corpse. When the original image had been snapped, the curtains of Mitterrand's room had been drawn, but by studying the intensity of the light leaking through a small gap and the angle at which it hit the opposite wall, they determined the time of day that the photo had been taken. A quick cross-check of the security diary revealed the name of the Presidential policeman on duty. He confessed, instantly losing both his job and a handsome state pension.

For the past 32 years Mitterrand had been conducting an affair with Anne Pingeot and this union had produced an illegitimate child, a daughter called Mazarine. In fact, a year before his death, Mitterrand had 'allowed' the paparazzi to photograph him and Mazarine outside a fashionable Parisian eatery. During Mitterrand's funeral in Jarnac (his birth place) around his graveside were gathered his wife Danielle and their sons, and no more than two yards away, his mistress Anne Pingeot and their daughter Mazarine. The French were fascinated to see all of them together. It was pure theatre and wouldn't have looked out of place had it been incorporated into the plot of a TV soap opera.

Anyway, my first few months raced by and I learnt as much French as I could, which still wasn't a whole lot. AP Television News were a small group of individuals squashed into a glass-fronted goldfish bowl office. The print journalists in the main office would often spend hours staring into it. Of course, the print service had existed long before the TV arm of had even been thought of, but despite us being two years old, we were still viewed with a certain amount of suspicion. As I covered more and more outside events such as street demonstrations and rallies (the French like a good street demo) or press conferences and political announcements, my face became part of the regular press pack and I began making friends with the Parisian media. As I slowly managed to figure out where I was going and what to do, my French-speaking producers stepped back and weren't always there to escort me.

Accredited members of the French press, along with many other European countries, are treated with respect and a valid press card got you into museums for free and nearly into any event you wanted. No matter the subject, being an agency meant that you went out and did whatever the job was: there was no cherry-picking and opting for the best assignment. Each morning there was a phone meeting with London where the Paris producer(s) would map out the day's events, and if the European desk in London thought any of them were of interest, then we'd cover them and send over the footage later in the day. Naturally, some things had been on the calendar for a while but the daily meeting was the only way to find out what was really going on.

One Sunday afternoon I watched a film on M6 which was to change my view of the French forever: *La Grande Vadrouille*. Released in 1966, it starred a number of big French names and a certain Terry-Thomas. A link with the UK had been found, and although I didn't understand a word, the story was wonderfully funny and off-beat. It reminded me of afternoons listening to radio comedy in the Shiplake dormitory. After three months in my grotty bedsit, I had a word with the lettings agency and they found me a proper apartment at 87 Boulevard Voltaire in the 11th arrondissement.

Passing through a pair of large wooden doors into a courtyard, it opened up to reveal a south-facing apartment building six floors high. My apartment was on the second floor and was owned by an Irishman called Billy who lived somewhere in the centre of France. He'd jumped on a train and come up to town to welcome me, which was rather nice. We got on very well and No 87 hit the spot. "Any problems, just give me a ring - much better than dealing with the agency" he said. He then took me over the road to a small bistrot called *Le Played* and introduced me to its owner, Jean-Claude.

The apartment had a compact but very bright kitchen, a reasonably sized bedroom and a tiny bathroom where it was possible to shit, shower and brush your teeth all at the same time. The walls of the living/dining room were canary yellow and two pairs of floor-to-ceiling windows opened out onto a view of the courtyard. Except for the tiled floor of the kitchen and bathroom, everywhere else was beautiful uniformed dark parquet. A charming Italian woman, her French husband and their children lived downstairs and I'd often knock on her door and ask her to kindly translate letters etc. She was a delight.

I then settled into French domestic life by borrowing a Filipino cleaning lady from a soon-to-be girlfriend. This diminutive and constantly-smiling woman was a cleaning marvel. She had a great sense of humour, spoke zero French and sent as much money as she could back home to her husband and kids. Before a year was up she informed me that she was going away for a hysterectomy and I never saw her again.

No 87 was just up the road from the Bataclan, the music venue which suffered that horrendous terrorist attack in November 2015 with the loss of 130 lives. I'd walk past it at least once a week and often drank coffee in the adjoining cafe. That attack shocked me to the very core, and watching from the UK made it even worse.

My canary yellow living room cropped up a few years later after I'd moved to an apartment in the centre of town. A monitor in our goldfish bowl office had been tuned into the BBC's World Service TV when that shade of yellow put in an appearance. In shot, and being interviewed, was David Shayler the former MI5 employee/turned whistle-blower. Along with his then girlfriend and former colleague Annie Machon, the pair of them skipped the UK and had gone to Holland, later moving to France and into my old apartment in Boulevard Voltaire. In 2009 it was reported that

Shayler was living in a squat in Abinger Hammer, Surrey, just a few miles down the road from where I am currently writing this. He was living as a 6ft transvestite squatter called Delores Kane who believes he is the Messiah.

As the summer of 1997 came around, I had a slightly better understanding of French news and had covered a wide variety of events ranging from politics, street demonstrations, strikes and fashion shows. I was more than comfortable with my surroundings, though my French still was pretty much non-existent and still relying on colleagues to help out. Whatever, it was a fun time though I was working far too much. Originally AP London had me sign a contract in which I was expected to fulfil a certain number of days per year, with any days over the agreed amount being rewarded in either overtime payment or time off in lieu. At the current rate that AP Paris was using me, by the time that September came around I'd be a free man and ready to rack up lots of freelance cash, so London told Paris to "slow down".

On one assignment, I'd met the BBC and its staff cameraman Rob, and had also become friends with some of the American writers from the AP office. We hung out together and enjoyed late balmy evenings sat around tiny pavement tables, drinking wine and eating the most glorious food. Dressed in shorts and a t-shirt gone midnight was a lifestyle that suited me. It was the last day of August 1997 when things went pear-shaped. Royally pear-shaped.

In Rue des Prouvaires, in the Les Halles district of the 1st arrondissement, was Le Gros Minet, an intimate family-run restaurant. Chris, one of the American AP writers, lived around the corner and knew the restaurant and its owner very well. Other than English, Chris spoke 4 languages fluently: French, Italian, German and Spanish. His mother was French and his father American. The speciality at Le Gros Minet was *confit de canard* and I couldn't get enough of it. Whenever I visited, I'd order the same thing every time as it was just too good.

Now well past midnight, and along with Rob the BBC cameraman, Chris, myself and a bunch of others, were sat at our pavement table laughing and drinking without so much as a care in the world. Two streets away, the noisy Rue de Rivoli was blocked solid with bumper-to-bumper French holidaymakers returning home after their annual month in the sun. We'd had a very good meal, copious amounts of wine and the owner had just delivered a tray-full of coffees and calvados - on the house. You know that lovely warm feeling after a really good meal, you're replete and ready wander home, slide between a pair of cool sheets and surrender to Morpheus? I was certainly looking forward to jumping on the last metro to Saint-Ambroise, my closest stop to No 87, but then Rob's mobile phone rang.

If it's possible for someone's skin tone to go from 'healthy summer pink' to 'terrified ashen grey' in a matter of seconds, then this was Rob's time to shine. Whatever was being relayed was causing his face to rapidly discolour. He muttered something into the phone, folded it and put it in a pocket, threw a handful of Francs onto the table, and turning to me said "Your phone is about to ring". With that, he headed off into the night. We were all gently lit but, now with the added confusion, what the hell was all that about? Chris began making phone calls as my mobile then chirped into life. It was the DNO at AP London who was in a bit of a flap, "Princess Di's been involved in a car crash over there, Dodi Al Fayed is dead and we need someone on the case *now*!"

Protocol in such situations follows a strict procedure: the local police contact the local Interior ministry who contact British Embassy who contacts the Foreign Office in London who then contacts Buck House. Buck House then reverts to the Foreign Office who inform the host broadcaster (the BBC) who then contacts their representatives on the ground abroad, and once the BBC have it, then every fu*ker knows about it.

French Francs were being dumped onto the table outside Le Gros Minet like confetti at a summer wedding. The owner was thanked and we all split. "I'll see you at the office!" Chris yelled at me. He was going home first to collect a few things. Nicely pissed, I was running up Rue de Roule towards the Rue de Rivoli and in desperate need of a taxi. My press card sat behind a plastic window in my wallet, and stepping out into the bad-tempered traffic, I waved my press card like a police badge trying to hail a taxi. What the hell was I thinking? This was before separate bus and taxi lanes had been introduced to Rue de Rivoli so traffic was 3 abreast. Eventually, I found a taxi and managed to get the driver to understand that I wanted him to take me to the office but to wait as I would be coming back down.

Once through the 6th-floor office door I found Yves, my opposite number, already there and sorting his camera kit. He said he'd do a tour of the hospitals so I volunteered to go down to the tunnel to film the accident spot. Other divisions of the Paris office were filling up with equally alcohol-enriched journalists hauled out of bars, off partners and out of bed, now busy reading the wires in an effort to understand what the hell what was going on. Chris arrived and fired up his computer, "Give me a call from down there and let me know what's going on?"

Jumping into the waiting taxi I asked him to drive to the Pont de l'Alma. As I sobered up in the back of his cab, I rang the DNO in London and briefed them as to what Yves and I were doing and that we'd be in touch separately. The police had sealed off roads in and around the tunnel so I had to run the rest of the way towards the mass of blue flashing lights. I hadn't taken a tripod, just my camera and a rucksack with spare batteries and tapes. A collection of late-night tourists and locals gathered on top of the underpass as a mass of rescue vehicles and officials busied themselves inside the tunnel. I bumped into someone I knew who gave me a quick rundown: "Her car's on the right, see it? It's a fucking mess. Got to go, good luck!"

The wide Cours Albert 1st has a steel and concrete separator running down the middle (much like an urban motorway), splitting the four lanes into two pairs. It's a fast road and great for getting into and out of town, to and from the west. I wandered across the closed roadway and jumped up onto the separator. From this elevated position here I could see right down into the tunnel and to the carnage within. Emergency vehicles were parked around Diana's Mercedes but the wreck was clearly visible. I filmed everything I could: police, rescue teams, on-lookers, wide shots, medium shots and tight shots. After 15 minutes or so I figured that I'd got enough and rang London who informed me that Diana had been transferred to a hospital on the left bank and that Yves was camped outside with other members of the press. I was to return to the office ASAP and send whatever I had to London by satellite.

I found a taxi in the deserted backstreets, and as we headed towards the office, I clearly remember reminding London there were only two of us on the ground at the moment and where the hell is the bureau chief and all our other producers? Once back in the goldfish bowl I ejected the tape and slotted it into a playout machine. The phones were ringing off the hook and every one was someone from a different desk in the same London office. It was obvious that coordination had gone to pot and that London was beginning to panic.

So that I could think straight, I disconnected all of the phones bar one so that I could deal with one person: the DNO, and gave them a detailed description of what I'd shot. A message came back saying that BBC and CNN were going to take the footage live if they could. With the satellite now open, I rewound the tape to the start, cued it up to 2 seconds before the first images and waited for a 'go' from London. All monitors in the goldfish bowl were tuned to 24 hour news channels: BBC World Service, CNN and LCI, French 24hr news. I heard the voice on the other end of the phone say 'go!', I pressed 'play', and after a three second delay, I saw my pictures from the cassette appear on both the BBC and CNN screens. Some of the French journalists from AP's wire service, along with Chris, came in and watched the tape playout. It was identical to what French TV was broadcasting but the reality and proximity of it all was overwhelming.

AP had an agreement with a motorcycle courier company who, when I called them at 3am using my bad French, stepped up to the plate and supplied a fantastic rider who shuttled tapes to and from Yves who was still outside the Pitié-Salpêtrière hospital.

London's next request wasn't far behind: "Can you get yourself to the Ritz Hotel?" Swapping out some camera batteries and putting a spare tape into my rucksack, I set off in another taxi, the alcohol I'd consumed earlier now converting itself into sweat and exiting my body. 10 minutes later I was standing on front of the Ritz Hotel in Place Vendome, from where Diana and the others had left a few hours previously. More public and press had gathered and it was fast approaching 4am. International voices of radio and TV journalists could be heard everywhere as they updated their audiences live on air. I went about my business and collected as many different views of the scene that I could, and at just gone 4am the phone rang.

It was the DNO, "Diana has just been pronounced dead". This may sound odd but as this was being relayed, inside I folded like a pack of cards. This poor woman had been hounded by the gutter press and had paid the ultimate price. Inside my head I heard "Well, that's it sunshine, you can forget all about sleep …" I discussed the options with the DNO, "Where the *hell* is the bureau chief and the producers? Everyone else seems to be fully staffed but there are two cameramen from AP and we really a dedicated person in the office to coordinate." I then made a decision, "I'll ring round for a freelancer to take over from me and I'll coordinate from the office. Oh, and if our permanent staff are pretending to be asleep then it's up to you to get us some backup from elsewhere." The DNO, whom I knew well, agreed.

This update was relayed to members of the London staff who were slowly drifting into work. It was true, two cameramen were keeping AP's operation afloat while every other broadcaster had camera crews spread across the city, producers aplenty and offices full of willing hands, so London needed get on with it and find bodies to help out. The nature and speed of the news industry trains people to see the overall picture with much wider eyes. Admittedly, it can sound brusque or pompous to the outsider, but it's all done with the intention of finding the most effective solution as quickly as possible.

Back in the goldfish bowl I'd rung around and found a freelancer. More footage from Yves was biked in and more tapes and charged batteries were being sent out. With the freelancer out on the streets, rushes from both cameramen were being played over the satellite to London, and like the machine that just wouldn't stop eating, the system consumed every last image we fed it. On one of his many runs, the courier stopped off and picked up some freshly baked croissants and bottles of orange juice from one of the bakeries now opening. He dropped some off with Yves and the freelancer and gave the rest to me.

Dark nighttime footage under street lighting turned into early morning sunlight footage. The guys outside were doing a great job and the biker was making sure everything was delivered as fast as possible. I had made a note of all the footage as I just knew I'd be editing with it later. Finally, six and half hours after we started this, at exactly 8.30 a three-man crew from Rome walked into the office and I could have kissed them. In fact, I think I did. The bureau chief (a wonderful American lady called Trish) asked for a rundown of what we'd been doing since the beginning and where our limited assets were. She was shocked to hear that 3 cameramen and a biker had held AP's operation afloat until now. "Where's Bill and everyone else?" she asked. If the French language was slow in coming to me then a Gallic shrug wasn't, so I gave her one of those. Once up to speed, she checked in with London and I went for a 30-minute lie down in an empty office of the 6th floor.

A tad dazed and sleepy, half an hour later I wandered downstairs only to find that Bill the bureau chief was now in residence and spurting some bullshit excuse about "having switched his phone off". What utter rubbish. He'd been following events until the early hours but fancied some shut-eye before he took over in the morning. By mid-morning, another crew had arrived, and this time from London. What struck me was that the Rome crew (who flew 852 miles) beat the London crew by three hours - and they only had to get on a train and travel 233 miles. "Can I go home for a break?" I asked Bill. "No, we need you" came the reply. Yeah, for the last 8 hours we've been working like one-armed wallpaper hangers but where were *you*?

Now in the driving seat, Bill had been digging through background information on Henri Paul, Diana's driver. He found an address and told me to film the outside of Paul's apartment and to take the young (female) trainee 'G' with me. I'd been living off coffee, fags and rollercoaster levels of adrenaline but it was now midday and I was spent. Ever-helpful Bill had written down Henri Paul's address and now 'G' was guiding me through the busy Parisian traffic. We found the address and I asked her to wait in the car while I took my camera and went for a walk. As soon as I saw Paul's name on the letterboxes I knew it was lunchtime. That's it, mind made up. I was going to take a break and switch my phone off. In fact, I was going to have a sit-down *steak frites avec de la sauce moutarde* and of course whatever 'G' wanted. 24 years later 'G' and I are still in touch. She later married a cameraman, and with their 2 kids, they still live in Paris.

We left the car in underground parking, and with the camera over my shoulder, the two of us walked to the nearest bistro where the TV inside was playing wall-to-wall Diana reaction. "So how did you know it was the wrong house?" asked 'G'. "Well", I began "Henri Paul was a single man and a driver working for the owner of the Ritz Hotel, Mohamed Al Fayed." She nodded. "The nameplate on the letterbox I saw just now is for a Dr & Mrs Henri Paul." Does that answer your question?" She smiled and we ordered from the menu. She questioned why we could sit and have a relaxed lunch while there was still so much to do. I went on to explain that:

a) I'd been on the go all night without a proper break and I was f*cked
b) there was enough going on elsewhere so we wouldn't be missed for a while and
c) Bill was dyslexic

When I finally switched my phone back on I wasn't putting up with any of Bill's "Where have you been?" nonsense, so returned 'G' to the office and left her with a wink as I was re-tasked to the Pitié-Salpêtrière Hospital - the mobile edit van needed an editor. The scenes at the hospital were quite moving. Hundreds of French were up against crowd control barriers surrounding the TV crews, all hoping to get a view of the hearse and the Royal Party. They threw abuse at many of my colleagues, accusing them of killing Diana. "No madame," said a Stuart Nimmo, a long-time expat British cameraman "that'll be the gutter press, and besides, at the time of the accident she was being driven *by* and pursued *by* you, the French." Stuart and I remain mates even today and whenever I could, I'd always booked him for two-camera shoots for the BBC, but I'll get to that later.

I had now been up for 36 hours, Charles was back on UK soil with his ex-wife's body and I was back in the office. Although there were still tons of questions that had to be answered this side of the Channel, for now the story moved to London. An inquest would soon be underway but my immediate requirement was sleep. Fresh crews had arrived and were busy elsewhere in the city, Yves had left the hospital and gone home and I'd had enough. "That's it, I'm done", I announced, glaring at those in the office, "sort the rest of it out yourselves". As I left the goldfish bowl, no one challenged my decision and Bill (very wisely) kept his trap shut.

The following month or so (unsurprisingly) was nothing but Diana coverage: interviews with French politicians who gave opinionated statements if only to get on TV, writers launching into poetic laments, conspiracy theorists only too eager to tell us whodunnit, lawyers who shared their specialist knowledge whilst looking at us over the tops of their glasses, and members of the public who pointed the blame squarely at the world's media (by the way, if you're going to generalise then shouldn't we include those thoughtless bastards at Railway Monthly and Catering News?). It's all well and good shouting at the media, but the catalyst behind such hunger was the public who bought sensationalist newspapers and glossy magazines which scrutinised the life of this poor creature on every turn of the page. I've already stated my lack of involvement and unwillingness to become part of such dreadful behaviour by the populist media.

The coroner was releasing Henri Paul's body from the city morgue so we all rushed over to the L'Institut Médico-Légal for an afternoon of eye-spy. All plates of French motor vehicles display a pair of numbers which indicate the region from which the vehicle is registered. For example, as Paris is in department 75, all vehicles registered in Paris carry 75 on their plates, but we were looking for a private ambulance with 29 (Quimper) as Paul was being interred in Lorient, Brittany. In a small café over the road from the morgue, a couple of dozen press settled down with coffees, beers and then a game of 'baby foot' (table football). The immigrant owner of the café must have thought that his ship had come in, the cash was pouring into his till and he couldn't work fast enough to keep everyone refreshed. By 6pm, the L'Institut Médico-Légal had closed its doors for 'outgoings' so we all went home. In truth, Henri Paul's body had been smuggled out some time ago so we'd all been wasting our time, but the café owner had had his 15 minutes of fame.

As with media all over, the French has its own domestic print (newspapers), radio and television outlets, but like every major capital city, it also plays host to numerous foreign agencies and broadcasters. When major events happen, the national broadcaster becomes the *host* broadcaster and supplies its international guests with their images. A big event in France would be covered by State broadcaster TF1, and they'd supply the images to everyone else (in the UK it's normally the BBC). However, during 'Diana' it worked slightly differently with the host broadcaster only supplying images to French media and a foreign agency would supply images to everyone else. This facility is called the 'pool' camera: French pool (for all French outlets), and International pool (for everyone else).

Henri Paul's funeral was due to take place in Lorient at the end of September and the Associated Press had been chosen as the international pool camera and I was given the job of filming everything up close and personal - so no pressure then. An APTV news crew, along with the mobile satellite van, drove the five hours cross-country to Lorient but I opted to take the train. I arrived early the day before and was stuck with a sudden case of injustice. In under 24 hours, the world's press was to descend onto this port town where shipbuilding and the French navy went hand in hand, but from tomorrow it would be known as the burial place of Diana's driver. All I had was a pair of jeans, a clean shirt and a pair of walking shoes but felt badly equipped for the job ahead. Walking into town, I found an inexpensive clothing shop where I bought the cheapest dark suit I could find, a white shirt and a black tie. No way was I going to cover this event in jeans and I felt better for it, though my colleagues thought I was stupid.

With the reluctant approval of the Paul family, it had been agreed that the 4 members of the press would be shown into the church once family and guests had taken their places but *before* the coffin had been placed before the altar. We could film the pallbearers as they entered the church and rested the coffin on the trestles, after which we would be ushered out the back door. I'd then hand over my tape to our producer who'd send it to London for onward distribution across the globe. Forty-five minutes later I'd make my way round to the graveside where the same group of press would set up to one side of the grave. We'd film the arrival of the family, watch the coffin as it was again placed on trestles and then we'd leave the grieving family to continue with the ceremony in private. Nice and respectful and just the way I like it.

As I remember it, there were four of us in total: two TV cameras (TF1 and AP - me) and two stills photographers (French agency and AP). In the church, we stood back from the trestles in full view of the congregation as waves of hate came our way. The music started, everyone stood and we recorded the procession and placing of Henri Paul's casket. As the pallbearers stepped back and bowed, a voice behind us whispered, "*s'il vous plait*" and the four of us quietly turned around and left the church by a side door. Outside in the September sun I realised that I was uncomfortable being uncomfortable doing something uncomfortable.

Walking round to the graveside, I joined the other 3 pressmen and we got ready for the next bit. I had a look into the grave: it was a very square affair with sharp lines, beautifully cut and lined with concrete that had been painted white. The coffin arrived followed by Paul's family and friends. It was positioned on the trestles, and when we'd got what we wanted, the "*s'il vous plait*" came again from behind us. We respectfully turned and took the long way round and out of the cemetery. What was galling was that Henri Paul was being buried in a corner of the cemetery, yet poking up from behind a wall was a TV camera on the end of a hydraulic pole. This poor innocent family couldn't even conduct a peaceful ceremony without some guttersnipe zooming in for every last tear and expression of grief. I handed in my second tape, collected my overnight bag from the crew van and jumped on the next TGV back to Paris.

Of course, there were other stories in France that didn't involve the Princess and her untimely demise. We covered champagne stories, political upheaval (how to make something out of nothing), national strikes and a story about new words being introduced into the official French language. It was now autumn and the annual grape harvest was on the cards so we visited a number of top-notch winemakers across the land. Normally, the owners of these establishments would give you a bottle to take away by way of a "thank you for the free promotion" kind of thing.

Château Pape Clément is in Pessac near Bordeaux, and Bill and I went on assignment to film the story of them having an old Pope (Pape) buried beneath the chateau. We overnighted and the next day I was up early to shoot some stunning images of an orange dawn breaking over the vineyard. Once finished, the owner handed over eight bottles of plonk: four red and white white. As we got on the Paris-bound train Bill said, "Shit! This stuff ain't cheap!" It tasted glorious and within 2 weeks I'd worked my way through the lot. In comparison, if you visit a champagne producer they'll offer you one small glass of bubbly to sip on the way in and sod all product to take away with you.

A couple of months after Diana's accident, I was booked to shoot a live satellite interview with Ritz Hotel owner, and father of Dodi Al Fayed, Mohamed Al Fayed from inside his top floor private suite in Place

Vendôme. The rooms afforded a magnificent view over Paris and we ferried all the kit up in the lift, setting up the camera, lights and the sound kit. Cables were thrown out of the window, gathered up and plugged into the satellite truck down at street level. After checking that all was working and that the bird (slang for 'satellite') was up and London could see and hear us, in came the famous Egyptian. No matter your views on him, his hold on Harrods, the way Private Eye lambasted him or how the British Government treated him, he'd lost a child in accident in full view of the world and its media. He spoke well and answered the interviewer's questions appropriately, with passion and good argument. Once the interview was over, he presented the crew with large bars of Toblerone as a 'thank you'. I found him to be very pleasant but you could see what the last few months had done to him: he was very, very drawn and emotionally fatigued.

In the film calendar, the Cannes Film Festival is a huge deal and during my one and only trip to the Festival, I was to make my debut on BBC Radio 4. Sony Broadcast has released a new piece of television editing kit and I had the honour of taking it down to Cannes and using it in anger for the first time. It was a huge metal box with a giant spinning disk inside, so rather than edit tape to tape, the footage was recorded stored and edited on this disk. Once through security at the Palais des Festivals et des Congrès, I installed it in our cramped office/edit suite area in the basement. Bearing in mind that I'd had the length of the train ride to read the instruction manual and figure out how this thing worked, and no opportunity to switch it on, I was in no position to start using it. Of course 'shoot first' Bill was expecting me to be fluent and left our office unit with "Well hurry up and make to work!" Try as I might, it just wasn't making any sense.

AP had already taken a tape editing suite to Cannes, but rather than bring a second as back up, some bright spark suggested that we took Sony's disc machine instead. What they *hadn't* counted on was a much-needed training session. When Bill returned to the unit I explained that I needed more time to learn this thing, at which point he hit the roof, "Just get it working as we don't have a second tape edit suite!" I screamed back something along the lines of "Well whose catastrophic idea was that then, yours?" He then launched into an uncontrolled verbal shit-fit. Of course, being the more experienced technician, I spelt out the reasons as to why it was a silly idea to have brought the damn thing in the first place. The exchange grew louder and my argument more impassioned. The door to our space was opened by a demure BBC Radio journalist who was at pains to inform us that due to the inadequate thickness of material separating our two units, her genteel Radio 4 audience had been party to "quite an unusual report".

She'd begun with a review of the film she'd seen the night before, but midway, a tirade of verbal obscenities had joined in live on air. Fame at last! Clutching the award to my chest "I'd like to thank …"

I had to dig Bill out of another hole during the festival when we were granted an interview one of the stars of 'Mrs Brown', the story of a recently widowed Queen Victoria and her relationship with Scotsman John Brown, a trusted estate servant. Sheltering from the hot summer sun under a purpose-built open sided tent on the beach, I set up my camera kit and we awaited the arrival of Billy Connolly. Being an American, Bill hadn't got a clue as to who Connolly was so I gave him a quick synopsis of the Big Yin's career to date.

Connolly arrived and sat down. I pinned a tie mic to his shirt as Bill explained the interview format. Connolly had us in fits from the start but soon brought himself into check and got down to the reason the was here, to plug the film. American shock-jock Howard Stern was also in town promoting *his* new film 'Private Parts'.

An erect Howard Stern in rude health.

So as to make the biggest promotional splash possible, his film's PR mob had installed a 30-foot inflatable version of Stern and sailed it out 100 yards offshore so it could be seen by absolutely everyone.

Our interview with Connolly was going well until I spotted something untoward and had to bring proceedings to a halt. I apologised and started to move the camera to one side, but when Connolly asked what the problem was, I pointed to the giant inflatable Stern out on the pontoon. The damn thing had sprung a leak and was slowly listing to one side. Stern's head was gently collapsing onto its shoulder and as soon as Connolly had turned round for a look, he burst into laughter with "Oh Christ! Howard's having a stroke!" It took a while to restart the interview as none of us could stop laughing, but eventually we got it in the can and that was that. We said goodbye to Connolly, shook hands and the film's PR flunky took him off down the beach for his next appointment. Happy days.

The larger of the two islands in Paris' River Seine is Île de la Cité and here you'll find Notre Dame, the Conciergerie and the Palais de Justice (the Paris equivalent of London's Old Bailey). Once again, filthy rich lawyers had gathered to contest another Diana ruling or cry over yet another infantile argument, and of course, the press was there to catch every last drop of it. The Palais de Justice sits behind huge metal gates topped with gold leaf and the compound is guarded by the police. The courtyard opens to an expansive stone staircase which rises up to three large entrance doors to this magnificent building. On the left of the courtyard is a narrow passageway which leads to the public entrance, and this is where the press were currently gathered, barred from entering the main courtyard until a verdict had been given. I was bored. We were all bored. Over the past three months we'd all been here at least twice a week but now it was becoming rather long in the tooth.

I have, and always have had, a wicked sense of fun, often edging towards gallows humour and I'll make no bones about it. Working as a member of the press out on the streets meant that pretty much every day we were accosted by the public wanting to know what we were doing. When we were up against the clock and just wanted to get the job done and back to the edit suite, our replies could be bad tempered and brusque: "Do we come and interrupt you at *your* place of work? Yes? No?" This frequently led to the offended inquisitor sheepishly heading off grumbling to themselves. I admit that those instances were rare, but we weren't civil servants and weren't paid by the State. We were just private individuals under stress who wanted to get the job done and get home. Although we realised we were a novelty street act to the general public, being stopped day in day out could get a tad boring.

Paris is, if you can picture it, full of little old ladies. Take your pick of any of *les Grandes Dames* who live in the city centre - they always have done and always will. Taking an afternoon stroll down to their local convenience shop to stock up on essentials, they'd get a bit of exercise and chat to a few of their chums along the way ... and some would fall upon a small British television news crew, standing around on a street corner. Always dressed to perfection, these delicate examples of an age gone by would wander up to us, a baguette and a bottle of red poking out of their canvas shopping bag, and ask *"Bonjour, qu'est-ce que vous faites ici?"* (Hello, what are you doing here?) No matter the weather or the pressure we were under, we always made sure these diminutive treasures were handled with the utmost respect. In such situations I would bend down and tell them *"Nous faisons un porno"* (We're making a porn film), followed by a wink. Some giggled with. Some ran.

Anyway, back to yet another Diana enquiry and the group of bored press at the Palais de Justice. Cupping my hand around the ear of a French colleague, I suggested that we livened things up with some high jinx. He agreed so I told him my plan. The press were in their default positions, standing around smoking or starting more unnecessary rumours. Whatever, everyone just wanted to get going. My idea was that as we were both cameramen, the pair of us would (all of a sudden) pick up our cameras and run through the passageway and into the courtyard as if something urgent was happening. Naturally, being excited sheep and thinking that something was up, the remaining press pack would do the same and come haring around the corner after us.

We waited a few minutes and then, quick as a flash bent down, picked up our cameras and ran at full tilt through the passageway. Even as we covered the 20 yards or so to the courtyard, we could hear the sound of people swearing, gathering up equipment, spitting out cigarettes and telling their colleagues to "hurry up!" In the courtyard, the pair of us stood with our cameras by our feet with huge smiles on our faces. Once the press pack realised they'd been suckered, they skidded to a halt. Whilst there were plenty of laughs, there was also the odd grumpy insult. No matter, we'd enjoyed ourselves and brought a little happiness to those less fortunate.

At that time, France's homegrown shit-stain was leader of the National Front Party, Jean-Marie Le Pen. His daughter Marine was a candidate in the upcoming elections, standing for a seat in the town of Mantes La Jolie, an hour's drive to the west of Paris. London producer 'K' had been brought over to Paris to help out in the run-up to the elections and she and I went to cover the Le Pens as they campaigned around Mantes. The pair were due to arrive at the town's church and a large crowd had already gathered, so we joined them in the glorious May sunshine.

A sleek black car with tinted windows swept into the parking bay, the rear doors opened and father and daughter stepped out, one from each side. A smiling Jean-Marie waved to the crowd, slipped on his jacket, shook hands with a few admirers and then all hell let loose. A voice in the crowd appeared to taunt the nationalist who, spotting his prey, made his way over to the church, cornered the Socialist candidate Annette Peulvast-Bergeal and pinned her against a wall. Grabbing and twisting her tricolour sash in his fist, he smashed her upper body into the stonework, and at the same time, his uncouth mouth was unloading all sorts of profanities just inches away from her face. Holding my camera high above the scene I hoped that the height and angle was enough to capture everything that was unfolding. So that I couldn't film this blatant act of physical abuse, a Le Pen supporter made a grab for the camera's hanging shoulder strap. My producer 'K', a diminutive woman, laid into this guy with all she'd got, trying to stop his attempt at sabotage. The mood of the townsfolk changed and Le Pen's bodyguard lashed out at a youth a few minutes later. To protect them, their security detail pushed father and daughter into a café. The shutters came down as they hid from a small angry crowd who were now pelting the windows with eggs. At the same time, details of Le Pen's antics were being released across French media and, of course, everyone in our office back in Paris was keen to see what we had.

Once back and with tape in hand (and I wish this didn't sound so dramatic), our French colleagues from the print and photo departments flooded into our small space just to take a look at what I'd shot. Although the Le Pens were known as a nasty lot, our colleagues were appalled by what they saw. You could clearly see Jean-Marie Le Pen assault the Socialist candidate. By the time the French evening news begun at 8pm, our images from Mantes had been circulated everywhere. The next day the Police Nationale asked for a copy of the rushes as a complaint had been made against Le Pen and they intended on using my tape as evidence.

For the next few months Le Pen kept himself busy doing the rounds of TV and radio shows screaming "we know it's all fake, the people who took those images manipulated them. Someone is complicit in this whole affair!" To keep me out of the spotlight until things cooled down, AP sent me to cover the handover in Hong Kong ...

To be honest, I didn't really enjoy myself over there. The assignments manager was unreasonable when it came to handing out working schedules. 18 hour days were commonplace and freelancers were given insufficient rest periods. No longer a member of AP management but now a lowly freelancer, I was immediately given night shift, part of a crew operating three cameras on the roof of the city's theatre which overlooked the waterfront. We were to do all the live shots before, during and after the handover ceremony. Once Chris Patton had handed the keys over to China, the weather outside turned nasty with storm-force winds and driving horizontal rain. After hours and hours of this, at around 4am, the water level on the roof of the theatre could potentially cause a massive short-circuit. I called the production office on the comms line and suggested we switched everything off. Although the flat roof had drainage pipes, they weren't dealing with the situation well enough, and our mass of electrical cables and connectors were now floating. Eventually, after all of our clients cancelled their bookings due to this tropical storm, the production office saw sense and closed down the roof operation. We covered all the kit with plastic sheeting and went back to the hotel - I needed my bed.

The centre of Hong Kong is a mass of busy roads spanned by pedestrian walkways. The sun was just coming up but the rain was still coming down. Hong Kong's streets appeared deserted as I squelched my way back to the hotel, but as I reached the central point of a pedestrian bridge, a convoy of Chinese Army trucks came into view. I stopped and watched them pass beneath me. Identical trucks, each open to the elements and full of sardine-packed soldiers wearing rain capes and standing stock still, one arm across their chests holding an automatic weapon, their other hand clutching the railing down the side of the vehicle. Once past me they carried on towards the old British Military base that had been vacated just a few hours beforehand - the Red Army had well and truly arrived.

I was quite pleased to return to Paris after Hong Kong, though there was one surprising moment which involved a trip to Kowloon on the Star Ferry. In one of those busy markets I found a t-shirt with an illustration of a galloping horse by Xu Beihong. As a child, my parents had two prints of Beihong's horses, one either side of the fireplace in Cobham but here I was on the other side of the world hugging a t-shirt with the same image. It's shrunk a bit now, but I still have it.

To fast forward the Le Pen story: in 2000 Le Pen was suspended from the European Parliament following prosecution for the physical assault of Peulvast-Bergeal which ultimately led to him losing his seat in the European parliament in 2003. The Versailles appeals court then banned him from seeking office for one year. My footage from Mantes La Jolie can be seen on YouTube if you're interested.

It was fast approaching the end of 1997 and there were three months left on my contract. Naturally, in the February of '98 I was half expecting it to simply roll over. I dropped an email to the higher-ups in London asking their intentions for the next 12 months but received nothing in return. I'd almost forgiven Bill for playing dead when we needed him most in August, and showing me his support, he too wrote to London, asking them what was happening with my contract. Surprisingly, this was also met with resounding silence.

In December, along with 'G' our trainee, I flew to Marseille for next year's FIFA World Cup Draw. As an agency we didn't have broadcasting rights so weren't allowed to film inside the Vélodrome, so covered what was going on outside in the street: footy fans, drunk footy fans and obnoxiously drunk footy fans. Before departure from Paris, the office had booked us a compact ECO car, the cheaper the better. On arrival at Marseille Provence Airport the young lady at the hire company told us that the ECO car was no longer available but she *did* have something else we could have for the same price: a huge black Mercedes. This was sheer luxury.

After a longish night filming, 'G' and I got a few hours shuteye and the following morning set off for the airport and our return flight to Paris. As we drove up the A7, I couldn't help but notice up ahead what looked like flying debris and plumes of smoke. Sure enough there had been a pile up and the car in front was braking hard. I immediately stuck my right arm out to protect 'G' and slammed on the brakes. The Merc's first-class system brought us to a halt well behind the car ahead ... but then I looked in the rear view mirror. A small white car was getting bigger and in an instant my brain told me that this was going to hurt. Sure enough, it ploughed into us with one hell of a thump pushing us into the car in front - and then it all went quiet. Checking to see that 'G' was OK, I made sure we could at least get the doors open but decided we should stay in the car as we waited for the emergency services. Unknown to us there were 12 cars involved and that we were number 11.

The Sapeur Pompiers (the fire service) arrived and the *sapeur* who ran up to us gave me a thumb's up and stopped to ask if we were both OK. At this point I saw a face I recognised, it was one of the AP photographers. They'd been in their own hire car some way behind us, and as the crawling traffic made it's way past the wreckage, one of the photographers had recognised our Mercedes. The day before they'd been green with envy after seeing us driving around in this palatial vehicle. Of course, being ever-ready news photographers, one of them leapt out and started taking photos. He checked we were both OK, wound the film back onto the bobbin inside the camera, ejected the roll of exposed film and gave it to me as a present. Back in Paris I had it developed and the Merc was a write-off.

'G' and I were led over to a Police wagon and interviewed where she did the talking for me and translated my answers. The two cops were really friendly and especially enjoyed the part (with relish) where they told us that the driver of the car who had slammed into the rear of us was a driving instructor, "Oh, him? He's already lost his job, you can sure of that!" The form filling began and one of them asked me my place of birth, to which I answered "Twickenham". His face lit up as he was a keen rugby player and proceeded to roll up his trouser legs to reveal his collection of scars.

We called Bill in Paris and he suggested that for insurance purposes we should go and get ourselves checked out in hospital. After several hours we were released from A&E and took a taxi to pick up our kit from the transport company who'd dragged the wrecked vehicles off the motorway. At the airport we were booked on to the last plane back to Paris, and typically, we both fell asleep in the departure hall, waking up as the 'gate closing' announcements were being made. As we now know, the World Cup draw was fixed and that the hosts met Brazil in the finals *wasn't* by chance. As a sporting nation, the French went *way* down in my estimation after that was uncovered.

My sister Debbie rang from the UK with some good news about our childhood home: Westdean's gardens were open to the public and would I like to go back and have a wander? Debbie had telephoned the current owner and explained who we were and that their brother would be coming over from Paris, so could we please have a cheeky private viewing around the house? Debs was good at that sort of thing and the lady of the house agreed. With Debbie's husband Steve and our other sister Jenny, here we were all together at our childhood home for the first time in over 25 years.

The new owner was somewhat taken aback to have 3 hyperactive adults running about the place, sticking their noses everywhere and announcing "Well that wasn't like that in *our* day." The memories were flooding back in full colour and it was magical. The hostess was an absolute sweetheart. We took photos all over the house and recreated some old black and white images from the 60s. There was one of me on Jenny's lap when I was a toddler and another of Debbie sitting on the front steps looking through a tennis racket (of course we'd thought this this one through and brought a tennis racket with us). We couldn't have been made to feel any more welcome and left full of memories, happy that our old house was being quite so well looked after.

Back in Paris I was to get up close and personal with and Ilich Ramírez Sánchez. Now that name might not mean anything to you as is, but if I was to use his nickname it might ring a bell: Carlos The Jackal. In 1994 Carlos was a wanted man, hiding out in the Sudan. Following acts of terrorism in the French capital, *les flics* badly wanted a word. During his time in the Sudan, Carlos required a surgical procedure on his testicles, whilst behind the scenes, the French did a deal with the Sudanese government: the Sudanese would give him an extra dose of general anaesthetic, and once he was well and truly under, they were to hand him over to agents of the DST (the French version of our MI5), who flew him to Paris for trial. It worked, and over the next three years Carlos was in and out of court. In December 1997 he was found guilty and sentenced to life imprisonment *without* the possibility of parole. Finally, the French (and I make no apology for this) had got him by the balls.

On the day of sentencing, along with the usual collection of French and International Press, I was outside the Palais de Justice's vehicle entrance on Quai des Orfèvres, where prison vans shuttle the criminal elements through giant wooden doors and into the Palais. With such a high-profile individual on his way, the cops were taking no risks and the streets leading up to the courthouse were flooded with gun-wielding, hooded, anonymous firearms officers.

Sitting on a low wall opposite the wooden doors, the press corps waited, smoked and chatted. A helicopter from the Gendarmerie appeared over the rooftops on the Left Bank, while down on the street, two-tone sirens announced the arrival of a swathe of Police vehicles, followed closely by the prison van and an assortment of others. With their side doors wide open, hooded marksmen leant out, scouring the pavements for possible attackers. We started filming this well rehearsed show of strength as it made its way along Quais de Grands Augustins and then turned right over Pont Neuf.

Within seconds the cavalcade arrived in front of us. From unmarked vans, balaclava'd marksmen jumped out to take up assigned positions around the convoy. It looked fab on camera until their plan went to hell in a handcart.

Every Police movement like this required advance planning and split-second timing, but today's exercise just didn't go as expected. When a convoy reaches the Quai des Orfèvres, the lead vehicle would radio ahead so that the Palais' huge wooden access gates would be open in time for the prison van to simply drive straight through and into the courtyard. Job done. As a cameraman back in London I'd seen this done many times when filming in Newgate Street, on the north side of the Old Bailey. Metropolitan Police vans swept around the corner and whisked assorted naughty boys (and girls) through its big black doors. It lasted seconds but the performance went like clockwork.

Looking through my viewfinder I'd framed up on the prison van but as drew level, it ground to a complete halt. The Palais' wooden doors weren't open and now the van's arse was stuck out in the street. The trigger-happy cops went into synchronised meltdown, hopping about the place, their eyes poking through their balaclavas sent us the message that went *"mon dieu, this isn't supposed to be happening!"* The upper portion of the prison van was smoked glass covered in a protective steel mesh. However, from the inside, ventilation windows could be opened - and one was. With a defiant display of fist-shaking whilst yelling obscenities about the French government, Carlos was giving his first public speech in years. Despite the best efforts of the uniformed Police, we ran up to the rear of the vehicle to capture what this notorious international terrorist had to say. We managed to grab several seconds of his impromptu tirade before the gates opened and the van finally drove into the courtyard.

I can't quite recall my first Christmas as an expat: whether I spent it in Paris or came home to the UK and to Debbie, Jenny and the rest of my family. Come the New Year, still nothing from London and my new contract. Bill's core temperature was rising steadily as he needed me for the coming year but London was definitely stalling. To be honest, I was in no mood to simply trot home as I was enjoying Paris and all it's trappings.

With a fortnight to run on the current contract (I'd finished the allotted days long before so was now on a daily rate) I received a call from Reg in Norwich Street - they were ready to talk. I expensed a first-class return Eurostar ticket (which went down very well) and took a taxi from London's Waterloo International to the AP office. Andy and Reg sat me down and went through the details. It was fairly obvious that on a global scale the company had overspent in a number of areas and that things had to change. I sympathised but said that it was neither my fault nor my problem as I was supplying them with a first-rate service at a very competitive price.

They announced their offer for the coming year: my contract days were to be increased by 18% but the money *wasn't* moving upwards. Since September, they had me on an expensive freelance rate and weren't happy with how Paris were spending. Well, Bill was using up my contract days like a lottery winner working their way through their prize money so what did they expect?

I listened to their offer, said nothing and returned to Paris. The following day Bill was eager to hear all about it. I gave him a rundown of the details to which he said "Great! So you'll stay?" I told him that only a mad man would accept an increase in days and with no increase in pay. I returned to my bright yellow flat, crossed the road and visited Jean-Claude in *Le Played*.

A stocky Frenchman who'd lived in London in the 60s, Jean-Claude was a keen music lover who'd decorated the walls of his bistrot with vinyl records and their colourful sleeves. The food was so-so, the beer was fair to middling but I felt comfortable here. I spent many, many hours leaning against the zinc bar as Jean-Claude taught me French. He was a delight and the first real friend I'd made in the city outside of the office.

I considered my options:

a) Take the deal and be even more knackered at the end of it.
b) Put my tail between my legs and return to the UK.
c) Stay in Paris and go freelance.

The next morning I gave London an ultimatum: we'd continue on the same contract as the previous year or offer me a realistic financial incentive to match the new contract, but failing that, I would be leaving the following Friday.

Going Solo

"That's a little unreasonable", AP London whined down the phone. "To be fair," I began, "I asked you for a decision on my contract at the start of last November but heard nothing for three months. Now with a fortnight to run, you offer me a contract with an increase in days but *no* increase in salary. Tell me something, have *you* all had pay rises this year?"

Once Bill heard that I would be leaving at the end of the week, he turned puce with rage. Graciously, he backed me to the hilt arguing that London had been playing the long game, hoping that I'd succumb to desperation by accepting a late offer. "We just don't have the money" they told him. The week soon ended with no change in offer, and on the Friday night I called a taxi on the company account and loaded up my camera kit. Giving the driver my address, I followed it home on my motorbike. The weekend *sans-boulot* was spent eating sushi in Bastille and propping up the bar at Jean-Claude's. A plan of action was called for, and now was the ideal time to thinking about one.

My first Monday morning as a freelancer was both daunting and strangely refreshing. I was clear of an inflexible and demanding taskmaster but still not entirely sure as to where I was going to earn a crust. It was bitterly cold outside, but as I stood at the huge living room windows, patches of clear blue sky could be seen between the travelling clouds. The muffled sound of car horns from frustrated drivers out on Boulevard Voltaire gave way to the foreign voices of immigrants as they wheeled their sack-trolleys of wholesale clothing from double-parked wagons into shady sweatshops.

Resplendent in my dressing gown, giving my neighbours an idea of what was to come, my phone rang. It was Bill, "Can you come in today, we need you." I had a feeling this would happen. Although AP had run out of contract money, they had very deep pockets when it came to ad-hoc freelance hire. Over the next six months I was in great demand and earning three times what I had before. London was quite happy to cut me off at the knees one minute, but more than happy to pay me (handsomely) as a freelancer. I was now in a position where I could pick and choose whether I worked or not, but realised I couldn't take the piss as one day they'd replace me, and after six months they did just that. However, in the interim period, I'd taken the BBC and CNN out for lunch and been in touch with a few foreign contacts I knew from London: Germany's ProSeiben, Finland's YLE and Austrian channel ORF.

Astrid, a client from Germany's ProSeiben, rang to ask if I could work with her on a game show. I'd worked with Astrid in London years ago and she was now working on a light entertainment show based in Munich. The premise of ProSeiben's show was a hybrid of Cilla Black's 'Blind Date': a young couple would be paired up in the Munich studio and a camera crew would follow them around on their 'date'. This particular date was in Paris so it made sense to hire a local crew rather than bring one from Germany. I hired a car, and with my favourite sound operator Didier, we drove to Charles de Gaulle airport to collect Astrid and the young couple. It was lovely to see Astrid again: pretty, funny, talented, fluent in three languages and she hadn't aged one bit. I'd always fancied her something rotten but she was married.

She introduced us to the young couple and it was obviously a case of Mr Bean vs Gwyneth Paltrow. We spent the day driving around Paris filming the couple as they walked, talked, ate ice cream and went on gentle sightseeing visits. It was evident that he was well out of his depth and she'd just picked the wrong guy. As the first day of the 'date' drew to a close, I was thinking that it would be such a shame to let this gorgeous German girl go home without her experiencing a good night out in Paris. The young male was called Carsten and he was going to have an early night so (on the quiet) I invited the German girl out. She accepted, so all I had to do now was drop Didier back at his motorbike, take Astrid and Carsten back to their hotel, get rid of my kit and we'd be off. Sadly, Astrid got wind of my intentions and with a very firm "Don't even think about it!" dragged the disappointed German girl out of my car. I could be very naughty when I wanted to be.

Astrid and I worked together again in February 1999 when an avalanche left 12 people dead and 20 cabins destroyed in the village of Le Tour near the popular ski resort of Chamonix. Now working at the news department of N24 (now WELT), Astrid flew in the company news camera helicopter from Berlin with her two colleagues: the pilot and the aerial cameraman. I took the TGV to Annecy where I hired a car and met the whirly bird at Chamonix's helipad. On landing, Astrid stepped out and gave me a hug. She told me they were going to fly over the avalanche site and see what footage they could get and they'd be back in a hour. French airspace is controlled by the military who allowed them (and others) to hover a few hundred feet above the rescue choppers but not to get in anyone's way.

Safety back at the helipad, I picked the three of them up and Astrid was to go live on the next N24 news bulletin. Due to the magnitude of the story, a number of mobile satellite vans had rolled into the town so N24 organised some slots and off we went. The first thing they did was to play their helicopter footage to Berlin and afterwards, I'd operate the camera for her live report. As a bonus, it also happened to be the aerial cameraman's birthday so the four of us went out for fondue in a cosy restaurant. The next day I drove them to the helipad, the pilot warmed up the machine, I kissed Astrid goodbye and off they went.

In researching this section I asked Mr Google to find Astrid, and sure enough he did. In May of 2018, she was out cycling with her husband and a couple of friends when she was hit by a car driven by an 81-year-old. She died of her injuries aged 51. I'd worked with her in London, Paris and Chamonix and she was a truly lovely girl. I was very lucky to have known her and she was a total sweetie. Bless her.

The Associated Press was a good and reliable source of income but the television news industry was (and still is) a case of *'finish when you finish'*. There were no set working hours, and if you said you were available then you could be called at 2am and they'd expect you to be wherever they wanted you to be - and on time. I can't remember how many dinners I postponed and ladies I disappointed due to last minute calls to duty.

I'd started working for other outlets, and at the time there were three television news agencies: AP, Reuters and WTN (World Television News). They all had their own clients so everyone rushed to whatever news event it was, film what they could and beat the competition in filing it first. Ron was the Paris bureau chief of WTN and we got on very well. AP were in the process of buying WTN so Ron was facing redundancy. We'd meet at his smart apartment just south of Place de la République and discuss how to make money. He was a top-notch TV news producer and knew the ground like a pro, so I would take up the slack with a creative/technical role. The FIFA World Cup was taking place in France in a few months so Ron decided that together we should open a company. We did and called it 'The Press Box'.

TV broadcasters from all over the planet were to converge on France for the event and all were going to need satellite slots in order to do live links to their audiences back home. Paris, Marseilles, Lyon, Lille, Bordeaux ... wherever a World Cup match was being played, visiting news crews would need a satellite route out. Ron had done his homework and realised that The Press Box could sell satellite space to Sky News using AP's mobile satellite dishes. I spoke to AP's bookings department (whom I knew of old) and they offered us a deal which was roughly "if you can guarantee selling X number of bookings, then we'll charged you a reduced rate so can charge yours client what you want". Effectively, we'd get a silly knock-down price, but to be honest, AP really didn't think we could put much business their way so didn't give it a second thought.

I contacted an old friend of mine, the bookings lady at Sky News. She flew over from Heathrow and we took her around several of the World Cup locations, showed her the pre-arranged press locations and the 'view' the camera would see. If you're reporting from outside a stadium, it's important that you see the stadium in question and not a blank wall, a housing estate or an abattoir. AP had sent me a list of locations and photos of what their live cameras would be pointing at so at least we could show Sky what to expect.

Sitting three-abreast on an early evening return flight from Marseilles, Ron and I needed some kind of guarantee that Sky would sign with us and that a deal could be struck. On an Air France napkin, Sky's bookings lady wrote out a list of dates, times and other requirements. She then signed it and handed it to Ron. On landing back in Paris we escorted her across the terminal and to her return flight to the UK.

The next day I emailed AP's London bookings department with everything that Sky had asked for. They were stunned. They'd given us such a good deal, we'd made it work in our favour. When the World Cup started, Sky's teams turned up in various locations around France and were guaranteed satellite booking slots everywhere. As the tournament progressed, they rang and asked for more bookings which I faxed through to AP. Thanks to Ron's business acumen and my contacts at Sky and AP, neither of us did a thing during the entire tournament except watching the cash roll in and spending a large chunk of it drinking in bars and eating in posh restaurants.

As a cameraman it felt really very strange to be slap bang in the middle of the world's most popular televised sporting event where I'd be front and centre, but here I was wondering which wine would compliment which meal and looking forward to my evening date. Back at AP Paris, Bill and my former-colleagues were run ragged as I just sat on the sidelines, "You couldn't really ignore this one could you, eh Bill?"

Chris, the American journalist who'd been part of the group the night Diana died, had dreams of becoming a television news reporter and asked me if he could accompany me on a shoot and practice a PTC (piece to camera). We selected the May 1st parade. Europe-wide, May 1st is heralded as 'Workers' Day', a celebration of labourers and the working classes. It is also renowned as the day that France's aforementioned shit-stain, Jean-Marie Le Pen and his National Front neanderthals, turns out in full force for one giant knuckle-dragging stomp around town. The press would follow the march up to the rally point in front of the Paris Opera where speeches, flag-waving and general tub-thumping began. I shot what I needed of the rally and then set Chris up for a practice piece to camera. For a first-timer, he wasn't at all bad.

Over the coming weeks, we did a few more practice PTCs on other stories which culminated in me editing a showreel for him. Before flying to California to visit his mum, he FedEx'd the showreel to CNN in Atlanta and they arranged a meeting. On his return trip home to Paris, he stopped over in Atlanta for a face-to-face interview with CNN, and due to his language and journalistic skills, he impressed them enough to be offered the position as Berlin bureau chief. I was really happy for him but sorry to see him go as we'd become firm friends. Chris had an apartment in the 1st arrondissement that everyone loved, so before handing in his notice I asked if he could introduce me to the landlady so I might take over at 91 rue St Honoré, just around the corner from the now infamous Gros Minet restaurant. Sure enough, I met his landlady and took her out for coffee. Turning on the British charm (yes, I used to have some of that), she was won over and the apartment was mine.

Waving goodbye to my bright yellow flat in Boulevard Voltaire, I moved into this fab new 2nd floor apartment right in the centre of town. My sisters Debbie and Jenny came to visit and I introduced them to all my chums in the neighbourhood. It was about now that I began getting the odd freelance shift at the BBC.

On a Friday morning I was called by a BBC Paris producer asking me if I was available and could I make my way to the coast and Les Sables-d'Olonne, in the Vendée region (north of La Rochelle). 24yr old Ellen MacArthur was racing solo in the *Vendée Globe* round-the-world race and it looked like she was going to finish second. Naturally, the British press were tripping over themselves to get images of this plucky young girl. She'd been living and training in France for years so the French sailing fraternity already knew her very well.

Taking a TGV from Gare Montparnasse, I headed to the seaside with my kit. The BBC crew met me at the marina and told me that I was to board a small boat and go out into the Atlantic to look for Ellen. I wasn't to be alone as there would be three official boats leaving the dockside: one with her parents aboard, one full of race officials and me on the press boat. The quayside was awash with shops and restaurants so I quickly had something to eat and bought a very expensive set of bright red waterproofs - with the blessing of the BBC. Their staff cameraman Rob had been posted to Washington DC so he'd been replaced with another. He was to stay ashore, shoot from his position and then whatever we both managed to film, would be combined into the edit with the reporter for the night time bulletin.

Resplendent in my spangly new sailing togs, I said goodbye to the BBC team, stepped aboard a rusty old boat and it chugged off into the setting sun behind the other 2 official vessels. To get from the marina to open sea takes a good few minutes as all vessels have to navigate a large S-shaped breakwater. A Frenchman had won the overall event the day before, but the railings of the breakwater now were full of hundreds of people all waving Union Jacks. French and Brits together waiting for this 5-foot wonder woman who'd sailed around the world single-handedly and was about to take second spot. On my tub was our captain, his mate, a French press photographer and me, and that was it. We followed the other two boats, and once clear of the smooth water inside the breakwater, we became victims of the cold and choppy Atlantic.

Stowing my camera and rucksack in the cabin, I stood aft, holding onto an upright whilst trying to retain my balance and whatever sandwich I'd eaten 30 minutes ago. I'm not a huge fan of boats but now was not the time to ask to get off. The diesel engine thumped rhythmically, the sun set, the sky turned black and a thick fog surrounded us. Oh goody. Within an hour we were, to quote the skipper, "*complètement perdus!*" (completely lost). He got on the radio and started yelling at some poor sod on the other end. "We're going back to port", he announced. Thankfully we were still close enough to shore that I could get a signal on my mobile so I forewarned the BBC producer. She went ballistic and began shouting and swearing. I had to remind her that I wasn't in charge of this little outing and therefore not part of the decision making process, so don't shoot the messenger.

The little boat swung around in the fog and headed back to port. Resigned to the fact that the news bulletin wasn't going to be as picture-rich as we first thought, the captain waved at me, calling me into the wheelhouse. For the past few minutes, with the radio tuned into race control, he'd been listening to a collection of English voices. Ellen MacArthur and race officials were exchanging messages over the airwaves. Neither he, his mate nor the French photographer understood what was being said, but I did. Although my French still wasn't good, I translated what I could into basic French: numbers, times that sort of thing. These snippets of information turned the captain's face into a beaming smile as he swung the little boat round once more and headed back out into the fog. I wish I'd kept my bloody trap shut.

Now separated from the two other official boats, we made our way further out into the Atlantic. The fog began to lift a little and through an open patch above our heads flew a TV news helicopter. I tapped the captain on his shoulder and pointed at the helicopter. He nodded and pointed the bow in the same general direction. As the fog gave way to clearer air, on the horizon we could see a flotilla bathed in light. Sticking vertically out from the centre of this gathering was a huge off-white sail belonging to Kingfisher, MacArthur's boat. Gingerly making our way to the bow, the press photographer and I cradled our cameras, sat down and braced ourselves for what was coming. Kingfisher was surrounded by four RIBs, security boats trying to keep the dozens of onlookers out of the way. However, being part of the official convoy our captain managed to secure a spot just off Kingfisher's stern. There were bumps and scrapes aplenty with the security RIBs pushing well-wishers and gawkers out of the way and I remember the bow of our boat riding up over the side of one boat with a huge 'crack'. They very quickly made room for us.

With my feet pushing hard against the chrome railings and my back wedged fast against a bulkhead, I started filming. Our captain had positioned the boat right next to Ellen's parents and the surrounding water was choppy white foam caused by a mass of propellors. Although we were bobbing around like a cork, I managed to keep Ellen in my viewfinder and rolled the tape. On deck she reached into a box, produced two distress flares and slammed the firing pins into Kingfisher's deck. Whoosh! Two sprays of sparks and smoke flew upwards above her head lighting up the immediate area. She screamed in triumph and that was my shot of the day.

The armada followed Ellen back into port where she received a tremendous reception from the public along the breakwater. The walls now heaving with people waving flags, cheering and blowing kisses. Our little press boat split off from the main group and tied up well away from all the action and flashguns. I said thank you and goodbye to the captain and the BBC Paris bureau chief met me at the top of the ramp where I handed him my cassette. Within the hour the BBC News opened with my shot of Ellen and the flares. Now *that* was a good day.

There was, unsurprisingly, an Irish pub around the corner from my new apartment. My French still wasn't fluid so it was nice to be able to go and speak my mother tongue and *practice* French in a convivial no-mans-land. The Flann O'Brien had a steady flow of regular expats of whom a number became friends. Jim Rowlands was one of the regulars of note: a Welshman with a guitar around his neck, he was often positioned in front of the toilets where he'd sing until closing time. I should add that this wasn't just an ad-hoc virtuoso performance but a paid gig and the toilet area was the only place (space-wise) he could fit. Whilst in full flow (and yes, he's got a proper voice on him) a small group would spend many a happy hour pulling faces, trying to make him laugh. Jim is now married and still lives in France (Middle Earth I believe). We're still in touch today but I miss those nights down at Flanns, though I'd encourage you to jump onto Spotify and listen to him.

I made friends with another local who lived round the corner, Paul Egan. Someone else in the 'regulars' group was Catrin, a smiling wide eyed girl of Welsh extraction. She and Paul hit it off and were married a few years later. After time spent in the US, the couple now live in the UK, and as I write this, Paul is preparing for Catrin's 50th birthday. I've offered to edit video messages from her friends into some form compilation and the couple remain some of my closest friends to this day. Distance is no barrier when retaining such a bond.

My lunch date with John, the CNN Paris Bureau Chief, paid off. As a multi-skilled operator he could see my potential. Their staff cameraman at the time could only shoot, he didn't edit and he certainly wasn't interested in learning. Kurt (let's call him that) was a particularly difficult individual who loved you when you stepped in to do jobs he didn't want to do, but let fly a tsunami of vitriol when you didn't.

The G8 member nations were holding a summit meeting in Cologne and CNN were to cover the event. Most of the team were plucked from their dedicated White House crew, pre-approved and accredited personnel who had special clearance, spending their days following 'El Pres' about the planet. A month before the summit, CNN Paris asked me if I'd be available to hop over to Cologne and help their White House crew as Clinton was giving them an interview. I handed over my passport so that the summit organisers, the German Police and the American Secret Service could check to see if I was safe enough to be let anywhere near the big man.

Travel day arrived, and with my kit packed, CNN Paris' contract logistics company took me and Kurt out to Orly airport. All Paris-based journalists who were flying to Cologne were to travel together in a chartered aircraft so we congregated in the private Pavillon d'Honneur, the VIP terminal away from the main airport building (I was here some time ago following the Marseille hijack).

The following morning in Cologne, after a questionable breakfast of rubbery meat and eggs, the two of us from the Paris office met up with the CNN White House crew. The interview was to take place in a function room of a government building and the Secret Service insisted that we start rigging all our equipment at least six hours in advance. Once finished, we were bundled into an ante-room as the Secret Service swept the room with portable devices. Once cleared we were allowed back in to take up our positions as a stream of huge suited men wearing sunglasses flooded the place. They parted and in stepped Bill Clinton and was welcomed by CNN's interviewer, Wolf Blitzer. Once happy, the men in suits blended into the background, into what was now, the most heavily guarded function room in the world.

The interview lasted a good 45 minutes, during which time I had many opportunities to study Bill: he was a total pro at answering questions, smooth and commanding and could side-step the trickiest of subjects with proficient ease.

With the interview over, a White House photographer appeared and a Clinton aide corralled our group into a line for a photo that now sits deep in the bowels of the Clinton Presidential Library. With that done we were lined up as we were going to be introduced to Bill. I've often asked myself the question "what would I say to such a personality should I be given the opportunity to meet one?" Would I be allowed to speak to him or should I just curtsy!? The controversial Monica Lewinsky business was only a short while ago so maybe I should mention the dry cleaning? No, probably best not.

He came down the line enthusiastically shaking everyone's hands, engaging them in short conversation if only for a couple of seconds. I was desperately trying to think of something so say to the most powerful man on the planet.

I'm a tad shorter than Bill but felt minuscule as his Presidential form arrived slap bang in front of me. He held out his right hand, I clasped it and we shook. He asked my name. "Oh a Brit?" he said on hearing the accent. "Yes Mr President, I flew in from Paris just for this". Just like a true pro who knows how to work a crowd, he never broke eye contact with me for the seconds we spoke. Still shaking hands, he tapped my right shoulder with his left "Well thanks for coming all this way Stuart, I appreciate it" and then moved down to the next one in the line. What a pro. You don't forget stuff like that.

A couple of months later CNN Paris received copies of 'that' photograph from the White House, but Kurt had decided that I wasn't going to get one. "You're a freelancer and as you're not CNN staff, you're not entitled to a copy", he barked. Bemused, I parried with "but I'm in the bloody photo you dipstick!" John overheard Kurt's childish ranting and told him not to be such an arse. Begrudgingly a copy was handed over …

… though I still wish I'd asked Bill about the dry cleaning.

That White House photo, though I have replaced Kurt's face with something that better suits his personality.

184

Vacanza Italiana

It was 1998 and Serbian leader Slobodan Milosevic had decided that Kosovo should be emptied of all Kosovar Albanians. It was as simple as that. His ethnic cleansing project continued into 1999 when NATO told him to stop, which of course he didn't. After a show of hands, NATO finally took action and President Clinton, along with NATO counterparts, set about a plan of action and what to do about Milosevic, though many Albanians had to die before any decisive action was taken. History has taught us that tinpot dictators need to be dealt with swiftly, but in reality it's never as easy as that.

For a week John had me camped out in Rambouillet, to the southwest of Paris, in whose Chateau saw where Americans, Brits and other NATO members thrashing out what could be done to avoid an all-out war between the Federal Republic of Yugoslavia and the Kosovar Albanians. Daily briefings from a feisty Madeleine Albright did nothing to shed any positive light on the situation.

Rumours were soon filtering into newsrooms that unless an agreement could be reached, NATO, in an attempt to punish the nefarious Serbian dictator, was to launch a bombing campaign against Belgrade. Back at the Paris bureau, together with Georgina a freelance VT editor, I was summoned into John's office where we were asked if we'd travel to Italy and a US airbase to keep an eye out for any movements. As freelancers this is what we prayed for, an open ended assignment. We'd already had a week at Rambouillet and now being handed a couple more with a nice expenses-paid trip to Italy and a comfy bed in a decent hotel. Kurt was away on a fortnight's holiday and nothing was going to drag him back from that.

Aviano airbase is about an hour's drive north of Venice. Built in 1911, it sits at the foot of the Dolomite Mountains and picturesque does not even begin to describe its location, the horizon was one long range of peaks. The airbase had somewhat of a chequered history, including the Nazis taking control during WW2. However, once over with, the Americans signed a deal with the Italian government of the time and Uncle Sam has retained a presence there ever since.

Just 12 months ago, an American Prowler electronic warfare aircraft (pictured p185) from Aviano, with its crew of four, was involved in a tragic flying accident. The pilot, flying too low and too fast through the mountains, clipped a cable car support with the tail fin. It sliced through the steel wire sending a gondola with 20 people aboard, 260 feet into the ravine below. It was a terribly messy affair and once back at Aviano, the pilot destroyed the aircraft's on-board video recording. Even more extraordinary was that the American government tried to exonerate the crew. Eventually, it was proved that this was nothing but a blatant act of stupidity by a Marine pilot, and such was the level of external pressure, the US eventually jailed the pilot and awarded each of the victim's families $1.6m. "You might administer the base" the Italian government told the US, "but you're still guests in our country".

Now at Venice's Marco Polo airport, John, Georgina and I gathered our kit and associated crap from baggage reclaim and hauled it through customs and into the arrivals hall where we met our local contact. Once you get clear of Venice airport, and its constant throng of tourists making their way to the ferries, the drive to Aviano in springtime is really very pretty. The Dolomites came into view, and stopping briefly at the hotel to drop off our luggage, we continued to the airbase.

Unmistakably, the big brash entrance gates were populated by camouflaged square-headed people in sunglasses wielding huge guns and carrying mirrors at the end of long sticks. Shouty over-sized Stars and Stripes fluttered from everything they could be attached to and of course there was the constant whine of jet engines and the smell of aviation exhaust. It was certainly no surprise that we'd arrived where Americans could be found. A group of Prowler aircraft were parked a little way from the entrance, ground crews in sleeveless yellow tabards walked along their wings, one diligently cleaning cockpit windshields while others plugged and unplugged refuelling lines, but all attending to the aircraft's needs.

Directly in front of the main gate on a patch of grubby municipal land, our Italian fixer introduced us to the newest member of our crew: a camping car, or as the boys and girls on the base would call it, an RV. For the time being we were the only TV crew present but it was still early days.

While John and the fixer went off to make contact with the USAF Press Officer with copies of our passports and media accreditation, Georgina and I started making ourselves comfortable in the RV. I found somewhere to plug in my battery charger, store the lighting kit and spare tape stock while Georgina rigged her editing kit. Thanks to the advances in technology, the mobile edit suite had now been reduced to a suitcase: two folding lids with the editing gubbins underneath. A few hours later, with the sun going down, the reunited crew headed off to the hotel in town as it was time to check out the local bars and find some scoff. As luck would have it, John was part Italian so he would be translating the menus from here on in.

The next morning it rained. In fact, it hoofed it down for the next *two* days. The RV sank up to its axels and we had to make a special trip into town to buy wellies and plastic ponchos. Such was the ferocity of the downpour that the gate personnel were now dressed in flowing plastic kaftans and nothing on the airbase took to the skies. It was a grotty 48 hours as we sat in the RV listening to Italian radio and the BBC World Service and eating crisps. Lots of crisps.

Our attempt to remain as solo artistes was broken by a facilities company who had thoughtfully brought along their mobile satellite dish. This meant that we could hire it in 15 minute bookings and send edited video footage or do live links back to CNN in Atlanta. In the coming days, a host of other TV stations were to join us on our prime patch of mud so that dish was to make an awful lot of money.

Ten days later and we'd settled into our new way of life: still doing hourly live reports, visiting the local area to film interviews with officials and report on military briefings from USAF Press Officers. The trattoria waiting staff in Aviano were fast becoming friends and each morning I'd visit the little newsagent over the road, exchange greetings with the old man behind the counter, have a coffee and buy the International Herald Tribune. This was all very jolly and quite acceptable, especially as we were being paid. Sadly, all good things must come to an end as our peace was about to be shattered. Some new information came my way which brought the shutters down on my little Italian '*vacanza*'. Kurt, CNN Paris' staff cameraman who'd been on holiday, was insisting that he joined the action, had booked himself a plane ticket and would be arriving at Venice airport the following afternoon. Oh goody. The walking colonoscopy was inbound and I couldn't wait.

Rather than do a straight swap and replace me with Kurt, John had an inkling that things were warming up NATO-wise and that we were about to get busy, so decided that his best course of action would be to keep all capable personnel close to hand. Georgina could only edit and Kurt could only shoot - whereas I could do both. It would be useful to have someone who could step in and take over when the others needed a break. John had his proposal signed off by the CNN bean-counters in Atlanta so there was no need to pack my bags just yet.

On arrival at Aviano, His Royal Highness stepped out of his carriage, and totally ignoring Georgina and I, went straight over to speak to John. To be honest neither of us were particular fans of this character. Born in Romania in the late 50s, he and his family had escaped the Communist regime and arrived in France as refugees. Now a full French citizen, he lauded about the place, dressing only in expensive clothes and patronised absolutely everyone - apart from John - displaying traces of his Communist DNA at gold medal standard.

He tiptoed through the mud in his costly shoes and indicated to us that he required an audience. "I've been discussing the situation with John and I want to talk to you both." Georgina and I made our way to the RV, found a seat and settled down for whatever was coming. "I suggest that we adopt a one-day-on, one-day-off type of thing and John agrees with me." Georgina and I nodded. "Now I'm taking tomorrow off so Stuart you work and I'll work on Saturday." I sat there a little bemused by his pronouncement and asked, "Let me get this right. You've been sunning yourself on holiday for two weeks, whereas Georgina and I are now into our 11th straight day and you want tomorrow off?"

It was at this point that the shouting began, "I am the senior cameraman here - the staff cameraman - you are the freelancer and you will do what I say or you will go home. Is that clear?" Even Georgina gulped. I suggested that we give Georgina the day off tomorrow and I'd take her place … "You will do what I say!" he replied. Sometime later John took me to one side and explained "Look, that's what he's like. Pay no attention, it's just his way."

"Fair enough" I replied "I may not be a gynaecologist, but I know a c*nt when I see one."

Day 12 started exactly the same as the previous 11 with brekkie, my coffee/ newspaper outing and then the drive to our muddy patch of Italian real estate. At the airbase we'd been joined by a few more TV stations who were eagerly claiming a stake of available land: Brits, Americans, French, Dutch, Italian and Danish TV. The one thing about such international events is that the same faces pitch up time after time as it morphs into a huge social occasion. I bumped into an old mate in the middle of a pitched battle between NATO troops and locals in Mitrovica, a northern Kosovo town on the border with Serbia. As tear gas canisters flew, we stopped and had one of those "so, what have you been up to recently?" conversations, but I'll get to that later.

Back in the mud bath I recognised members of a Danish TV station who'd been with us during the summit talks at Rambouillet. Then a Dutch producer wandered over and reminded me that we'd also met somewhere. It was turning into a game of 'match the face to the event'. John appeared, and taking me by the elbow said "We've all been invited onto the base so we're to report to the main gate later on this afternoon." At last, something was going to happen.

Around 6pm, along with the other crews, we boarded a soulless grey military transport bus which was waved through the gate by heavily armed personnel. It drove along roadways bordered by neatly manicured grass, past admin buildings, the commissary (a US forces grocery shop), a gym, the swimming pool, a cinema and then along taxiways flanked by giant sealed hangers complete with armed guards and finally to one with its doors wide open.

The bus pulled up and we were invited to descend and gather within. Another Stars and Stripes (the size of a tennis court) adorned the back wall and the hanger's floor space had been surgically cleaned within an inch of its life. Thoughtfully, they'd laid out several dozen chairs, a couple of fold-away tables dressed with napkins and covered with acres of finger food. Oh, and Coca Cola, lots of Coca Cola (I'm so proud that British Forces run on tea). Along with our friendly USAF Press Officers, some junior ranks had been roped in to show us were the 'rest rooms' could be found and to help us should there be anything else we needed. Now seated, the media hubbub died down as an officer made a few house-keeping announcements. The first one gave the game away, "As of now, the use of mobile communication devices is strictly forbidden. We ask that you surrender them immediately." Air Force personnel mingled with the press corps and stopped them from making that last call to the office, collecting all mobile phones and issuing receipts in exchange for toothy smiles. Once unarmed, we were free to help ourselves to the food and drink.

It was getting dark and the hanger floodlights sparked into life. A loudspeaker relayed a live radio announcement by Bill Clinton from the White House: as no workable agreement had been reached, Milosevic and his merry men were to face the full wrath of NATO. The overall tone of Bill's message being that it's all Slobodan's fault, so suck it up. As soon as the address came to and end, our American hosts whooped and applauded. We waited a matter of minutes before a further announcement was made by the officer, "Ladies and gentlemen, please make yourselves as comfortable as possible by using the restrooms and then proceed to board the bus. We will be away from this facility for some time." Like naughty school children, we lined up by the toilets, left what deposits we could and made our way to the waiting transport.

In the distance, the whine of jet engines could be heard as somewhere out on this vast airfield, flight crews were making final checks by dotting i's and crossing t's, readying a mass of strike aircraft for a busy nightshift ahead. On board the bus, I threw a glance at John which was met with a grin the width of the Ponte Vecchio. This was all getting rather exciting. With a smidgen of ambient light still available, the bus passed a fleet of enormous Globemaster transport planes. The sheer size of these things is breathtaking. One of them had its rear door open and you could have loaded my Paris apartment building into it and still have room to spare. The bus rocked to a halt and we were asked to step down as a line of junior ranks holding torches ushered us onto a grass strip parallel to the runway. A member of the air force Press department stretched out his arms, "Along this line please ladies and gentlemen. There is plenty of room for everyone but please do not move from this position." A junior rating ran down the line issuing packets of disposable foam earplugs.

At the end of the runway to our left, lights appeared followed by the unmistakable roar of jet engines. We'd only just managed to get our cameras set up when the first plane came barreling towards us. It drew level, its nose pitched up and flames from the afterburner licked the tarmac. Leaving the ground, it retracted its undercarriage, extinguished its lights and effortlessly, though noisily, clawed its way into the night's sky. The air crackled and spat with sound announcing the NATO-style launch party of punishment. We were not alone as other bases around Europe were to equal Aviano's display of power and aggression.

Additional American aircraft and their flight crews had been redeployed to Aviano from other US bases across Europe and beyond. F-16s, F-15s, Prowlers and Warthogs all took to the skies. Then, like a Hollywood diva, it rolled into view. An aircraft spotter's wet dream: the B-117 Nighthawk Stealth Fighter. Behind us, the angular Nighthawks left their bombproof hangers as we all swung our cameras around to get a good shot. "No you can't film those!" screamed the Air Force personnel, "Keep your cameras pointed towards the runway!" As it happened, 20 minutes later they were a lot closer and rolling for take off right in front of us.

The aircraft kept coming and the sky was now peppered with bomb-laden dots racing away from us towards Belgrade. To get everything off the ground took 90 minutes which was staggering. How many aircraft was that? Military planning (when it works) is exquisite. The flight time to Belgrade was approximately 45 minutes, so by the time the last plane had left Aviano, a long line of white landing lights was already strung out in the sky to our left, indicating the return of the first wave. One by one they touched down, fuel tanks thirsty for more go-go juice and empty bomb racks in need of re-arming.

The Dolomites were now ghostly silhouettes but no one could honestly recall how many planes had taken off. We'd got more than enough footage so it was time for the Air Force to return our telephones and deposit us outside the main gates. John and I (still buzzing) wandered over to the RV, if not a little deaf, from what we'd just witnessed. We shot a very quick piece to camera and I handed Georgina my tapes with which she cut a news package and sent it to Atlanta. The thing is, by confiscating our phones, the Air Force's intention was to keep this event as quiet as possible, however the company with the mobile satellite dish had also brought a camera so throughout the entire operation they'd been broadcasting the event live from right outside Aviano's main gate. Every news channel on the planet had tuned into these live pictures so the Serbs knew that NATO was on its way. It gave the Serbian government a 45 minute heads up and time to scatter, make for the underground bunkers.

Another wave of attack aircraft was now racing over our heads, but back in the RV John's phone didn't stop ringing. Who was calling? Was it our masters at CNN in Atlanta? No, it was that silly little man Kurt back in his hotel room. He'd been watching proceedings live on TV and had decided he didn't want a day off after all. I saw him at breakfast the next day and doubted that a thesaurus contained enough words to describe how angry he was.

One Last Time

My mate Chris, now CNN's Berlin bureau chief, rang with a proposition: "how do you fancy three months in Berlin working on the 10th anniversary of the fall of the Berlin Wall?" I put my Parisian life on hold, packed my kit and set off for former East Germany. We had heaps of fun over those 90 days and shot many fascinating news stories: tales of desperate people who'd slipped past border guards and away to safety, those who escaped Communism by swimming to freedom in the dead of a winter's night or others who'd been smuggled out, hidden in the frame of Trabant passenger seat. I was shocked to hear, first hand, all about the Stasi and their methods when spying on their citizens and what happened if someone broke the rules. I learnt so much, met some really extraordinary individuals ... the local girls were lovely too.

We went over the border to Poland where we met and interviewed Lech Wałęsa (left). I liked Poland and I think Poland liked me. Once back in Germany, Chris and I traveled all over the former East and our CNN masters lapped up our reports, but on returning to Berlin I was 'borrowed' for an interview. A CNN crew were flying in from Atlanta for the huge 10th Anniversary Ceremony and, at the Adlon Hotel, had secured an interview with former Russian President Mikhail Gorbachev. Although they'd brought a large crew, they needed another camera operator so Chris released me for the day.

Arriving to set up our temporary TV studio in a large function room at the hotel next to the Brandenburg Gate, every last bit of kit was double-checked, especially the dual translation system: Gorbachev didn't speak English and the journalist didn't speak Russian, so the 2 translation people hooked up to a mass of cables, microphones and headsets, needed to have clear communications that worked. With the kit up and working, we had time to kill so I went for a wander. I snaffled a copy of the International Herald Tribune newspaper and settled into an armchair way in the back of the reception area of the hotel. There were security details from governments everywhere, all identical plain-clothed armed brick shit-houses, but as I was wearing a pass, no one really bothered me. Not only was Gorbachev in town, but George Bush senior and Helmut Kohl made up the three amigos who'd brokered the tearing down of the Wall a decade ago. One by one, the three retired heads of state arrived in the lobby, and on seeing one another after so long, hugged each other as I just sat in any armchair watching all this unfold. A rare privilege indeed.

With Gorbachev on site I went back upstairs and gave the head's-up to my CNN colleagues. We fired up the lights, checked the colour balance of the cameras one final time, tested the microphones and confirmed that the translation people were happy. The door opened and in stepped a small white-haired man, followed by a bear of a man in a suit two sizes too small for him. The bear shut the door and stood in front of it, and of course the small white-haired man was Gorbachev. His wife Raisa had only died a few months previously but what struck me was the way he walked round the room shaking hands and introducing himself to absolutely everyone: the sound man, the junior producer, the senior producer, the guys who rigged the lights, the two cameraman (me and an American chap) and then, of course, the journalist.

My camera was positioned over Gorbachev's left shoulder so I was to film the interviewer, Christiane Amanpour, while my American colleague was to film Gorbachev. The interview went well, though I couldn't understand any of his replies. He got up, buttoned his jacket, shook the journalist's hand and proceeded to tour the room again, in reverse, shaking everyone by the hand once more. The bear opened the door and Gorbachev slipped out.

I returned to my life in Paris, I drank with my mates in Flann's, spoilt myself rotten with meals out and late night dinners with chums, went to parties and out on dates. Honestly, I kind of missed Berlin but my life was here, and even if there *was* a deal on the table (which there wasn't), I was having a hard enough time learning French let alone switching to guttural German.

A year later, Chris rang and offered me another job: "How about you and me going into Kosovo?" Just like that, as casual as you would ask a mate to go for a beer. He detailed the trip and without too much persuasion I agreed to go.

It was February 2000 and the weather was suitably icy. Chris and I flew into Skopje independently, meeting up at the hotel. The next day we were to head across the border into a highly volatile country where we'd meet our Albanian translator. Keeping the peace were KFOR and UNMIK

(Kosovo Force and United Nations Interim Administration Mission in Kosovo, respectively). NATO's bombing of Serbia was still fresh but some parts to the north of Kosovo were still very much divided, Mitrovica for example. Kosovar Albanians lived south of the River Ibar and Kosovar Serbs to the north.

As you approach the boundary line with any conflict zone, it always carries a look of being 'highly dodgy' - which it normally is. After a couple of hours on the road we arrived in the capital Pristina and checked into the aptly named Grand Hotel. Kosovar military uniformed personnel hugging AK47s lay across the sofas in reception while fat men in ill-fitting suits and sunglasses gave me the second clue as to this place being in the top 10 of 'just a tad suspect'. We met up with our local translator/producer. Thankfully his English was top notch, he enjoyed a good laugh and he looked after us well enough.

The fine people of Pristina had organised a peace march which was to leave the city centre and end in the northern town of Mitrovica, 25 miles away. Here, they were to wave their beloved Albanian flag in the faces of the Serb Albanians on the opposite bank of the River Ibar. On a snowy and freezing Saturday morning we set off in a hire van which came ready to roll with a local driver. Along the northerly road to Mitrovica we stopped periodically so I could hop out and film the thousands of happy smiling Kosovar Albanians all marching together. The fact the current temperatures were in the minus camp *and* was going take them 4 hours to get there (and back) didn't seem to bother them one bit.

Being half French, Chris found and made friends with the French UN troops, and as our translator disappeared to talk to the locals, I tagged along behind Chris for something to do. It was here that I managed to compere the famous MREs: the French vs the rest of NATO. Those bland cardboard boxes that I had ripped into in Bosnia contained packet and tinned muck designed to keep the soldier 'on the go' but was not paired with any recognisable taste. French MREs had a small (and I mean 'small') bottle of wine - in Bosnia we were lucky to get powdered orange juice. The French also travelled with rolls of fluffy white toilet roll - we had folded sheets of tracing paper. When the French went to war, they did it in style.

The southern sector of Mitrovica was patrolled by Canadian, British and French troops, but today the French were to be camped out *on* the bridge, the Brits were on the road *leading up* to the bridge and the Canadians were stationed *either side* of the bridge. The throng of flag-waving Kosovar Albanians were on their way and the taunting Serbs on the northern river bank were waiting for them. Of course, there was no way either side could physically get to one another but a military presence had to be kept - especially along the 200 meter gap spanning the bridge.

As the morning rolled into the afternoon, the Pristina marchers arrived and congregated on the south bank. Their number quickly grew and soon they became more than a tad rowdy. A British officer stood atop an APC (armoured patrol car), and flanked by his interpreter, made several requests through a loudhailer:

The European Pushing and Shoving Championships,
spoilt only by the French and their teargas.

"We are with you and we understand your situation but you must remain peaceful. If you do, I will ask the French not to use tear gas. We are with you in your struggle."

I was towards the middle of the bridge watching the angry hoards getting themselves into a state when I bumped into Nigel, the BBC cameraman from Vitez and South Africa. It was lovely to see him again so we put our cameras on the ground and had a good old catch up. It's always good to bump into colleagues in the middle of nowhere, though I had a feeling someone I knew was going to pop up here at some time or other. The crowd were now gagging for a punch up and missiles were being thrown. Lumps of paving stone were coming from the Albanians in front of us so we figured we ought to curtail our chinwag and get to work.

As the Kosovars surged forwards, the British forces attempted to block them. In somewhat of a panic, Nigel and I both bent down, picked up our cameras and immediately ran into each other. We laughed at this stupidity as his journalist, Kate Adie, was yelling for Nigel to come and film the tussle that was going on between the civilians and the British troops. I followed suit and raced after Nigel, shooting the physical pushing and shoving. It was all getting a bit nasty. The British soldiers were wearing normal uniform with berets and not sporting riot kit. This was their strategy, as full body armour might have provoked more of a reaction from the Albanians, so down-play it and keep it friendly.

The French, fed up of being left out of the proceedings, then started firing tear gas canisters into the crowd. Tempers flared and the demonstrators split into several directions. I was swept along with one group who ended up in a field next to the bridge, and as the field was *lower* than the roadway, it started to fill up with throat-clogging gas. Huge bearded Canadian Pathfinders were plucking demonstrators by the collars and hauling them out of the teary soup. Holding my camera above my head, a couple of Pathfinders dragged me up to their level and into clean air. Limp and unconscious Albanians were stretchered left and right having been injured in the crush or overcome by gas. The noise of the battle rose as the British tried to hold everyone back but were simply outnumbered. I skirted round the edge and made my way back towards the action hoping to get an angle behind the protestors and film the military pushing for all it was worth. More fizzing gas canisters tipped into the crowd as Albanian and British heads collided, civilian pummelled against solider in an effort to break through and get to their Serb enemy over the bridge. My battery light was flashing, I was almost out of tape, my eyes were red raw and stung to high heaven, my nose was running like an open tap and I was coughing. Time to beat a tactful retreat.

I found Chris, wrapped in a warm jacket and enjoying a coffee, in a small café just along the way. If there's going to be a pitched street battle, then the owner of this café wasn't going miss out on making some ready cash. My mouth had an odd, metallic flavour rolling around it, I absolutely stank of gas but Chris was happily sitting, watching the full-scale riot no more than 50 yards up the road. I'd filmed more than enough so decided we had sufficient to illustrate the news report. I splashed my face with handfuls of bottled water and the rolling tears and snot soon abated and I was able to enjoy a coffee. The French delivered yet more volleys of tear gas into the angry crowd, which now included the British military who were now *very* pissed off with them. Chris ordered another coffee, smiled and made notes in the chilly February air. From that day onwards, I gave him the nickname 'two lumps'.

At breakfast the next day I sat with Nigel and Kate and we brought each other up to date with what we'd been doing over the past few years. After brekkie our little CNN crew were going out on patrol, guests of the Americans, so I bid my farewells and toddled off.

Chris and I were to meet the US Commander and his men at their barracks on the outskirts of town, but being a local Kosovar, our translator wasn't allowed to come along. Chris sat with the Commander upfront in the lead Humvee, whereas I filmed from a following one. The patrol rattled through open countryside, tiny hamlets and up through the hills. We stopped and filmed plenty of goodwill handshakes between the American Commander and the local populace, then onwards to a Russian army base. Russia had been asked to join the peacekeeping mission to patrol the Serb population. Typically, the Ruskies had run out of food and were now begging off the American UN troops, though we weren't allowed to film that.

Our road trip culminated in a tank firing exercise. We were delivered to a field of thick mud which had been rented from a farmer. The Americans had installed huge wooden targets on a hillside about half a mile away. Sure enough, three Abrams tanks slid into the field and began setting up for firing practice. We were introduced to the Tank Commander and I was invited to shoot whatever was wanted. I crawled all over these giant metal things and there were times when I couldn't physically walk as my boots were caked in mud. Then the firing started.

Packing a punch - American heavy metal takes it out on flimsy wooden targets.

Each tank had a barrel from which spewed 120mm shells and above that, the standard .50 calibre machine gun. The crews fired their weapons in turn, but when a practice shell left the barrel, the atmospheric compression that rippled behind the tank thudded into me to the point I honestly thought that my heart had stopped beating just for a second.

I'd shot loads of really good stuff, and as the day drew to a close, the Tank Commander organised some fun: the three Abrams were going to fire simultaneously so he gave me a few minutes to prepare my shot. I wanted a view down the line of barrels so the tank crews watched as I placed my tripod, framed the shot, hit 'record' and gave them a 'thumbs up'. I then ran as fast as the mud would allow me to somewhere behind the firing line. All three barrels fired pretty much at the same time but that particular shockwave caused me to wince as it shook my internal organs from one side to the other. It's been 22 years since that morning on the tank range but I still think that footage was some of the best I have ever shot.

On another day we covered a story which was to bring the trip down to a really uncomfortable level: an American serviceman had been arrested for the rape and murder of a 12 year old local girl. For the peacekeepers this was a PR disaster, and by the time we got to the barracks the accused was either elsewhere in Kosovo or had been flown to a US base in Germany. Whenever the military are involved, you're not going to get the whole truth quite that easily.

Within the month it was time to go home. We shot a quick story in the morning - again in thick mud. Chris and I arrived at Skopje's most expensive marbled-floored hotel and trudged our way to reception as hotel staff winced at the trail of mud we left behind. On checking in, Chris left his credit card details for both rooms and upstairs I lowered myself into the deepest and longest hot soak known to man.

After some mental arithmetic, I realised that in the course of five years I'd lost five friends - all of them in conflict zones. In 2001 in Paris, I celebrated my 40th birthday and decided that Kosovo would be my last conflict zone. I was happy with that decision and have never regretted it. It's like crossing a road with your eyes shut: you'll get away with it once, maybe twice, but any more than that and the percentages against you begin to add up.

Pick 'n Mix

Still deep within CNN's pockets, I was out of town on a story with one of their Paris-based reporters. I forget the subject but as we drove back into town just after lunch, our driver switched the car radio to France Info and turned up the volume: "a light aircraft had hit one of the twin towers in New York."

By the time we made it back to the CNN office in rue de Berri, one look at how that storyline had changed brought terror to all of us. No light aircraft, two passenger jets. "Go home", John the Bureau Chief told me. "The story's over there for now but I'll call you when we know what's going on." Like millions around the world, once home I sat glued to my television, aghast at what had happened. The next day I was called back to CNN where, for the next few weeks, we were kept busy with reactions and press conferences from Paris.

Jean-Claude, the cafe owner at *'Le Played'* had sold up and moved to a larger and fancier place further along Boulevard Voltaire, so I'd dip in and see him for lunch now and again. On one day when I fancied a good lunch, I threw my leg over the bike and sped off to the 11th arrondissement but he wasn't there. His restaurant had been bought by a Portuguese family and Jean-Claude had disappeared, assumed retired. Still, it was a pleasure to have known him.

One odd booking that came in was the press launch of the TV series 'Band of Brothers'. The invited media met at Saint Lazare train station and were corralled onto a private train heading for Caen and the Normandy Beaches. Onboard were a number of celebs and film executives, and once on the move, the press would be invited into various compartments to conduct interviews. I was assigned to David Schwimmer, who looked as comfortable as a man facing a firing squad.

The film production company had persuaded the authorities at the Colleville-sur-Mer Normandy American Cemetery, to erect a tent in which to welcome the press. If you've yet to visit this cemetery then you're in for a shock. Set on the shoreline of the famous beaches, under it's perfectly manicured lawns lie 9,388 American dead, their white crosses in perfectly symmetrical lines. This memorial was built for solemn reflection, it is emotionally powerful and a humbling sight to behold. Now, as a giant Stars and Stripes fluttered high above the tree line and the sun shone across those resting places, in typical bad taste some bright spark had installed a TV in the press tent which was now playing loud excerpts from 'Saving Private

Ryan' which could be heard across the estate (the film starts in the every same cemetery). Hollywood just had to go one step too far.

In 2002 BBC Birmingham was given my name by my Parisian colleagues. A department in the Midlands were making a 30 minute documentary about Violette Szabo (of 'Carve Her Name With Pride' fame) as new information had come to light, so after a long chat on the phone with the director, I was sent the shooting schedule. In all, I was to be away from Paris for 4 days and headed off to a little French village to meet up with the team. Szabo had been a member of the Special Operations Executive (SOE) and operated in occupied France during WW2. In the true spirit of spy craft, the director and presenter met me off the train both decked out in hats and sunglasses, skulking from doorway to doorway. Straight away I knew I was going to get along with this pair.

We met up with Bob Maloubier, who'd been a member of SOE and had parachuted into France with Violette. He was also one of the last people to see her before she was captured by the Nazis. Earlier in this record, I mentioned that I would link my mother to events in France at this time, so here goes: my mother had a background part in 'Carve Her Name With Pride', the film about Violette Szabo. You can see her in the London club scene where Violette meets Bob for the first time, and here I was now talking to the *real life* Bob.

Left: Virginia McKenna walks past Mum (seated foreground) in the film 'Carve Her Name With Pride', and right, the real life Bob Maloubier.

We filmed in the villages where the SOE agents operated, on the exact spot where Bob said goodbye to Violette for the last time and inside Limoges prison where Violette was held before being transferred to Fresnes prison on the outskirts of Paris. It was at Limoges where Bob and the local *maquis* had planned to stop the vehicle carrying Violette and snatch her away from the Nazis. Sadly, it was not to be. Violette had been spirited away a couple of hours earlier and sent to Paris. She was tortured and then sent to Ravensbrück concentration camp in Germany where she was eventually executed with two other agents, Denise Bloch and Lilian Rolfe.

Bob carried on the good fight, at the end of hostilities he took the German surrender at a local hotel and survived the war. I met him a number of times after 2002 and visited him at his house for a photo shoot, then took him out for lunch. He was a great talker and had stories aplenty. He lived to the ripe old age of 92, dying in 2015 and I was deeply touched when Bob's widow asked if she could use my black and white photo (p199) for the official announcement and ceremony at Les Invalides.

The BBC programme proved popular, getting its initial airing on BBC Two then another on BBC One. It went on to win a Royal Television Award for Best Regional Documentary. As a final note on this, for Mother's Day of 2021, I managed to get mum a credit for that film on the IMDB website. She might have only appeared in one film, but I made sure it was recognised.

Here's a fact you might not know: the French like a good riot. Oh yes. In October and November 2005 there was a three-week period of unsociable behaviour which broke out in the suburbs of Paris, spreading to other French cities.

These riots involved youths of predominantly north African and Arab heritage, who launched violent attacks, burning cars and destroying private property. The unrest began in Clichy-sous-Bois where police were investigating a reported break-in at a building site. Pursued by the cops, a group of youths had scattered in order to avoid capture, three of them hiding in an electrical substation where two had died from electrocution. The incident sparked an enquiry into youth unemployment and Police harassment in and around the poorer housing estates, and thus, three weeks of cross-country rioting kicked off.

Nightly television news reports showed images of blazing vehicles and pitched running street battles between riot Police and angry, overexcited youths. With CNN running out of cash, I was now working pretty much full time for the BBC and filming little sorties like this inside the tinderbox housing estates was on my radar. The BBC were planning an evening sortie where TV, radio and online would go up to Aulnay-sous-Bois and report on an evening's rioting.

One night we were to spend time trawling the streets of Aulnay in the company car. We'd organised a security bod to drive the car, a Renault Espace, but we'd have to drive it to the location in the first place. The team were made up of myself (camera), the TV journalist, a senior producer, a radio journalist (who doubled up as the BBC online writer) and the work experience bod. I drove us up the motorway heading to our agreed *rendez-vous* point with the Police press relations person at Aulnay's '*caserne*' (the fire station). Along the motorway were convoys of riot Police vehicles and coach loads of heavily tooled-up reinforcements. On meeting our local security man the senior producer went over to the Police press liaison officer to discuss what was happening. Of course, the Police would rather we weren't there but tough, we were.

It had been decided that we'd take a tour of the local area to see what-was-what, but once out from behind the safety of the Police cordon, we were on our own. Our security chap was now behind the wheel and he drove us out from behind the line of cops and we headed down the hill towards the town centre. Coming up through the dark to meet us was a group of angry rioters, armed with bricks and petrol bombs. I opened the sunroof and squeezed my top half outside, then brought the camera up and onto my shoulder and pressed 'record'.

I had been living in France eight years now and my language skills had improved dramatically so I could *parlay* with the natives - however basic. I shouted down to the driver suggesting that we take a slow pass along the street and I'd let him know if I was uncomfortable about anything, in which case he should floor the accelerator and get us out of there. The other four members of the BBC team sat quietly in the Espace when on our first pass, from out of the shadows, came a group of youths with their faces covered by scarves and bandanas. Hurling a mixture of both rocks and abuse, the car's body panels were being ruined, glass was smashing and the high-pitched screaming coming from inside the car was now louder than the actual assault outside. My top half was firmly wedged outside the vehicle as the security man sped off down the road in an effort to outrun the angry group. We made it back to the cordon as the cops gave us knowing smirks from as our tattered vehicle limped over the line. It is interesting to note that the screaming wasn't coming from the women in our team, but from the three males, one of whom was the work experience lad who is now a BBC foreign correspondent. I so wish I could tell you his name.

When I wasn't working, at lunchtimes I'd eat locally and kept seeing this stunning blonde woman sitting at a pavement table of my favourite bistro, Le Taverne de l'Arbre Sec. So began a period of regular afternoon coffee sessions as I waited for this gorgeous vision to appear. One day I opted for a late lunch on the patio, so choosing a spot midway along the tables I waited. Sure enough she arrived and sat a couple of tables away. We smiled at each other in recognition, struck up a conversation and found out a little more about each other. She was a single mother who lived out of town, her name was Frédérique and she worked just down the road. The relationship blossomed and was to last 10 wonderful years ...

A new Bureau Chief arrived at the BBC, Alan. An utterly charming Scottish gent whose demeanour was such a breath of fresh air after the last correspondent who'd now moved upwards in the Corporation. Alan was unhurried and plodded his way through life at his own speed. In the middle of the afternoon, and without notice, he'd often disappear home for a bath. During his tenure at the Rue de Faubourg Saint Honoré office, I spent many a happy hour in his company, shooting and editing all sorts of stories. There was also a new cameraman, an Australian whom I shall introduce properly shortly.

As a freelancer at the BBC, I got a call if:

- if their staff cameraman/editor was off or busy.
- if Brussels (the BBC's European hub) needed a helping hand.
- if any of the BBC's other outlets (Panorama, HardTalk, Newsnight etc) needed a cameraman.

In the middle of a car park in Arras is a small black metal door, and behind that door, a concrete staircase - narrow and dangerously steep, descending into the earth a *very* long way. At the time, the BBC had a London-based correspondent who was into all things World War, be it 1 or 2. I drove to Arras and met him in the car park. The first of our two-day jaunt was spent behind this door, and what we were shown was utterly fascinating.

One of the town's municipal key holders unlocked the door as a local historian led the pair of us down into the gloom. Lightbulbs hung in festoons stretching the length of the staircase, but after a minute or so slowly padding our way down, we arrived on solid ground. The historian asked us to stay where we were as he wandered off into the darkness to find the master light switch. A click later and we found ourselves standing in a cavernous chalk-white underground chamber.

First World War British soldiers had dug a virtual cathedral-space out of the chalk, and more was to be revealed. Long narrow tunnels had been dug into the walls of the gallery, running in all directions which took the soldiers and their armaments to and from the frontline. The historian, together with a select group of chums, had been slowly working along a few of these tunnels to discover where they led and what was at the other end. One tunnel contained a narrow gauge railway the soldiers used to supply the needy at the front and to bring back the wounded. The lighting the team had installed only stretched a few meters into these tunnels, and not knowing what was out there in the dark, we were advised to not wander off too far.

It was a squeeze but walking down these tunnels was fascinating. Chalk had been chipped away to make rudimentary ledges for candle holders, and some were still holding the remains of stubby wax lumps. All along the passageways, soldiers had carved their names, ranks and regiments while others had scratched limericks and good luck messages. Down one tunnel we found what looked like a rubbish tip, departing soldiers had dumped everything they no longer needed: tin cans, canteens of cutlery, clothing and webbing.

The historian showed us where the current 'dig' had reached, but of course we wanted something new so could we go further down into the darkness, past the point where the lighting stopped? Initially the historian was reluctant but eventually agreed to going a few steps further. Using the light attached to my camera and a torch, we slowly made our way down one tunnel which the historian said, "no one had been down since the war ended 87 years ago." This is what we wanted, something undiscovered and we wanted to stumble across a surprise or two. It was strangely moving to be the first people since the end of WW1 to find this undiscovered detritus lying where it fell. The historian gave us a running commentary as he gently picked up a number of items. He told us what they were and what he thought they were used for and, if possible, who it had belonged to.

It was cold, eerily quiet and I was loving it. Working my way down a narrow passageway I'd stop to read the names and the funny little ditties that generation had left behind. This wasn't a book off a shelf, nor a documentary on the small screen, but history that I could touch and experience first hand: the temperature, the smell the total and absolute silence. Before too long it was time to gather up our bits and pieces, switch the lights out, mount the staircase and regroup in the car park 200 feet above our heads. As the chamber lights were extinguished and the labyrinth of tunnels disappeared from view, I couldn't help but think of all the thousands of men who'd been through here during the Great War and how many of them were still lying in the mud at the end of those tunnels.

From out of the blue I received a call from ABC Australia who were in need of a bi-lingual cameraman. David Bowie was to play Paris for one night at the Stade de France. A journalist and cameraman were flying over from Australia to interview Bowie the morning after the show and they needed a second cameraman. I was to meet the jet-lagged twosome at one of those little private bijoux hotels that Paris tucks away out of plain sight.

The smiling hotel manager welcomed us at the door and steered our little group towards a quiet lounge room that had been reserved for the interview. Bowie's assistant came to say hello and asked us how long it would take us before we were ready. Now, unlike the Gorbachev interview in Berlin where the trusted CNN staff cameraman filmed the VIP, in *this* setup the Aussie journalist wanted his staff cameraman to shoot him and I was to film Bowie. This was odd. Once we'd lit the interview space, we were ready to go so the journalist rang Bowie's assistant on the internal phone system. It was now 10am and only 12 hours ago Bowie had been on stage, so to see someone like this up for a TV interview quite so early the following morning was impressive.

In Bowie came and I was, unsurprisingly, nervous. He was carrying a cup of something hot and chewing a piece of gum. Shaking the journalist's hand he sat in the chair opposite me. "I suppose I should get rid of this?" said Bowie, removing the gum from his mouth. He looked around the room until his eyes fell upon me, or rather the fireplace behind me. He cocked his head to one side - the international sign for 'please move' - and threw the gum. Moving smartly to one side, the gum flew past my shoulder and landed in the grate. The interview was fantastic and I sat mesmerised by this Rock God for 45 minutes. There are very few celebrities who really impressed me but Bowie was one of them.

Another of those in the music biz who lived up to their reputation was Charles Aznavour: a global phenomenon with a career spanning 70 years. He sang in nine languages and sold somewhere in the region of 200 million records. Amenian TV was coming to town to interview Aznavour (he had Armenian roots) and they needed someone to shoot the interview using two cameras. In the 60s and 70s Aznavour appeared regularly on British TV and his records dominated the radio waves. Now I had the chance to meet this global superstar.

I drove over to his management offices in the swanky 16th arrondissement and met the Armenian TV reporter. Aznavour's manager showed us to a meeting room and I began setting up the cameras the reporter had brought with him. I was still fiddling about with cables and lights when a diminutive grey-haired chap walked into the room. "Hello", he said. Aznavour had arrived and the Armenian TV reporter began a bowing and scrapping ritual which looked a bit out of place, but still, we were dealing with an international Demi-God here.

The interview was conducted in Armenian, so of course I didn't understand a word of it. Once finished, I began coiling cables and folding lighting stands. However, rather than rush off, Aznavour and I started chatting as he began to tell me about his passion outside of music: photography. Would I be interested in having a look at his camera kit? Apparently, he never traveled without it. Happily forgetting my de-rigging for a moment, he led me through the plush offices to a visitor's room where his hat, coat and camera bag were located. He opened the well-travelled bag and carefully removed each item, as one by one, we discussed its merits. He was highly knowledgeable about photography and we exchanged opinions and ideas.

Eventually, a flustered office minion was dispatched to retrieve him. Our chat drew to a close and I returned to continue packing up. Just as I was closing the last bag, Aznavour stuck his head round the door to say goodbye and graciously stopped for a photo. What an utterly charming man.

BBC's HardTalk was a regular visitor to Paris and (for now) I was the freelancer *du jour*. Each show required two cameras and a sound operator so that's an easy one to staff: my favourites were Stuart Nimmo and soundman Didier. We shot all sorts of hard-hitting interviews, mainly with politicians. Rafic Hariri was Prime Minister of The Lebanon (twice) and had a swanky Parisan pad hidden behind two large wooden doors on Place d'Iéna. I sent the crew names and my car registration to HardTalk in London who forwarded them to Hariri's security detail.

Once through the ram-proof wooden doors we were met by three equally solid South African bodyguards who proved strict but friendly. We unloaded the car and were allowed to park inside the compound (there's a photo of his Parisian residence on Wikipedia). Dare I say it but Hariri's place was a smudge gaudy, dripping in gold and assorted tat. Visitors were greeted at the front door by a pair of stuffed lions in heraldic pose, and once inside, every flat surface was covered with heavy gold photo frames with equally shiny images of his grinning family on private yachts and private beaches around the world.

Tea, coffee and bottled water were supplied as we very carefully placed our kit around this uber-expensive palace. Every lighting stand and tripod was delicately positioned and every cable laid out with infinite care. Hariri was a formidable presence and he played a huge role in reconstructing Beirut, the Lebanese capital. He was the first post-civil war prime minister and the most influential and wealthiest Lebanese politician, and here I was in his Parisian sanctuary shaking his hand.

The interview was, as expected, centred on how he was going to get the Lebanon back on track and running the way he wanted it. HardTalk runs for a little under 30 minutes so we'd shoot for about 40 minutes and afterwards might re-record the introduction, a question or two or re-stage the final 'thank you' handshake. Once we stopped rolling, the guest would normally relax and chat to the interviewer before buggering off, but not Hariri. He disappeared out of sight for a while but reappeared holding a large golden tray. Careful stepping over cables etc., he offered each member of the crew fresh Lebanese pastries. The Prime Minister of The Lebanon was acting as waiter in his own home. Returning to shake us all by the hand, he and said his goodbyes and was off. A couple of years later, in 2006, whist driving through Beirut, along with 22 others including some of his bodyguard, he was killed by a car bomb.

"Hello, good evening and welcome" will immediately remind a certain generation of Sir David Frost. His BBC Sunday late morning show 'Frost On Sunday' was the pre-cursor to Andrew Marr and the Frost team were coming to Paris to interview French Foreign Minister, Dominique De Villepin. The production office in London rang me on the Friday around lunchtime to ask if I was available to film that night, I was but it proved difficult to find a sound recordist who was also available at such short notice.

Over the road from me lived Colin, a Scotsman who worked at an English language training school. This was really cheeky but I offered him some folding money if he'd help me out and act as my sound recordist. I assured him that I'd set up the sound kit and all he had to do was stick the headphones on and give the impression that he knew what he was doing. He agreed, so I faxed my press card and Colin's passport details to the Quai d'Orsay (the French Foreign Ministry), we loaded the kit into a taxi and off we went.

Through security and now in a beautifully ornate reception room, Colin and I began setting up, only Colin hadn't got a clue what to do so I asked him to unravel cables and move stuff about and generally help with bits and pieces. The Frost team arrived, and surprisingly, they were only two of them: David Frost and his producer. We introduced each other and Frost prepared for the interview.

Thankfully, I'd finished setting up the camera, lights and sound kit, everything was ready to go, so neither Frost nor his producer knew that Colin was totally ignorant to the workings of television. When Foreign Minister De Villepin arrived, I attached both his and Frost's microphones, Colin popped on the headphones and I 'helped' him with the audio levels and the interview got going. Once it was all over, Frost stopped for a photo and left the building with the producer now clutching the cassette. It was now 9pm and Colin and I giggled like school kids as we packed up, jumped in a taxi, went home and I dipped into a cash point to settle the bill. On the Monday morning the producer emailed to thank Colin and myself for a job well done. I watched the interview a few days later and breathed a sigh of relief that I'd got away with that one.

In April 2004 I saw a headline on the BBC website announcing '*Expedition Global Eagle: an attempt to fly an autogyro around the world*'. No doubt you'll have seen an autogyro as they were made famous by Wing Commander Ken Wallis who flew 'Little Nellie' in the 1967 James Bond film 'You Only Live Twice'. Warrant Officer Barry Jones, an Army Air

Corps (AAC) Lynx helicopter pilot, was to fly one from Middle Wallop in Hampshire and head east through Europe, the Middle East and onwards.

Jones (BJ to his friends) was hoping to raise funds for three charities: the Dyslexia Institute, the NSPCC and the Red Cross. Backed by a small support team of AAC soldiers from Dishforth who were to follow in a maintenance van, Jones was to leave the UK on 26th April and fly to Ostend in Belgium. I decided to take some time out, drive up to Ostend, meet this chap and photograph him and his machine. If I could get him and the cause some press coverage, then I would. Admittedly, the Ostend hop was only BJ's first waypoint but it meant that he'd crossed the channel and was on his way. Everyone *loves* a story like this.

After the minimal of research, I found the Dishforth HQ telephone number, called, told them who I was and what I wanted to do and they couldn't have been more helpful. They gave me the name of the hotel where BJ and the team were staying, so I called ahead, booked a room and jumped on a train. It was dark by the time I arrived but found BJ and the team in the bar.

I ploughed straight in "Hi, I've been on the phone to Dishforth and I'm here to cover your story." Again, they couldn't have been more helpful. Over the next four days the weather closed in so as BJ was grounded, I got to know the team.

On the 29th April the support team saw a gap in the weather for the following day so they loaded the maintenance truck and headed off to the next stop, Friedrichshaven in Germany.

On the morning of the 30th I drove BJ up to the airport where he loaded his kit into the autogyro and filed a flight plan. We shook hands, he started the engine, taxied and he was off. The moment he was out of sight I rang the Dishforth HQ and let them know, then headed back to Paris.

In June BJ reached India, but due to torrential monsoons, was forced to store the autogyro in a hanger until the weather improved. He returned to the UK on a commercial flight and waited until October before returning to India where it was found that the rain water had risen so high that it had destroyed Global Eagle, along with the expedition's dreams. I'm still in touch with BJ today but really wish the project hadn't come to such a sad end.

In November of 2004, the BBC booked me to join their Newsnight crew for a four camera interview with then President Jacques Chirac. Apart from the President, I was one of two French speakers on the team. After the interview and as we were packing up, Monsieur le President was chatting to the programme's host, Gavin Esler. Our 'studio' inside the Elysées Palace was in one of those majestic '*meet-and-greet*' reception rooms you see on the news. It was heaving with antique bling, so every care was taken not to smack into a vase or whatever, priced at something outrageous. As I was taking my camera kit apart, the President loomed up in my peripheral vision. He was on his way out of the room but stopped and asked me "Excuse me, have you seen the official photographer?" Somewhat shyly I replied "No, Monsieur le President, I haven't".

"Well, let's go and look for him together - two are better than one", and with that he took me by the elbow and led me out of the room and into the inner recesses of the Elysée.

Through a collection of smaller reception rooms and a rabbit warren of corridors, we arrived in a sumptuous ballroom. The walls of this revered building contained mystery doors giving access to hidden staircases and secret staff entrances and exits. As we walked through the ground floor of the Palace we chatted and he asked me how I spoke such good French (!?). I told him that I lived 2 kms further down the same road, which I did. "Oh really?" He replied, "Well don't worry, if any of your post gets delivered here by mistake, I'll make sure it gets sent on to you" followed by a wink.

As our search for the photographer continued, staff passed us in the corridors, busy with Palace duties. Some laden down with trays of cutlery, others with perfectly ironed table linen. Chirac was 6'2" and as his lofty figure loomed around dimly lit corners, he stopped and asked each smartly uniformed staffer if they'd seen the official photographer. No one had seen him but he thanked each one of them. "Oh well," he said turning to me "let's go back".

Lo and behold, while we were out on our tour, the Palace photographer had arrived. Monsieur le President placed his hand on my shoulder "Thank you for your help", turned and strode towards the photographer to take control of organising the post-interview photo.

Chirac served as Paris Mayor, French Prime Minister (twice) and then President (again, twice). OK, he was a serial philanderer and the only President to be convicted of corruption, but he exhibited something that today's politicians sadly lack - genuine charm, even towards a British cameraman dressed in jeans who spoke French.

Ish.

The black and white image over the page is Robert Doisneau's iconic image '*Le Baiser de l'hôtel de ville*' (Kiss by the town hall). Published in Life Magazine in June 1950, it featured a couple kissing on the pavement along a busy Rue de Rivoli, and has since become an international symbol of love.

However, the identity of the kissing couple remained a mystery for the next 42 years. In 1992, Jean and Denise Lavergne, believed that they were the couple in the photograph and took Doisneau to court for "taking their picture without their knowledge" (under French law, an individual retains the rights to their own likeness).

Now standing before the judge, Doisneau was forced to reveal the identity of the real couple. He admitted that he'd posed the shot but used another couple entirely, namely Françoise Delbart (20) and Jacques Carteaud (23). On the day, he approached Delbart and Carteaud and asked them if they would kiss for the camera, to which they agreed. Françoise Delbart corroborated this whilst standing in front of the judge. The ruling went against the lying Lavergnes and Doisneau was exonerated.

Shortly after the original photo session in March 1950, Doisneau sent Françoise Delbart a signed copy of the photograph. Now 55 years later and married, Françoise (now Bornet) was putting this piece of photographic history up for auction.

"To Stuart, a friendly kiss on the cheek. F Bornet"

On April 20th 2005, I shot an interview for the BBC with Françoise at the very spot this iconic shot was taken. She told me what she remembered about that day, her recollections of her then-boyfriend Jacques Carteaud and how Doisneau had tried the same shot in two other locations before deciding on the town hall.

Once the interview had come to an end, Françoise settled at a pavement café table and we ordered coffees. A few doors down was a typical Parisian gift shop, so I dipped into it and bought a cheap copy of 'Le Baiser' which Françoise then very kindly signed for me: "To Stuart, a friendly kiss on the cheek. F Bornet".

Five days later, her original print signed by Doisneau, sold at auction with the hammer coming down at £160,000. Admittedly, my copy is valued at considerably less but has been equally treasured and on my wall ever since.

Jailbird

The BBC staff cameraman was missing and could I help look for him? Of course. The Australian was one of my best mates and if there was something wrong then I'd help find him.

Over the past two years we'd become firm friends and I supported him when his Mum had died in Australia, I'd given him a bed when his wife threw him out (eventually leaving him and taking their child with her) and I generally stuck by him as he got back on his feet. He had just started dating a cute and youthful French BBC lady producer, so life for him was getting back to the fairly straight and level. His new girlfriend had called me to say that he was missing, but last night thought that he'd headed down to the 'Les Halles' area of Paris, which was right on my doorstep.

Frédérique and I were now an item and she was coming over for the night, so I locked my front door and made a note of what time I needed to be home. She had her own key so could let herself in. I crossed over to Les Halles and within seconds I'd spotted the Australian's scooter. It was that quick, so I rang the BBC and gave them the news that his bike was here. "He's not answering his mobile or home phone so could you go up to his apartment and check if he's there?" I arranged to pick up a set of keys from his cleaning lady and headed over. The AP studio manager of the time said he'd come and help, so he jumped on *his* scooter and we met up in the 18th arrondissement.

Once inside the ground floor apartment and started looking for clues. It wasn't a big place but clearly he wasn't here. The studio manager rifled through a few kitchen drawers looking for anything that might help us and stumbled across a small white packet full of powder: oh right, cocaine. We were just deciding whether we should flush it down the toilet when there was a knock at the door. As the studio manager slid the wrap into his pocket, I opened the front door. Two business-like shotgun barrels were pointing straight at me, and between two burly uniformed flics was the Australian, handcuffed and clearly in distress. A stubby plain-clothed cop in a black later jacket started barking instructions, telling me to back away from the door. As I moved, I saw a handful of armed cops making their way across the grass of the communal gardens and heading for the large glass patio doors.

Both the studio manager and I were throughly searched, and of course the paper packet was found on him so he was handcuffed. I was clean so was told to "sit down and shut up". The stubby plain-clothed cop was obviously the boss and clearly in a filthy mood. He began quizzing the studio manager who really didn't understand what he was being asked, but being the good samaritan that I am, explained to this moody Rottweiler that out of the three of us, I spoke the better French so could I help translate? I did what I could and a short while later the Rottweiler pointed at me, then to the front door and barked "get out".

It was obvious that the Australian was in bits and that the newly arrested studio manager was also in a state of shock. I stopped and asked the grumpy cop where he was taking the pair of them so at least I could inform their next of kin that they wouldn't be home for dinner. Before I knew what was happening, the Rottweiler grunted to a subordinate who spun me around and placed me in cuffs too. The three of us were then led outside and paraded in front of a large group of immigrants, now enjoying the sight of three handcuffed white guys being loaded into Police cars. There were vehicles everywhere, both marked and unmarked. This wasn't the result of some bloke getting caught with a bit of dope in his pockets, this was another level entirely and was obviously some 'major league shit'.

With my hands behind my back, and now sandwiched between two over-excited uniformed officers, one engaged me in small talk: "Do you think you're going to like French prison food?" For reasons I couldn't explain, I started laughing. I'd done nothing wrong, I had no drugs about my person so this was turning into a totally surreal situation. The convoy, blues and twos going like the clappers, made it from the 18th arrondissement and down to the Police station at Chatelet in the 1st arrondissement in 7 minutes, I know because I was looking at the clock on the dash of the Police car. On any normal day it would take a civilian car at least 25 minutes, but this was the drug squad and they were in a hurry. We arrived at the Police station, no more than three minutes walk from my apartment, though my bile was still up in the 18th arrondissement.

Hauled out of the cars, we were again paraded in front of the mass of youthful immigrants hanging around Les Halles and led into the Police station. We were taken upstairs, sat on wooden benches and told not to talk. We did anyway. "Keep quiet!!" bawled the cop standing over us. The Australian was led away and the studio manager and I were individually processed, led downstairs, uncuffed and told to strip. "You have 30 seconds to get undressed" barked a cop. I then had my backside thoroughly searched, which for someone who had done nothing wrong and had nothing found on him was decidedly uncalled for.

My clothes were handed back and the backside investigator snapped "You have 30 seconds to get dressed!" I was again cuffed to make the short 10 pace walk to my cell where they uncuffed me and ushered me in. The studio manager ended up in an adjoining cell but I had no idea where the Australian was. My perspex-fronted box was two meters behind a thick perspex wall which separated the holding cells from the station's reception area. A desk Sergeant was on duty out front and I could clearly see people coming and going through the front door. Time ticked by, and as the afternoon turned into early evening, I was joined by two other hardened criminals: a shoplifter and a pickpocket. Dinner was a sandwich and a carton of juice, and if you wanted to go to the loo then you asked permission and you'd be led to a filthy toilet where, under supervision, with the open door you did your business.

Frédérique should have arrived at mine hours ago and God knows what was going through her head. In reality she'd become really quite worried as she'd not heard from me and my phone was diverting to the message service. She rifled through paperwork scattered across my desk and came across the BBC's senior Paris producer's business card so she gave them a call. The Corporation's understanding was thus: one of their number had gone missing, his bike had been found in Les Halles, Stuart and another guy had gone up to the Australian's apartment and neither had been heard of since.

Throughout the world, the BBC have contacts at levels you wouldn't believe and the Paris producers had been ringing various French government ministries to find out who knew what. One of the best contacts in the BBC arsenal was an anti-terrorist judge, so a call was put through to his office. So, the latest understand was that the three of us were being held under suspicion of being accomplices in an ongoing drugs investigation in or around the 1st arrondissement and that no more details were to be given for the time being. My girlfriend put two and two together and told the BBC "If the Australian was arrested locally then I think I know where they are".

I was sitting in my cell getting to know my new chums when I happened to look up at the entrance the moment that Frédérique walked in. Once at the desk she demanded to know if they were holding me in the cells. I could see the non-plussed desk sergeant shaking his head. In a flash I was up on my feet, banging on the perspex and shouting at the top of my lungs to attract her attention. The lights were off in the cell but it was worth a go. Eventually she saw my white arms waving from the shadows. Pointing in my direction she screamed "He's not here? then who the fu*k is *that* then?!" The sergeant whipped around the desk and forcibly ejected her from the premises giving her a mouthful in the process.

It was impossible to sleep as the thin stinky blanket I'd been given didn't offer any warmth. The night shift kept switching on the cell lights to check they hadn't lost any of us, which was relaxing. When the wall clock in the entrance ticked round to 4am, the cell lights came on again, my name was called, I was cuffed and led upstairs for my official interview. The female plain-clothed officer had me uncuffed, offered me a seat and I asked if I wanted any water, and I could have as much as I wanted. Listing the course of events in my best French, it soon became clear that my story matched that of the studio manager. "You know," she said with a wry smile, "I'm pretty sure this is a case of mistaken identity, so don't worry, you'll be out of here by this afternoon." She was one of those officers that had seen it all, now sporting a collection of facial scars from ploughing into vicious street battles with criminal elements.

She went through a few other boring bits of admin and I asked if I could use the toilet one more time and have some more water. I was allowed to visit the loo unaccompanied and then I sat beside her guzzling water as she typed the last of her report. She gave me a quick rundown of events and to why I found myself face to face with her at such an early hour: the previous day, at the port of Calais, an Australian smuggler had been caught with 100kg of drugs in a van and was promptly arrested. The Australian BBC cameraman had been in the park at Les Halles that night trying to score some a tiny bag of weed but had been caught in a sting operation by the local drug squad. Once in custody, and discovering that they too had an Australian, they immediately linked him to the Australian who'd been arrested in Calais earlier that day. The Rottweiler boss of the unit was convinced that he had another 'Mr Big' in his Police station. I began giggling. The female officer was forcibly controlling her own fit of laughter.

European legal containment laws state that if no proof has been found within the first 24 hours then the individual(s) must be released. We'd been arrested at 4pm the previous afternoon so we should be released at 4pm the following afternoon. However, the investigation was to continue unhindered until then. I explained to the officer that what they had in their cells were three insignificant TV types, one of whom just happened to be Australian. She nodded and smiled, I thanked her for her kindness and she offered me her hand, which I shook. Again, I was cuffed and escorted back to my cell. At 7am breakfast was served, but of course I was now so full of water I needed several trips to the loo, but at least I felt that an end to this ridiculous situation was in sight. As our stories had matched during our interviews, the studio manager was brought into my cell. He grinned, slid down the wall and settled next to me on the floor as I introduced him to my two cellmates. To keep our spirits up, we introduced our two French chums to the game of 'charades'. I explained the rules and we got going. There was much laughing that at one point the desk sergeant dispatched a minion to tell us to keep the noise down.

At just before 4pm I was invited to step out of my cell, I turned round and offered my hands for cuffing. The plain clothed smiled and waved a cursory hand. He led me up a narrow staircase "It's all over" he said "you're free to go but you just need to sign some papers." Over the past 24 hours (apart from the overnight interview officer) they had dished out blunt treatment with a side serving of sarcasm, but now these cops were courteous and respectful.

I was shown into the Rottweiler's office and he was on the phone. The look on his face said it all. We weren't the drug lords he thought we were and that his promotion was going to have to wait a while longer. Evidently he was finding it difficult to multitask, so pointing to a pen and a piece of paper on his desk, he continued grunting down the phone. Pent up anger welled up inside me, so signing the form 'M Mouse', I threw the pen back at him to display my disgust over the whole sorry affair, gave him a refresher course in traditional Anglo Saxon and stormed out of his office. The day shift desk Sergeant handed over my belongings, and as I turned to leave, I shouted to the studio manager that he too would be out in a minute. "Shut up" bawled the desk Sergeant. I stopped, smiled, wished the bad tempered man a "good afternoon" and Elvis left the building.

Outside in the sunshine I threaded my shoelaces, checked my wallet, powered up my mobile phone to ring my girlfriend. I then called the BBC and watched the Studio manager walk free. At the Taverne de l'Arbre Sec, two floors below my apartment, now joined by the Australian, the three ex-cons joined their wives and girlfriends and some of the BBC staff. It had been quite an experience and something I wasn't going to forget in a hurry.

A week later I was parking my scooter near my apartment. I stooped to put the chain around the rear wheel when I was forced into a double take. Coming out of my local bakery, a baguette sandwich in his hand, was the Rottweiler. I gave him the best Paddington stare I could muster. He saw me, held my gaze for a second and then looked at his feet as he walked along the opposite pavement. As he drew level with me I shouted "Bonjour commandant!!" to which he made no attempt to reply.

Within the year, the Australian and his new girlfriend had moved in together and a child was on the way. He opened an off-shore company and the pair of them set about cooking up a new way of assigning work for BBC freelancers. She'd hijack all in-coming enquiries but funnel all the freelance work his way. From then on, he'd handle the booking, engage the freelancer but take a healthy commission percentage in the process. Sadly, it soon became unworkable as he was eventually paying me a half day fee whilst I was putting in a full day's work. Greed had taken over.

After helping a mate rough some seriously rough times only to be shat on like that did make me wonder why I bothered in the first place.

Something In The Air

I fancied adding another string to my bow so branched out into press photography, covering news and features.

My initial contacts were found locally in France but then I spread my wings a little wider and contacted NTI, a picture agency in the UK and World Picture News (WPN) in New York. With the Anglophone agencies, I played my usual *'bi-lingual operator in a foreign country'* card which worked well. More and more French cameramen and photographers were speaking English but misunderstandings were still commonplace, so Anglophone agencies often preferred dealing with native English speakers. I'd been lucky enough to have done the odd photo spread for specialist aviation magazines in the UK and some lovely colour stuff for The Scotsman and The Irish Times, but I needed to impress the Americans with something. The 2005 edition of Paris International Airshow was going to be a memorable one, only I didn't know it just yet.

The first of the 'Press Days' was 48 hours away and the talk of the town was of the spanking new Airbus A380. It had made its maiden flight six weeks earlier and was due to display before both trade and the public at the Le Bourget airshow, so this is where I was going to strike it lucky. The Airbus PR machine had announced a planned arrival time and date for their double-decked behemoth and sent out an open invitation to the world's media to witness the first touchdown outside of their Toulouse HQ.

Access to Le Bourget would be granted under strict supervision, and that interested parties should "report to Gate L" at an allotted time.

Wanting to make a good impression with my first submission to WPN in New York, I needed something that would leap off the page. It was a lovely sunny day and on my scooter I weaved my way up through the traffic on the A1 and presented myself at Gate L.

I recognised a number of my fellow press corps, we shook hands and exchanged the usual pleasantries. Very soon the numbers had increased to over well 40 and the hungry group began hungrily circling a 16-seater minibus which we assumed would fit everyone and take us onto the airfield. A visibly harassed press officer was met with this heaving mass of impatient and eager media, going straight into meltdown. "There are far too many of you, the minibus isn't big enough!" She wasn't wrong. In fact, fewer than half are going to get onto that bus, and more importantly, as this visit is 'under supervision', those who *do* make it are going to be herded into the same pen and all going to get the same shot. In a flash I'd decided that this wasn't for me.

I've never liked following the crowd, so wherever possible, I've dipped out and tried to capture something different by looking for another angle, trying to find the unusual. If everyone was going to get the same image then where's the fun in that?

The assembled press had begun their familiar chorus of "I was here before you", so as to get a coveted seat in the minibus, the pushing and shoving started. After many years of working around Le Bourget I had a rough idea of the layout of the airfield so went back to my bike for a think. I had the arrival time for the aircraft so I was in no rush to find an alternative spot to shoot from.

The arriving air traffic was coming in from my left so I drove round the interior ring road until I found a point where the planes were directly over head. I pulled up in a temporary exhibitors car park which lay directly under the approach path of the active runway. Parking the bike I followed the centre line of the landing lights until I was up against the fence. Planes that were seconds from touching down passed right over my head so this was my spot. I lay on my back in the grass, and as plane after plane came in over my head, I checked the framing and exposure.

The A380 arrives at le Bourget, 2005.

Exhibitors who were still finishing the preparation of their stands, parked and stepped out of their cars, though a little confused by a chap lying in the grass with a camera in hand. I raised a palm in greeting as if it was perfectly normal that I should be there and a couple asked if I was all right. Without missing a beat I explained what I was doing but brought the conversation to a halt by pointing to the sky behind them. They spun around as the sky was filled as this giant came in right over our heads. 'Click'.

I went back to Gate L where I was let in by security, and after a good 20 minute walk, joined my press brethren by the side of the now parked A380. The crew, chief test pilot Jacques Rosay and co pilot Claude Lelaie who flew the giant from Toulouse, were now fielding questions from the press.

A few months earlier I'd been down at Airbus to film a piece for BBC Business about the A380 and had interviewed Rosay and Lelaie. I went over to say to Rosay (pictured below) and I reminded him of our first meeting in Toulouse. His memory clicked into gear, "Of course! How are you? Have you been inside?" I hadn't so he said "Come with me!" and he led me up the staircase and into the lower deck cabin area.

The A380 was still going through flight testing, so for now, no seats were installed but in their place were row upon row of water tanks which simulated the weight of a full passenger flight. We went upstairs, where halfway down the cabin was a desk, a bank of monitors and four seats where the flight engineers sat making notes and recording every movement made by this 573-tonne machine when in-flight. I could see that Jacques was a busy man so I thanked him for his time and left him to some corporate aviation bigwigs. By now I reckoned I'd got enough so made my way to the exit, jumped on my scooter and hoofed it back down the A1.

I downloaded the photographs, edited half a dozen of the best and sent them to WPN in New York.

The next day I was stunned to see that my photo of the A380 had made it to a few of the French newspapers, and later, into some magazines. WPN were delighted. In researching this section, I discovered that senior test pilot Jacques Rosay died in 2015 at the age of 66.

From somewhere along the line, someone mentioned 'The World Helicopter Championships' so I took a stab in the dark and contacted the French Helicopter Club. I spoke to a charming gentleman called Gerard, the event's PR officer, and he suggested that I meet him and the French helicopter team at Toussous Le Noble airfield to the south-west of Paris. The team were really lovely but for some reason no French photographers had shown the slightest bit of interest in the upcoming Championships in Rouen. I had a quick ride in a helicopter to take some aerial photos of the team practising, and before leaving, Gerard asked me if I'd like to get involved. A hotel room would be made available and he'd pay me to be the event's official photographer. Out of all the French aviation photographers in the country, they asked a Brit?

Frédérique lent me her car for the week and I set off for Rouen, arriving at the airport around midday. I found Gerard on site and he made a fuss of me, introducing me to the event organisers and to influential French aviators. The competitors were due to arrive shortly so I was told to get a feel for the place, pick up my day glow jacket, a staff pass and get ready.

Sure enough, just after lunchtime, the sky was full of helicopters arriving from elsewhere in France, from the UK, Germany, Switzerland, Belgium and Russia. The latter trailing plumes of thick black smoke behind them. Over the next three hours, machines of all kinds landed in the grass and rows of them now sported national flags which fluttered from rotor blades. Pilots and navigators decked out in team flying suits wandered the event area, saying "hello" to one another and catching up with old friends. The Brits had brought several machines, including a military team with their Gazelle (pictured p222). Of course, I made an immediate b-line for the Brits and have remained friends with David and Brenda (the team manager and competition judge respectively) to this day.

When the week was over I felt definite sadness as we all said goodbye. The teams flew off home and I was now 'well in' with the French and went on to be invited to the French Championships in Montbéliard and the European Championships in Poitiers and Le Touquet.

Paul Cooper, a fellow British photographer whom I'd met at the end of the tunnel during 'Diana', very kindly started giving me the odd freelance job. Through an ex-AP photo editor, I was also working with a French agency called 'Le Desk' and soon zipping about the place shooting a couple of guide books for the state-owned public transport operator RATP. The ex-AP photo editor co-owned the agency and he'd seen what I'd produced for the helicopters and asked if I'd like to work as one of the official photographers at the Paris International Airshow at Le Bourget? Naturally, I'd need to send a portfolio to the show organisers. I did and was promptly booked. Now this was a rarity for a strictly French-only club to admit a Brit, so I felt rather honoured.

Needless to say, the pair of us were worked into the ground over that week at Le Bourget. We covered press conferences, product launches, and we took profile shots of display pilots along with business and aviation leaders. However, the very first day it almost came crashing down when the organiser informed us that we, as freelancers, were not entitled to free food and liquid refreshment as it wasn't part of the deal. During such a major show, as anyone will tell you, luxuries such as food and drink are seriously expensive when bought from any of the on-site outlets. Being a forceful Frenchman, my mate took the lead by slamming his fist onto the table and raising his voice announcing that the pair of us had every right to partake of 'necessary refreshments'. He went to add that *"This was not brought up during contract negotiations and it is unfair. We're working harder than your staff photographers and unless we get food and drink - daily - we're off now! Bordel!"* It was true, the staff photographers were pampered beyond belief.

The senior photographer would pick up his kit, which included a huge 600mm zoom lens, and with a deck chair under his arm, would plop himself at the end of the runway effortlessly squeezing off close up shots of the best action all day long. Of course, his photos were met with gushing praise and graced the front covers, while my mate and I were on our feet all day, up and down the length of the show ground and against the clock to fill the show newspapers and magazines with content - and not getting fed or watered into the bargain was just as sore as our blisters.

After a quick union-style meeting, the organisers caved in and agreed to supply us with daily food and water. My mate had argued our point very well with his Gallic posturing and expletive-loaded tirade had clinched it.

All sorts of everything was coming in work-wise, and Michael Jackson at the Musée Grévin (the waxworks museum) was one that comes to mind. It was a Saturday morning on Boulevard Montmartre and Jackson's people had asked the Police to block the street off, a major 3-lane cross-town artery. The cops agreed and diverted the busy city traffic elsewhere. I believe that Wacko was in town on his 'Dangerous Tour' at the Stade de France but today a new waxwork model of him was being unveiled. We were ushered into the museum's theatre, with Jacko's adoring pre-pubescent fans filling the stalls and the press were slotted into the first two rows of the circle. Another one of Wacko's requests was that legendary mime artist Marcel Marceau was to greet him when he arrived. While we waited for the King of Pop, Marceau gave us a 20 minute mime show on stage. With his infamous costume and blancoed makeup, he launched into his act but we were quickly lost as no-one had the slightest idea what this 82 year-old was doing. He did, but we didn't. The years had not been kind to Marcel because he'd clearly lost the plot.

With the bizarre mime act finished, the over excited kids downstairs began to run out of puff as four hours later Jackson arrived. That's right kids, four hours late. This gaunt man gingerly stepped onto the stage and was met by a wave of adoring sound from these hysterical kids. Snide remarks from an abusive press pack were lost within the noise. People made speeches, Jackson waved a white glove and uttered thin sounds into a microphone and taking the now crazed adulation from the hoards of ear-splitting squealers. Most television camera lenses had 'doublers' which extended the focal length of the lens. So, let's take a closer look at Jackson's botched facial surgery. I flipped mine in and ... Christ on a bike! His nose was hanging on by a thread. All the camera ops were nudging each other, screwing their faces up in pain: this guy's face was literally coming apart at the seams.

The world-famous John Lennon touring exhibition was coming to town and a British production company had managed to score time with its curator and relentless promoter, Yoko Ono - but they needed a cameraman. I met them at the Palais de Tokyo but what got me was how young the crew were. Clearly, they hadn't done a great deal of preparation as they were all telling each other what to do: I refer to individuals such as these as 'chaos pixies'.

Ono duly arrived surrounded by bowing and scraping flunkies, revolving around her in a constant fuss-ball. The woman only had to give the slightest hint of lifting a finger and someone was there to deal with whatever it was she wanted. The presenter of the show was to accompany Ono as the pair of them walked around the exhibition stopping at various Lennon mementoes, with Ono then trotting out some anecdote or other. Ordinarily, you'd have scoped out the exhibition in advance and chosen your pieces before the interview started, but not this lot. They went from room to room, piece to piece, era to era and then back to where we started because they'd forgotten something. No one could decide the order of things to shoot and no one appeared to be in charge. The chaos pixies were in full flow and living up to their reputation.

We must have shot 40 individual pieces and Ono delivered a rambling story about every last one. On taking a break, I ejected a used 30 minute tape and handed it of the junior producers. "How long is the edited piece?" I asked. "Oh, about 5 minutes" she replied. They now had 90 minutes of footage for a 5-minute piece, so inserting tape number four into the camera, I sighed and off we went again.

The exhausting thing being that the entire shoot had to be conducted off the shoulder as I wasn't allowed to use a tripod. Walking around two people whilst zooming in, zooming out, panning left or right, tilting up or down, constantly focussing and on the move is exhausting. These cameras weighed over 15lbs (7kg) and had to sit in the sweet spot of your shoulder. Finally, just after lunch (which we never got) they wrapped on the Ono shoot with a grand total of 10 tapes. That's 5 hours of footage for a 5 minute piece, and even then the pall of chaos pixies were still trying to remember what was on each tape and as they filled in their logs - and only one of them had a pen.

Karel Beer, a British promoter, regularly brought comedy and music shows to Paris. Most of the comedians you currently see on TV these days came through the doors of the Hôtel du Nord or La Java to perform spots for the expats. Some of the musical acts Karel promoted included Hugh Cornwell (formerly of The Stranglers), Michelle Shocked, Richard Thompson and Jools Holland, along with his Rhythm and Blues Orchestra. The Holland shows were brilliant and there's nothing quite like the sound of a full band with a horn section. They opened with 'Double-O-Boogie' which is an absolute stomper.

Jools came to Paris twice, and prior to his second visit Karel needed some promo shots. Over to attend 'Retromobile', a classic and vintage car show, Jools agreed to some publicity photos so I met up with him at his boutique hotel on the Left Bank. We sat with a had coffee and talked about cars. If there's one thing he knows better than a keyboard, then it's classic motors.

My BBC chums in Paris had given my number to The Radio Times who needed some promo shots of Michael Palin to accompany his new programme "Michael Palin and The Women Who Loved Matisse". Palin would meet me at the Louvre the next day, and knowing that I'd need a hand, I rang my mate Colin from over the road, "Fancy an hour with Michael Palin tomorrow?"

Once at the Louvre, and due to copyright reasons, we couldn't photograph the *whole* Matisse painting so Palin would have to stand in front of it. He arrived bang on time with his PR assistant (his daughter) and once introductions had been made, she went off to make some phone calls.

Whenever faced with putting someone at their ease (and in this instance, it was my nerves that needed calming), starting a light conversation always helps to break the ice. However, today I had one to top them all. As I was making my last minutes preparations I asked, "You remember the final scene in 'The Meaning of Life', the restaurant in heaven shot at Elstree?"

He started by looking a little confused but he eventually nodded. "… and the Santas with their plastic tits, and you kitted out in a red dress?" He nodded and smiled, "Well for two weeks I sat just behind the backcloth flashing those stars in the background during the musical number." His face lit up, "Oh, well I never! What a coincidence! Yes, of course I remember those days and and it's always lovely to meet people who worked on our films!"

Of course, he didn't remember me personally and I wouldn't expect him to as I was only a tiny part of a giant cog, but I'd tapped into a rich vein of memories which struck a chord. For a while, we reminisced about the people, that scene and the time it took to put it all together.

The photo shoot went well enough and before we wrapped Palin suggested that we "do some serious ones." In fact, one of the 'serious' photos happens to be my favourite as it shows a side of Palin we rarely see - the scholar, the well-read, the educated.

The shoot over, his daughter came to retrieve him and whisked him off for lunch. Vigorously he shook my hand, "It was really lovely to meet you and I am delighted to have bumped into someone who worked on a Python film!" and with that he was off.

As soon as we were alone, Colin turned to me and said "You never told me you worked on a Python film?!"

"No" I replied, "I didn't, did I …"

Jason And The Aeronauts

Gerard, the PR man from the helicopters had another job for me out in Champagne country. A French Airforce base in Reims had fallen victim of recent government cuts and was soon to close but it planned to go out with a bang. 'Reims-Champagne Air Base' (Base 112) was to hold a huge farewell international airshow and had invited all and sundry to take part: from the UK came the 'Red Arrows', the Spanish sent their 'Patrulla Águila', the Royal Moroccan Air Force's 'Marche Verte' was putting in an appearance, along with the Swiss, the Dutch and the Belgians. It was planned to take place over the weekend of 27/28 July 2009, and Gerard offered me the role as the official photographer and I'd be required as of Thursday 25th.

That night in Reims, I dined *al fresco* with Gerard and his wife, chowing down on fabulous food and glorious wine. Through his contacts, he'd put me forward for the job and I my paymasters were Reims City Council. I was to start my coverage with the official event launch the next day, the press conference and then the two days of the airshow with access all areas.

The next morning I woke to hear that overnight Michael Jackson had died and the news channels were stuffed with it. Gerard and I met at his hotel and travelled to the press launch on the '*parvis*' (pavement) outside Reims' beautiful Cathedral and then onwards to a press conference at the town hall where it seemed that absolutely everyone *had* to give a speech. It was all over by 4pm so it was back to the hotel to download my files before another warm summer's evening meal with Gerard and his missus. Despite my constant reminders to Gerard about getting me a show pass, he still hadn't managed to hand one over, and if I didn't get one then I wasn't going to get onto the air base the next morning. Hoping that one would arrive with my breakfast croissant, I said goodnight to Gerard and his wife and went out for a last beer.

The city centre was buzzing, thanks to a mix of locals who were now joined by airshow personnel. Multiple languages could be heard through the hubbub and I bumped into display teams who'd travelled from all over. A small group soon developed in one bar as more alcohol arrived to fuel the constant good humour, and it was at this point that I fell upon a group of Dutchmen.

The Dutch Air Force's F-16 Solo Display Team of 8 was based at Leeuwarden Air Base. They were made up of the display pilot, the team manager and six aircraft engineers. Their summer months were spent touring Europe, wowing the crowds with their bright orange F-16 jet. Having just arrived in Reims following a display in the UK, they were looking forward to going home in a few days rest before next weekend's airshow. The pilot, Captain Ralph "Sheik" Aarts, flew the jet from show to show with the support crew slumming it in the back of the team van. It was getting rather late but the team were a fun bunch (though Ralph wasn't drinking), so as I'd had enough I wished them goodnight and headed for my pit.

Saturday was the first show day and I was due on-site at 10am so at sparrow's fart I rang and left another message on Gerard's phone reminding him about my pass. An hour later I tried again. By 11am I was getting worried. Display flying started at 1pm and with the spectator traffic, it would take at least 30-45 minutes to get there. Gerard called me 15 minutes later and apologised as he hadn't managed to get me a pass as he'd not seen anyone from the press office, at which point I started to smell a rat. I'd been by his side for the past 36 hours and we'd both been at the official launch *and* at the press conference: for someone who works full time with press and PR, he wasn't exactly filling me with confidence.

Well and truly buggered, I was stranded in Reims city centre with no way of getting *to* the airbase, let alone getting *onto* it. I walked out of the hotel and into the main square where, from an underground car park over the way, came a vehicle which slowed to pick up a chap in a green flying suit. It was the Dutch pilot and manager. I waved and shouted to get their attention. On reaching the car I explained my predicament: what a total f*ck up it all was but could they give me a lift to the air base? "Of course, jump in!"

The manager Chris (callsign "Omlet"), drove with Ralph the display pilot in the passenger seat, so like Lord Muck, I stretched out across the rear seats and thanked them for rescuing me. The car's windscreen had official stickers aplenty and therefore had access to the participant entrance gate which was on the other side of the airfield well away from the public. The two in the front wore military flying suits and proper show badges around their necks but all I had was a press pass from the Foreign Ministry in Paris, though it did say 'BBC' on it. At the entrance gate a pair of French military guardians took one look at the two flying personnel in the front and the stickers on the windscreen and waved us through. I couldn't believe it.

On parking up and, we walked towards a hanger where all the flying teams were gathered. I helped myself to a cup of coffee and some fresh pastries then settled down in one of the many sofas that had been sourced and spread around inside the hanger. The place looked like a giant secondhand furniture showroom.

I was just considering ringing Gerard when the Red Arrows walked in, loaded up with coffee and nibbles and squatted on several other sofas around me. "This is ridiculous", I thought. "here I am on a heavily guarded French military airforce base with millions of quid's worth of kit, the world's top military flying talent and yet *no one* has asked me who I am or can they see my official pass."

Ralph 'Sheik' Aarts (right) and his toy.

As Ralph and Chris left to prepare for their display, they invited me to join the team BBQ later on. Their bright orange jet was parked next to their stand so I couldn't really miss it. Despite enjoying the efforts of multinational teams trying their best to make coherent conversation using sign language and broken English, I had to get over to the other side of the airfield so wandered over to the shuttle buses and blagged a ride.

"Oh, you got in then?" said Gerard on spotting me, sheepishly handing me a pass. It was a busy first day and I shot everything that moved. Ralph, in the Dutch F-16, ripped his way up and down the display line with the afterburner on full chat. He'd disappear into the sky, and as he threw the plane into swallow dive, he released chaff to make a glorious streaking arc. On landing, he waved to the crowd as he taxied to his parking bay as I pushed my way through the sun drenched attendees, eager for the promised BBQ.

Sunday was another hot non-stop day where the Red Arrows stole the show. After a good seven hours on site I was ready for a shower and a good dinner. Gerard offered me a lift back to town, and now joined by his wife, we made small talk waiting our turn to leave the car park.

As if making some off-the-cuff announcement, Gerard casually told me that Reims council had had their own photographer on site for two days so I wasn't going to get paid. I thought I'd misheard him, but controlling my language because of Madame in the passenger seat, I questioned his last statement, "Hang on just a second, you booked me weeks ago, I've been here 4 days and now you're telling me I'm not getting paid? How long have you known about this?" With the awkwardness of a child not owning up to breaking a family heirloom, he danced around the subject. Whatever he said, I wasn't buying it so the rest of the trip to Reims was spent in an uncomfortable silence. At the hotel I unloaded my camera kit as he threw another little gem my way: "but could you send Reims council a copy of everything you've shot?" I was stunned by his audacity. "Seriously Gerard?!"

Over the coming weeks, Reims council rang a few times and sent a couple of emails enquiring after 'their photos'. I gently informed them that if they agreed to pay my bill in full, then I'd package everything up and send it by recorded post. This was met with a series of pleading phone calls from the Town Hall asking me to reconsider. I did my utmost to explain to the woman in Reims that Gerard had booked me and that I could supply her with a copy of the confirmation email and that only the deranged would think that I was about to hand over all that work for free. The cerebellum of your average French civil servant has been wired in such a way that it bypasses rational thought and sober logic, so she remained at a total loss as to why I wasn't prepared to give her all my photos gratis. That was the last I heard of Gerard too.

Another one of those '*I have no idea where they got my number from*' calls came in, "We're a London-based production company who make programmes for Sky Arts", said the voice on the other end. "We're making a series called 'The South Bank Show' and we've lined up an interview in Paris next week and wondered if you were available to shoot it?"

The schedule was emailed over and it was about this time that health and safety were starting to get their noses into everything. The reams of pages to do with risk assessments were mind-blowing and apparently you couldn't shoot a frame unless you'd informed someone in a hi-viz jacket that everything was in good working order and that you'd had your rabies jab. The name of the actor we were to interview rang a bell but I wasn't sure from where I'd heard it: Jason Isaacs.

The morning of the shoot was warm and sunny. Shops were opening, goods were arriving on sack trollies and street cleaners were hosing down the pavements as I carried my kit to the door of the address I'd been given.

Walking towards me was a tall man wearing sandals, shorts and t-shirt and he was laden with carrier bags. He'd obviously been to Rue Montorgueil, the popular pedestrian fruit and veg street. As he came closer I noticed that he was taking an interest in my kit piled up on the pavement. "Hi. Are you Stuart?" As it happened I was and this was Jason Isaacs. He was in Paris filming an adaptation of 'Rosemary's Baby' and for the next few evenings he was on a night shoots. Freshly arrived from the set he'd stopped at Rue Montorgueil to buy breakfast for himself and us.

The film's producers had rented him an apartment while he was in town, and inside I stacked my kit in a corner of the living room. We had to wait for the two production ladies currently inbound on the Eurostar, so Mr Isaacs emptied the shopping bags, plunged the strawberries and blueberries into water and I distributed various bowls and cutlery. We struck up a conversation about our respective lives: tricky for him at the moment as he had two daughters and that keeping them grounded and suitably educated while his job took him all over the world was difficult. I explained that I had a girlfriend who had a daughter and that she was pretty well settled at school blah blah blah.

The doorbell rang and the two London ladies joined us. With intros made, we sat down for brekkie and then to the job in hand: the interview. Some years ago Jason had played the role of Jackson Brody in 'Case Histories' and that today's shoot was a profile all about its author Kate Atkinson.

He gave a very polished interview and was a real gent. Once we'd finished we said our goodbyes and he went off to grab some sleep before that night's filming. He was under no obligation to buy us breakfast, let alone prepare and serve it too.

Strap In

Up to now, life had been fairly even-keeled and really quite fun. I'd moved out of the city centre and into the suburbs and a lovely 6th-floor apartment in an art-deco building in Asnières-sur-Seine. A brand new car sat in the road outside, I'd ploughed some money into the country house and in the November I bought a kitten - Peanut. Although I missed all my chums in central Paris, they were only a five-minute train ride away and I could easily walk to the AP studio from St Lazare and do any other little jobs I had.

My photographic work continued but it didn't pay as much as television. I did the launch of Alastair Campbell's book at WH Smiths in Rue de Rivoli - a tad desperate but I covered it. The European Helicopter Cup was being held at Le Touquet, so under management of another Frenchman, I was invited to be the official photographer for three days. My chums from the British Helicopter Team, David and Brenda flew in for the prize giving dinner so we sat together, drank and chatted.

I had a few other ad-hoc bookings from British clients including a couple of trips down to Toulouse where I took part in the media training of Airbus executives. A selection of corporate grown-ups were mock-interviewed by a seasoned journalist. They sat through fairly rough interviews and were expected to give a good account of themselves by not being tripped with those tricky curve-ball questions TV reporters often throw.

For reasons known only unto her, Frédérique decided that on Christmas Day 2013 was the day to end our 10 year relationship. Surprised? Yes of course. Within an hour of being told, I drove home to Asnières, and with my cat spent the remaining hours of Christmas Day watching wall-to-wall garbage on TV. I didn't bother telling any of my family in the UK for a while as I thought it best not to interrupt their festivities.

Early in the New Year, the Airbus media training people wanted me for a couple of days in Toulouse. For a change of scenery, I decided to treat myself to a mind-cleansing drive instead of taking the TGV. I found someone to come round for an hour each day to cat-sit Peanut and at 6am the next day, I hit the road. Once on the A10 motorway heading to Orleans, the road became quieter and unhurried. French motorways are paid-for (toll roads) so on top of fuel, a run to Toulouse might set you back a further £35 but (accidents and hold-ups dependant) they are by far the best means to get around. Besides, Airbus was paying and they weren't short of a bob or two. Here I was in beautiful crisp February weather, blue skies, sunglasses on and music at full blast driving down towards the Haute-Garonne. For the first time in a while, I felt positive.

Throughout the Spring and Summer of that year, the Airbus bookings and general studio work at AP continued, though not at the pace I would have liked. Come the autumn, I was talking to my sister Debbie who said "Well, I think it's time you came home. You've been there long enough and at least here you have family." She was right, it was time to acknowledge the fact that life here in France wasn't going to get any better and that maybe it was time to reinvent myself elsewhere. I think I just needed someone else to tell me. I'd been alone for a while and life was certainly missing something.

Debbie said that I could stay with her and husband Steve until I found somewhere permanent, but this was the thing that frightened me: what if I couldn't find anywhere? Landlords were notorious pet haters. I contacted a number of people putting out feelers and Debbie had also suggested that I find somewhere equidistant between her and my eldest sister Jenny. I called my cameraman mate Stuart, who was still living in central Paris, and asked if he knew of anyone in or around Surrey who had anywhere to rent. He forwarded my request to the Ski Club of Great Britain.

When my cat Peanut was a youngster, he loved the bath. Whilst I had my soak, he'd sit either on the lip of the bath or on the mat and wait for me to flick bubbles over the edge. As they ran down the side, he'd chase and try to swallow them. During one of these feline entertainment sessions, the phone rang and it was a chap from Dorking in Surrey. On the other end of the line was Ian who'd seen an announcement posted by the Ski Club and he went on to tell me that he had just what I was looking for: a bungalow in Dorking which also happens to be the mid-point between my two sisters. "Ahh, there is one thing", I said to Ian, "I have a cat ..." I waited for the pause and only too common apologetic reply of "Ah right, sorry, no pets" but was further surprised when I heard "Sure! No problem, bring it along!"

The next day I contacted a number of UK-based long-distance removal companies, eventually choosing a Suffolk-based company. They were simply brilliant and highly proficient in moving people out of the UK or moving expats back.

I then contacted the agent who managed my apartment and told her I was leaving. The basement *cave* was next. The *cave* was a God-send: a private lockable basement storage area which came with the flat, and as I didn't have the luxury of space where I was going, I was forced to make many difficult decisions as to what to throw out and what to keep. Bulging black rubbish bags full of memories were disposed of but it had to be done.

With the basement *cave* now empty and cleaned, I started on the apartment and made a list of furniture I was going to keep. The only thing I'd bring to the UK was my bed so the rest would have to go. I took photos of everything for sale and posted them online, and within ten days most of it had gone and Peanut and I were surrounded by towers of cardboard boxes, a single deckchair and the double bed. My mate Thierry, a watch repairer who lived around the corner, bought my dishwasher, my widescreen TV, the cooker *and* my scooter. The flat was spotless and I was proud that I'd looked after it quite so well. I loved that place - and I mean *loved* it.

Six floors up, it overlooked a park with a bandstand in the middle. In the distance you could see Sacre Coeur ... between May and October Peanut and I would sit on the balcony while I sipped on a glass of wine and he'd watch the kids playing downstairs. On the odd July 14th (Bastille Day) if it was just him and me, I'd sit in a deckchair with my bottle of wine and he'd sit next to me as together we'd watch the fireworks exploding in the skies all around us. To this day, come Guy Fawkes night, Peanut remains nonplussed about fireworks.

However, getting him across the border was causing me concern. One of the chaps in the local bistrot said "Leave it here, it's only a cat after all". Seriously? The French don't use the word *'pet'* but instead *'animale de companie'* - companion animal. There was no way on earth that I was going to give this little thing away and skip over the Channel. He was coming with me and that was that.

Within days, Peanut had his rabies jab, I'd got his passport and then booked the car onto the train at Calais. The removal lorry pulled up at the end of the road and its two-man team and I loaded my worldly possessions in around three hours, with Peanut sitting on the parquet flooring, bemused by what was happening to *his* apartment.

The keys were returned to a guardian, and to show how sorry I was to be leaving in such a rush, I left the owner my cash deposit I'd paid him three years earlier. Thierry had offered me a bed for my last night and Peanut spent most of it wandering around exploring every last nook and cranny. As I mentioned earlier, Thierry was a watch repairer who'd turned his back on a well-paid marketing job in order to concentrate on his passion. He was happier doing something he loved. That night he gave me the floor of his workshop and a blow-up mattress to sleep on, but now surrounded by hundreds of ticking timepieces, the racket was enough to drive anyone to distraction.

Ordinarily, a road trip to the UK would have filled me with pleasure. I'd be looking forward to seeing my family and enjoying some breathing space from Paris. Now aged 53, with my relationship finished and my work done, here I was driving out of France for good, heading to the UK with 18 years worth of memories, the minimum of possessions ... and a cat.

Once at At Calais the sign saying 'Animal Reception' turned my insides into knots, but if there was anything wrong with the paperwork or anything else, I'd just stay here until it was sorted. Walking into the reception portacabin, an agent smiled and asked to see my paperwork. I opened the door to Peanut's travel box and the agent waved a magic wand over his head. With a loud bleep the wand displayed his unique serial number which was checked against the paperwork. Two rubber stamps thumped down on Peanut's passport and everything was handed back: "Bon voyage monsieur". I couldn't believe it. Simple and painless.

Once on the train, I let Peanut out of his box to stretch his legs, and although his litter tray was on the back seat, he opted for the dark underside of the passenger seat. As we pulled into Folkestone I managed to coax him out and put him back into his box. He'd been in the damn thing for approaching 5 hours and was doing really well with no toilet accidents. In comparison, the moment you put Frédérique's cat anywhere *near* her travel box, it suffered from instant bowel evacuation. Now it was just a case of a couple of hours on the M20, around the M25, I'd soon be nursing a cup of tea and Peanut would be discovering his new surroundings and it would all be over.

The one thing that kept our family together was my sister Debbie: she organised get-togethers, Christmases, reunions, you name it. To say that I arrived from Paris without a care in the world would be a lie. Taking everything into account, I sat in her kitchen for an hour or so as all the emotion came flooding out. After seven hours in his travel box Peanut was tentatively exploring the garden and taking his first lungfuls of British air. Everything I'd worked for over the past 18 years was gone, my relationship, the country house and my livelihood. Before me lay an uncertain future with no financial stability. What next?

Feet First

Immediately, Debbie took control and started reorganising my life. Once you've lived in a country where complicated administration is on par with anaesthetic-free dental extractions, then the moment you experience anything approaching ease, you feel as though you've won a tiny battle. For example, opening a bank account in France is complicated, only because they make it so bloody problematic, but opening a bank account in the UK was simple. Debbie introduced me to the Nationwide in Guildford where we were in and out in 30 minutes, my debit card and cheque book were with me days later.

My sisters Debbie and Jenny ... and then all grown-ip and the other way around.

Organising a mobile phone contract didn't require sacrificing my first-born, it was so easy and stress-free. On previous visits to see my family, I couldn't wait to get back on the Eurostar and sod off back home to France to where belligerence and rudeness was normal. In fact, I'd lived in France for a ⅓ of my life and it was a sobering thought.

Being back in the UK wasn't too bad after all as services were simple to arrange. The next thing on my mind was getting some work. I'd been away for the best part of two decades so I was never going to slot back into where I left off - I had no immediate history, no one knew me and I really didn't know if I wanted to go back into television news. To be honest, the flame for that had long since extinguished and the industry was crawling with bottom feeders, ready to exploit the innocent or whomever just to get a story, and that wasn't for me.

I was now living miles outside the capital and to be honest, I didn't fancy two hours on a train every day. Over the Channel I'd been used to either living inside the city walls or at least within a matter of minutes from the action. To qualify as a quick responder you really needed to live within 30 minute radius and besides, on a Sunday the trains didn't run as the network ground to a halt so they can fix stuff.

Debbie and I visited my new abode in Dorking. Ian and Claire (the owners) and I got on straight away and their three kids seemed to have tons of character. Claire was expecting their 4th child, and assuming it arrived on time, then I could move in on January 2nd so the place was mine if I wanted it. The semi-detached bungalow was ideal and the three kids were excited at the prospect of a fur ball running about the place. I couldn't believe how lucky I'd been since I'd moved home: bank, communications and now accommodation. It was all slotting into place. I contacted my removal company in Suffolk, gave them a tentative date for them to drop off my boxed life.

Debbie and Steve had very kindly loaned me a spare room in their modest little house and I was rapidly filling it up with crap. Peanut seemed quite happy with his new digs but stuck close to me wherever I went. As Christmas approached there was some talk about the tree and it's decorations. Would Peanut rip the thing to shreds? I very much doubted it, and sure enough once it was up and all sparkly, he looked at it once and left well alone.

On January 2nd 2015 I moved into the bungalow and awaited my household possessions. I'd take regular trips into town to have a look at the place. In fact, before moving in I'd driven over to Dorking on a few occasions, parked in one of the public car parks and strolled up and down the high street. I sized up my local pub and pleased that I was close enough to town so able to walk nearly everywhere. I began contacting old clients and colleagues who did their best help me out work-wise. Peanut stayed inside for a few months while he got used to the place and after month or so, I let him outside and watched him as he hugged the exterior walls, exploring his new environment.

My cousin David, who played the Inspector in 'The Mouse Trap' all those years ago, was very ill with cancer. He and his wife lived about half an hour from me, but as he was home from hospital, I arranged to pop round and see him. The last time we saw each other was when we were both in the West End in the late 70s but it was really good to catch up. After an hour he made his excuses, said he was tired and could I come back another day? Of course I could.

A few months later David died but I was so very happy to have seen him one last time. Debbie and I went to his funeral at Woking Crematorium and it was the funniest funeral I'd ever been to. He had written the text for the ceremony himself and it was delivered by a friend of his, interspersed with musical segments. Being a *'thesp'*, a lot of David's peers had traveled miles to attend, including a colourful Su Pollard. There was standing room only but the crematoria had a side room with a video relay for ceremonies that were *really* well attended, and this one was. Crammed with non-stop laughter, David's text hit home and his jokes were brilliant.

In the September, Debbie and Steve's daughter Nicola married Simon in a gloriously stand-out ceremony near Swanage. Earlier in the year Debbie had been diagnosed with breast cancer, initially telling me about it during one of my regular dinners with her. As a family (along with friends) we alternated driving duties taking her into The Royal Surrey Hospital in Guildford for her daily zapping of radiotherapy. Convinced she was going to loose her hair before the wedding, there was much talk about wigs, but thankfully she kept every last follicle, and when she was cancer-free, it was a wonderful moment to savour.

Simon, Debbie's son-on-law, is now a successful cinematographer and when I first arrived home, he offered me some work. We did a couple of jobs which were easy enough and I was very grateful to him. One of these shoots was at London's Freemason's Hall, where the fashion industry was hosting its annual prize giving. Millionaire sponsors and business leaders gathered to heap praise on this year's graduates who'd been awarded prize money or full time employment. Before the start of proceedings, the production team asked me to "pop outside and get some shots of the building and of the guests arriving".

With my camera and tripod I worked my way through the crowds and out into Great Queen Street where I lined up a few shots. Over my shoulder I saw that I'd been joined by two kids from the production company. They stood directly directly behind me and watched my every move. Apparently their boss had dispatched them as I was 'an unknown quantity' and therefore they needed to check that I knew what I was doing. Though mildly amused, I also felt rather insulted as Simon had put my name forward because he knew I was more than capable of doing the job. No matter, after Westminster, The Cook Report, Bosnia, Kosovo, filming umpteen Heads of State, shooting and editing headline news stories for the world's most respected broadcasters, filming simply 100s of hours-worth of television news and Christ knows what else, I was now being shadowed by a couple of 12 year olds making sure that I could film a stationary building without fu*king it up. I know they were only doing their job, but even so. It was obvious that my age was a problem to the youth of the day.

My skills and experience were no longer needed by the industry I loved, and in which I'd like to think I'd made a good name for myself. My best before date had expired and I was now irrelevant. If you weren't in your 20s or 30s, then this industry had no time for you, and the youth made *quite* sure you knew it.

I applied for loads of full time jobs, but was never offered a position. I was, on the other hand, offered loads of interviews. One position I went for was the post of Studio Manager at Surrey University's TV facility, and on walking into the interview room the expressions on the faces of the board spoke volumes: "his CV is spot on but he's much older than we thought". An ex-BBC director asked me about a lighting scenario to which I gave a quite brilliant answer. For some reason she disagreed and started an argument, which I found slightly bizarre. It was fairly obvious that I had the experience they needed but University types tend to stick together, and within hours I was informed that I had not been selected.

The assumption being that I was now 'too old' or 'possessed too much experience' for the jobs I applied for. I was convinced that with my skills and industry knowledge, I would be in great demand, but sadly not.

Jason, the only school chum I'd kept in touch with from Shiplake, sent me a link to a job announcement for a photographic software company who were looking for a video producer to make tutorial clips.

I applied, sent in examples of my work and had a phone interview with the boss. On a Sunday evening in late April I received a firm offer and I could have wept. Finally, I'd got somewhere and been awarded a job on merit and my experience was, at last, wanted by at least someone.

Thankfully, I was to be based at home, and to begin with the work was enjoyable as it tested all my creative skills and problem-solving techniques, but fairly rapidly the boss (who was based in Dorset) soon showed her true colours: a control freak and a micromanager of gold medal standard. She had a lapdog in Berlin who'd been at the company for some time and nothing could be done without his say so. I was being managed by two people who often contradicted each other, which wasn't entirely helpful.

I'd be given a brief and start by writing a script which would be sent for approval. My boss and the Berliner would submit their changes individually rather than sending them over in one document. Then another company director (who was based in Australia) would be asked to comment on my work, and another list of changes would arrive. I was now being managed by *three* people who frequently contradicted each other. It was a bizarre way of working and it didn't seem to bother them. It was obviously 'change for the sake of changing' as each one of them tried to put their own footprint on whatever tutorial was being made.

Christmas 2016 and I was invited around to Debbie and Steve's for the seasonal celebrations and a meal. Both their kids were there, along with Nicola's husband Simon, but Debbie was in bed and in great discomfort. One by one we'd pop up to see how she was doing. On the Boxing Day she was taken into Guildford hospital and tests were arranged. She may have beaten breast cancer but the primary cancer was in the stomach and they didn't find it until it was too late. I visited her as many times as I could while she was at Guildford, and as she deteriorated, a bed in the Woking hospice was found. Debbie died on January 20th 2017 and my world was ripped apart. You accept the death of your parents as that is their final act as the those who brought you into this world, but not a sibling.

For a second time the family were back at Randall's Crematorium in Leatherhead and I took my place in the last row as I simply couldn't face being at the front with Steve, his kids, my other sister Jenny and the rest of the family. It was standing room only and I spent the entire ceremony looking up at the stained glass windows or down at my shoes. Only once did I look at the coffin.

The institutionalised bullying at work was becoming a nightmare. Every Sunday night I rolled around in bed worrying about the sniping emails that were likely to greet me the next morning. Sure enough, at start of play on the Monday, more fault finding, textual discipline arrived in which my colleagues had been cc'd. Should anything be out of place, then I'd be made an example of in an email "Why is it taking so long? This is not what I am paying you for". Well, if three people weren't sending in lists of notes one after another, that could well be the reason.

I had been asked to make contact with David, a photographer in Farnham as the company were going to use him for a number of video tutorials. Thankfully, David and I got on famously. We still do. Then after three years, my boss made me redundant. She had been spending too much money on other projects and simply ran out. She asked the accountants where she could make some savings and they suggested that as I wasn't directly part of the revenue stream, I should go. I was absolutely bloody furious. Still, she gave me six weeks notice before redundancy.

A few projects were still in the pipeline which needed tying up, and she brought me back as a freelancer for two months. Of course my German colleague kept changing his mind on absolutely everything thus delaying delivery of the finished product. One day I opened an email in which I had been cc'd and it was obvious that both he and the boss had been chatting, as in the bulk of the email she'd been talking about having me replaced as it was "taking too long to complete the work". I pressed 'reply all' and typed "I really don't think you wanted to add me to the list of recipients". An embarrassed email followed with apologies from Berlin.

No matter, if they insisted on prolonging each and every project by simply making countless tiny and unnecessary changes, then fair enough, I'll not disappoint them. I withdrew my services with immediate effect, followed by an explanation as to what a total pain in the arse it had been working for such unprofessional people who knowingly delayed every sodding project through constant and unnecessary change - and then blaming the poor sod trying to produce their content. However, my final act was to attach a couple of nice fat invoices which her company was duty-bound to settle.

Within days I contacted a few friends of old, and as luck would have it, a chap I worked with years ago came back to me with an idea. As soon as I'd heard from him, the following story came to mind: in the 90s, and being a keen pilot, this chum of mine had heard of an air rally in which a dozen or so light aircraft were to leave White Waltham airfield (2 miles south-west of Maidenhead) and fly to Australia. He'd sold the idea to the news department of London Weekend Television (LWT) so would I like to help him film the departure? On 25 March 1990, we swung by his office to pick up a camera kit and various accessories and headed off to the airfield. It was and a nice enough day and White Waltham was packed with aircraft and well-wishers. We were to film the start as the departing planes raced off down the runway, then capture a little colour of the event and high-tail it to the South Bank and hand the footage over to LWT.

Of course being air operations everything was reliant on wind direction, and as the wind had changed, the starting line had been hastily rearranged for *another* runway. The rally was being waved off by a celeb and now we *all* needed to get to the new runway. An airfield ops chap delivered us to the far end of the grass runway as the celeb, Richard Branson, arrived in a vintage Bentley. Well he would, wouldn't he?

On cue, Branson was due to fire a green Very light into the air to get the event underway. However, now all congregated at the starting line, a problem had developed with the first aircraft so everyone switched off their engines and waited. Me, my mate, the ops driver, Branson and the Bentley driver sat in the grass chatting and making daisy chains. It was quite surreal.

So after being made redundant in 2019 and I'd contacted the same chap about a job. He ran an aerial photographic company and suggested we got together for a chat as they were looking for someone to run their video department. A lunch-come-interview was organised I hadn't seen this guy since the 90s but it was great to see him again and to catch up. I was introduced to his business partner and the three of us went for lunch at the complex canteen, during which I gave him a rundown of what I'd been up to and he, in turn, told me about the job he had going.

After lunch, it was back to the office for a tour of the premises where I was shown the image library and a run-through of how the system worked followed by the security backup area for photo and video files. We then slipped into the board room where he began a further 45 minute hard-sell sales pitch to convince me to come and work for him. All in all I spent a little over four hours at his office. He finished with "Go away and think about it and come back to me in two days with a decision." So that's exactly what I did.

Two days later I called him but he wasn't available so I left a message and called the next day. He still wasn't available but replied with a text saying "Busy now but are you around over the weekend? I'll call you." I spent the weekend waiting for the call which never arrived. I tried the following week to get hold of him but he never returned my calls, nor my emails or texts and I then realised that I'd fallen foul of the latest craze doing the rounds: ghosting.

How bizarre.

Tale End

It was obvious that job opportunities for the over 50s in the UK were scarce. Despite filling in a mass of forms and sending my CV for *'professional critique'* (and I use that phrase sparingly), all I was getting in return was a spattering of left-field suggestions as to what to do next. My inbox was filed with *"it looks like you're a great fit to work as a carer ..."*. I didn't want to wipe bottoms in care homes or work in Lidl, though out of sheer frustration I *did* apply for a job at my local branch to stack shelves overnight. My CV was attached to the application and I was invited to sit an online English language test. Needless to say, I wasn't offered an interview. I mean, even Somalian Warlords appear to have more job stability.

On the spur of the moment I arranged a meeting with my local MP as I was keen to know his thoughts on the ever-expanding glut of over-50s sitting on the sidelines, just waiting for some over achieving 40 year old hiring manager to allow them back into the workplace. I firmly believe that you can tell a lot about an individual simply by their handshake, and his left me feeling that the outcome of this 10 minute meeting was likely to be a long walk down a windy beach to a café that was closed.

As I delivered my impassioned speech, I saw that I was losing my audience. The Honourable MP For His Own Interests rocked back in his chair, folded his arms and explained that, statistically speaking, the chances of a white male over 50 getting another full time job was slimmer than a vegan catwalk model. "If you ever get one, I'll be surprised." The meeting was over and I was escorted out of the council offices.

I spent the next 12 months doing my best to find freelance work, and then then Covid arrived. So many interviews for work and so many refusals. Had I wanted this level of rejection I would have joined an internet dating agency. Then fast forward to July 2021 when I was offered a full-time job at a FTSE 100 company where I now manage the creation and distribution of digital assets (and in turn) manage the working timetables of the creatives who produce them. So for now, I'm back in the game. Admittedly, I'm in a completely different comfort zone. As you get older, unless you've stuck it out with the same company for years, then offers of full time employment are going to be few and far between. I'm learning new skills everyday and I'm getting a monthly salary which pays the bills and keeps Peanut rolling in catnip. In July of 2022 I got a female kitten, Pickle. So both are enjoying life, though Peanut still isn't on good terms with the new recruit.

So there you have it. Over the years I've been lucky enough to have done some extraordinary things and met some equally extraordinary people, but I'm not going to end this collection of memories with any long-winded conclusions, and certainly no moralistic crap. Admittedly it's a fairly blunt way of ending things, but if there's nothing more to say, then shut up. Despite my ramblings and constant direction changes, I hope you've enjoyed the last 244 pages. I'm sorry if you didn't get a mention in this book, but it's OK, I'll not be upset if you don't mention me in yours.

There are plenty of anecdotes which I didn't include, despite those which really deserved an airing. However, my handy counter tells me that if this were an audiobook, then it would run for over 10 hours, so I think you've probably had *a)* enough and *b)* your money's worth. So to wrap things up, I set myself a challenge and I'll try and finish this exercise by using the word '*bollocks*', so here goes:

And It's Light's Out!

A fellow pupil at Shiplake had a sister who was blessed with the most wonderful bosom. She must have been around 17 when she accompanied her parents to visit her little brother at school. Word of this beauty and her two accomplices preceded her, as now a small group of us sat in the first floor bay windows looking down into the car park. Sure enough, she stepped out of her parent's car, her magnificent pair gently cosseted under a thick woollen jumper. After each of her brief visits to the school, excited juvenile conversations circulated between the 14 and 15 year olds, both gloriously infantile and pathetically naive.

Anyway, fast forward two or three years later to 1978 and I'd broken free of the shackles of education and was just waiting to get my break in the West End. My peers were still incarcerated in Oxfordshire waiting to find out if they'd be going up to University or joining the Army. For some reason I had this girl's phone number so I gave her a call and she invited me up to her place in Wandsworth. Back then, aged 20 or 21, she was shacked up with some hooray Henry city-type to whom I was introduced.

The moment I sat on the sofa, its leather backrest and seat cushions almost swallowed me up, trapping me where I fell. A mug of tea was thrust into one hand and we engaged in small talk when there was a knock at the door and her fella got up to answer it. Muffled voices could be heard coming from the entrance hall and then in came Oscar. A large and over-friendly

246

Alsatian, Oscar made his way across the sitting room floor at speed, his nose and my crotch came together faster than a newly married teenage couple. Trying to keep a hold of the steaming mug of tea whilst placating this friendly creature was multiskilling at its best, if not a prize-winning juggling act. The dog was called and it dutifully backed off. It was at this point that I saw its owner: world champion Formula One driver, James Hunt.

At the time, Hunt lived in Wimbledon, a matter of a few miles down the road, and this girl's chinless-wonder boyfriend was one of his trusted confidantes. Whilst driving for McLaren 2 years earlier in 1976, Hunt had won the F1 World Championship, and now stuck inside a sofa in Wandsworth, I was incapable of getting out of the damn thing to shake his hand. From that moment onwards I also lost the power of speech. James Hunt was now sitting in the same room and chatting to his mate. Whatever, I was awestruck.

Despite being a legendary ladies' man, it was said that his best friend was Oscar, his beloved German Shepherd. According to friends, Hunt's relationship with Oscar "seemed far closer than any human relationship he ever had. He was completely devoted to that dog." Oscar became a legend in his own right as he'd regularly accompany Hunt to high class restaurants in London's West End. The pair were once reported to have visited Langan's in Mayfair where they shared a spinach soufflé with entrecôte de veau, polished off with a cassis sorbet. In 1979, a year after I couldn't get out of that sofa, Hunt retired from driving and died in his sleep in 1993 aged 43.

Is That Your Minkey?

Years before overly-zealous security and ID passes came into existence, as a 16-year-old I knew that "Revenge of the Pink Panther" was being made at Shepperton Studios so I chanced my arm and rode my Puch Maxi scooter up to the main gate, waved at the security guard and in I went. Eventually I found my way to the sound stage where the nightclub scene was being shot (to be honest, there were signs everywhere). Next to the main soundproofed studio door was a smaller door through which people passed to access the dressing rooms and makeup. I opened one of these doors and to my left was the door to Stage A with Stage B to my right.

As I explained earlier, I'd spent four miserable years at Shiplake but found an escape listening to radio comedy every Saturday lunchtime in the dormitory. Lying on my bed with a radio and using a little earpiece, I'd soak up The Goons, Morecambe & Wise, The News Huddlines and anything else that was on offer - I survived off this stuff. The Goons were my staple fayre, Spike Milligan being my No 1, though Peter Sellers ran a very close second.

On the wall by the door to Stage A was a large bright red light along with a sign saying "Red light means No Entry!". A bell rang once to signal the end of shooting (two for "Rehearsing" and three for "Cameras Are Rolling"), the light went out and the steel door slid open. A troupe of technicians, makeup and wardrobe people filed out followed, in full costume, by Peter Sellers. He was the one I wanted to see and there he was right in front of me. I wasn't after an autograph, I only wanted to catch a glimpse of him if I could.

Sellers saw me, smiled and almost stopping said "Hello". That was it. Nothing more. I remained riveted to the spot, incapable of movement or reaction. Then, in a flurry of busy dressers and makeup people, he was ushered upstairs to his dressing room.

A Record Breaker

I made the Guinness Book of Records. Well not by name exactly, but I was certainly part of a record-breaking attempt by SNCF, the French national state-owned railway.

Les Frogs had spent an absolute fortune on a new stretch of railway track between Valence and Marseille. With it in place, they believed that they could set a new speed record for '*the highest average speed by a train over a distance of 1,000 km (621 miles)*'. With Jon, a mate of mine, to conduct the interviews, on May 26th 2001 we stepped onto the platform at Calais. Louis Gallois, Chairman of the SNCF, was due to board the record-breaking TGV to crow about his company's technical abilities, but that was later.

At either end of this train were the instantly recognisable pointy-nosed power units and between them were two passenger carriages (for guests and journalists), a technical carriage full of geeks looking at readout screens and a carriage where food and drink was prepared. The food and drink was to be delivered by a team of young, good looking serving staff who, as the train whizzed through France, needed to change into regional costumes as we went racing through the countryside.

Along with my fellow press colleagues, I filmed the atmosphere on the Calais platform, and as the minute hand clicked ever closer to 4pm, we were told to take our seats. The most important take-away message from the on-board briefing was "Don't get up out of your seat unless you really need to." Yes it was going to be a rough ride, and at exactly 4.30pm, the train pulled out of Calais. In the journalist's carriage we gripped the table edges as the group exchanged humorous one-liners.

There were tv screens displaying images from cameras that had been installed all over the train - inside the driver's compartment and outside on the train's body, looking forward, backwards and even one underneath looking at the wheels. An LED display gave us the distance travelled and the speed in KPH.

The ride was indeed fast and furious, as had been promised during the welcome briefing. Walking to the toilet proved to be both dangerous and exciting. The serving staff did their utmost to hand out snacks whilst quick changing into their required costumes and we managed to get an interview with SNCF Chairman, Louis Gallois. During interviews for anglophone media, it was always best if you could encourage whichever Frenchie it was to give their replies in English. Surrounded by toadying SNCF PR flunkies, Gallois said he would speak in English, yet he stumbled his way through basic shit even to the point where I was finding him difficult to understand. Jon suggested he switched to French, which he did with comparative ease.

Our arrival at Marseille's St Charles station was timed to perfection and met with huge fanfare. French national TV news started at 8pm so what better intro than a live shot of the train pulling into the station? It was a PR stunt which ran like a Swiss watch. One of the train drivers said that had they been allowed to really go for it, they could have knocked a further 20 minutes off the time, but it was all engineered to fit around the evening news bulletins. After the popping champagne celebrations on the platform and the press scrum the team of train drivers, we were invited to a chateau where the railway company forced-fed us alcohol and top-notch grub until the early hours.

The following morning, after very little sleep in a budget hotel, the delicate group of journalists presented themselves at Gare St Charles for the return trip. Decked out in sunglasses and speaking in very soft voices, we gingerly helped each other onto the train, only this one was a normal five hour scheduled TGV run up to Paris.

The official record reads:

The highest average speed by a train over a distance of 1,000 km (621 miles) is 306.37 km/h (190.37 mph), by a French SNCF TGV train between Calais and Marseille on 26 May 2001. The train, which was unmodified and therefore identical to Eurostar trains, covered the 1,067 km (663 miles) between the cities in 3 hours 29 minutes, reaching a maximum speed of 366 km/h (227 mph).

A Gentle Walk Around Chequers

I was given the job of shooting a Greenpeace 'action' at Chequers, the Prime Minister's country house in Buckinghamshire. Despite Greenpeace saying that it was a 'surprise', claiming that the Police knew nothing about it, it was all rubbish. Nearly every organisation has a mole and every mole updates the domestic security forces as to the movements' next 'action'.

The rendez-vous with the Greenpeace press contact was in a public car park, a 3 mile walk from Chequers. The place was buzzing with supporters, busy packing banners into rucksacks and gearing up for a trudge across the countryside where they hoped to spoil the PMs weekend, and that of his top-brass guests. Rather than carry my camera by the usual method of over my shoulder, I disconnected the lens from the camera and carefully put both into a rucksack so I could walk to the house without drawing attention to myself - as if the 200 other people 'out for a stroll' wouldn't do that themselves.

On cresting a hill, we saw the house about half a mile away surrounded by farmland. The supporters split into pre-organised groups and scattered. I stuck close to the press contact and we waited for the others to reach their launching positions: a third were way out in the woods to our left, and a third to our right. Now we'd sit amongst the trees and wait for the 'go'.

I assembled my camera, checked that it worked as a five minute warning was issued throughout the group. Leaning against a tree. I started filming the house, serenely nestled by a backdrop of trees, golden leaves and acres of ploughed fields.

The command was given and my group set off down the hill towards Chequers, with the others breaking from the left and right. I continued filming so at least I could get scenes of people streaming out of the woods. After a minute or so it was time to make tracks and join them, so I set off down the incline and into the field.

250

Of course, the Police had been watching all this buggering about with long lenses so they knew exactly what to expect - it's all a big game to both sides. A long stream of day-glo-vested riot Police came rushing out from their hidey-holes, spreading out in an effort to stop protestors from reaching the main house. Greenpeace disciples, their limbs flailing windmill style, were getting stuck in. Plod, on the other hand, was making merry with fists and batons, cuffing protestors and leading them off to waiting vans. Greenpeace's lesbian militant splinter group were also going for it hammer and tongs, their cloth banners daubed with slogans full of perfect grammar. It was a quintessential British afternoon.

As soon as the Police vans were full, and the bloodied walking wounded had retreated back up the hill, it was time to declare it a draw and head home for tea and medals. In a matter of hours, those arrested would be cautioned and freed, while officers would share a few off-duty pints with colleagues, regaling them with stories of how they gave some hippy a much deserved kick in the bollocks.

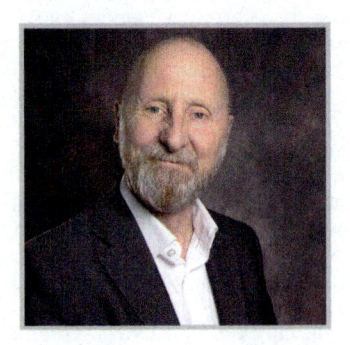

Fin

At this point, in any number of books of the same nature, you'd probably expect to find paragraphs of gushing thanks, as praise and gratitude are heaped upon those who helped write whatever it was that came before. Not here.

Hang on, that's not strictly true, as I suppose I should thank the pandemic which was the initial inspiration behind this. On my daily solo walks up through the woods, I'd listen to autobiographies of the rich and famous and thought, "Well, if that vain prick can write one, then so can I".

It took one year to get all this into some form of order, and then I'd be reminded of another event and would have to re-edit. A further year of tinkering and I thought I was happy. This is now version 6 and I *think* this is it. I'm sure you'll have heard the old expression in television and film that sometimes some of the best stuff *'ends up on the cutting room floor'*? As I was to discover, it's the same with books. Version 1 topped in at 330 pages long, and my copy now props the living room door open.

As I said at the start, this was a project to illustrate my life story as I have no one to hand anything on to when my time is up: no wife and no children. There has to be a trace of my existence left somewhere, so a bookshelf is probably the best place to be. Since I decided to fill these pages, I've spoken to friends and family who've helped remind me of a whole host of situations and events. One look at a photograph and I'm straight back there, right in the middle of it all.

I suppose I should ask myself if I've been lucky? Well yes, I've been *very* lucky simply by ending up in the right place at the right time. I've have had some fantastic jobs and experienced some extraordinary moments in history, and all without the obligatory degree that companies swear you need in order to earn a crust these days.

There are still lots of things I want to do, so I can assure you that this tome doesn't mark the end of anything, it just stops at the point where I am now.

So, if I could do it all again, would I?

Of course, but with a few minor changes, the details of which I'll leave you to ponder.

No further questions. Your witness.